AT A PLACE CALLED
Buckingham

HISTORIC SKETCHES OF BUCKINGHAM COUNTY, VIRGINIA

Volume Two

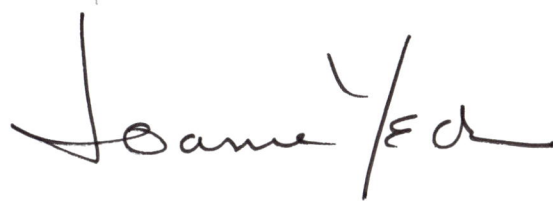

Also by Joanne L. Yeck

"At a Place Called Buckingham"...
Historic Sketches of Buckingham County, Virginia

The Jefferson Brothers

"AT A PLACE CALLED BUCKINGHAM"...

☙☜

Historic Sketches
of Buckingham County, Virginia

Volume Two

Joanne L. Yeck

Front Cover Photo: *Harper's New Monthly Magazine*, View of Columbia, Fluvanna County, c.1865

Copyright © 2015 by Joanne L. Yeck

All rights reserved. Printed in the United States of America.

No part of this book may be reproduced in any manner whatsoever without written permission except in the case of brief quotations embodied in critical articles and reviews.

Library of Congress Cataloging-In-Publication Data

Yeck, Joanne L.

"At a Place Called Buckingham"... Historic Sketches of Buckingham County, Virginia, Volume Two/by Joanne L. Yeck

p. cm.

Includes bibliographical references.

1. Virginia—Buckingham County—History. 2. Virginia—Buckingham County—Biography. 3. Plantation life—Virginia—Buckingham County. 4. Slavery—Virginia—Buckingham County. 5. Education—19th century—Virginia—Buckingham County. 6. Civilian Conservation Corps—Virginia. 7. Historic Buildings—Virginia—Buckingham County. 8. Historic Sites—Virginia—Buckingham County. I. Joanne L. Yeck, 1954 – II. Title.

F232.B96 Y43 2015

2011276195

ISBN 978-0-9839898-3-7

Designed by Carole Ohl

Printed by Greyden Press, LLC.

Published by Slate River Press Ltd., Kettering, OH

slateriverpress.com

For

All those who cherish
the history of Buckingham County

Contents

Preface ix

PART ONE: PLACES OF BUCKINGHAM COUNTY

Frontier Elegance: Bellmont 3

Stewards of the Poor: Buckingham County's Poorhouses 15

Ferrying across the James River 33

"Going to the Springs" in Buckingham County 47

Hospitality and Entertainment: Buckingham Hotel 67

Spirit and Industry:
Buckingham County and the Civilian Conservation Corp 85

MAYSVLLE GALLERY

Frances Benjamin Johnston:
The Village of Buckingham Court House 107

PART TWO: PEOPLE OF BUCKINGHAM COUNTY

Elijah G. Hanes and Humanity Hall Academy 129

Capt. Robert Henry Miller and Life at Millwood 153

Buckingham County's Mark Twain: George W. Bagby 173

The Man behind Alexander Hill: Alexander Moseley 191

Preserving Buckingham County's Past: William Gamaliel Shepard 215

A Life of Service: Louise Harrison McCraw 227

Minnie Garland (Harris) and Charles Milan Sanger, 1911
(SANGER FAMILY COLLECTION)

Preface

> "Your grandmother was born in Buckingham Court House. Not in the courthouse. But like Washington Courthouse in Ohio."
>
> Grandpa

That's how it started. A yellowing scrap of paper on which my amusing grandfather, Charles Milan Sanger, wrote the most basic information about his wife, Minnie Garland (Harris) Sanger. Indeed, Minnie was born in Buckingham County, Virginia on April 26, 1891. Her parents lived in a cabin near Muddy Creek, not far from Well Water and the home of her grandfather, John T. L. Woodson. As a toddler, Minnie was whisked away to Leon, Iowa. There she grew up and, eventually, the family ties to Virginia were broken. Beginning in 1995, I set out to rebuild those broken links, ultimately finding my way back to Jamestowne and the earliest days of the Virginia Colony.

Unearthing the history of Buckingham County, Virginia, as it turned out, was full of challenges, surprises, and many, many rewards. After twenty years of exploration, there remains much to discover. The Buckingham County well has not run dry. Boxes filled with family papers still turn up in attics. 19th-century letters appear out of nowhere, suddenly for sale on eBay. A cousin finds a priceless photo tucked in a family Bible.

In 2011, my book, *"At a Place Called Buckingham"* . . . *Historic Sketches of Buckingham County, Virginia*, celebrated the 250th anniversary of Buckingham County and offered me the opportunity to share some of what I had learned about the county while investigating my family roots. Following its publication, I continued to write historical articles for the *Buckingham Beacon*, eventually amassing enough material to warrant a second collection. As with the previous volume, those essays have been expanded and cited for this book.

In 2012, I launched Slate River Ramblings (slateriverramblings.com), a blog devoted to Buckingham County and its environs. The followers now constitute a lively and collaborative community. Their desire to preserve and protect the heritage of Buckingham County, which continues unabated, is both inspiring and gratifying. Their collective knowledge enriched this collection. My thanks to all of you.

Many colleagues, friends, and family members supported this project, including Spencer Adams, Winnie Adams, Ed Ayres, Pattie Bell, James Blake, Jean DeNoon Cable, John Stuart Clayton, Jr., Luella Coleman, Jim Cooke, Jean L. Cooper, Bill Davidson, Linda Hope Doerger, Betty Duncan, Greg Eanes, John Ayres Greenlee, Harry S. Holman, Cathy Isham, Carole Jensen, Larry Lamb, Gene Lightfoot, Ruby Loving, Martha Louis, Estaline Anderson McCraw, Shirley Mcmichen, Nancy Maxey, Jordan Miles, Richard S. Morris, Sandra Carrington Nelson, Richard Nicholas, Melissa Blake Palmore, Anne Robertson, William Q. O. Shelton, Lillian Smith, Ruby Talley Smith, Martha Stokes, Bob Vernon, Charles W. White, and Nancy Jamerson Wieland.

Special thanks go to Carlos Santos, publisher of the *Buckingham Beacon*, who originally published shorter versions of these essays; to Connie Geary, Scottsville Museum's digital archivist and webmaster, for her tireless efforts on behalf of Scottsville and its neighbor to the south; to Jeremy Winfrey for his impressive ability to connect the dots and his eagerness to share what he learns; to Margaret Thomas who not only served as my proofreader and fact checker but also frequently supplied records from Buckingham Courthouse and from the collection at Historic Buckingham's Housewright Museum; and to Mary Carolyn Mitton whose love for and knowledge of Buckingham runs deep.

Institutions safeguard history; however, it is the individuals who work in them that make research a pleasure. My thanks go to the staffs at the Library of Congress, The Huntington Library, Housewright Museum (Historic Buckingham), National Museum of American History (Smithsonian Institution), Scottsville Museum, Sheridan Libraries (Johns Hopkins

University), and the Virginia Historical Society. My ongoing gratitude goes especially to the expert staff at the Library of Virginia, who has assisted me over many years of research, and particularly to Dale Neighbors who did some extra digging for the images included in this volume.

At Dayton Metro Library, Greg Estes and Jeanne Waselewski facilitated many interlibrary loan requests. Searchable databases of historic newspapers including Chronicling America: Historic American Newspapers (Library of Congress), Virginia Chronicle (Library of Virginia), and the collection at GenealogyBank.com provided many 19th-century and early 20th-century accounts which appeared in *The Farmville Herald*, *The Times* (Richmond, Virginia), *Richmond Times-Dispatch*, and the *Richmond Whig*.

To my editor, Nancey Bridston Hocking, and to my graphic designer, Carole Ohl — once again your talents made the people and places of Buckingham County look their best.

A last word about the selection of essays…. Four of the six individuals featured in this volume were writers: an essayist, a newspaper editor, an historian, and a novelist. This is not because Buckingham County was an especially literary place; rather, it is because writers leave tracks where others do not. Importantly, these authors reflect Buckingham County as well as themselves. Their upbringings shine through their prose, especially the high value that Buckingham County's forefathers placed on education. In each case, these individuals were devoted to the culture of central Virginia and wanted the larger world to appreciate her glories. In the absence of public documents destroyed in the 1869 burning of Buckingham Courthouse and the paucity of personal papers such as correspondence and diaries, the writings of Dr. George W. Bagby, Alexander Moseley, William G. Shepard, and Louise Harrison McCraw offer us a privileged and personal window into Buckingham County's past.

Joanne Yeck
Kettering, Ohio

PART ONE

PLACES OF BUCKINGHAM COUNTY

Bellmont (Photo by Frances Benjamin Johnston, Library of Congress)

Frontier Elegance: Bellmont

In 1937, when Rosa "Garnett" Williams surveyed the dwelling house at Bellmont for the Virginia Historical Inventory, it was believed to be the oldest existing frame house, not only in Buckingham County, but in Virginia, west of Richmond. Mrs. Williams quickly pointed out that this could not be proved due to the loss of county records. Located roughly eight miles northeast of Dillwyn, off of Route 667 near the Cumberland County line, the home established by David Bell and his wife, Judith Cary, was without a doubt a very early and very elegant entry in what was to become Buckingham County.[1]

When Mrs. Williams surveyed the once lovely Bell home, it had passed its 180th anniversary and the "quaint old house" was in "a very deplorable condition." The decades had taken their toll on the Bell seat and the Great Depression made timely restoration unlikely. Describing the 18th-century house in great detail, she wrote: "It is situated on a knoll, and is surrounded by several of the original old oaks, there are also several boxwood and a large magnolia tree at the end of the porch. A small front porch with a large six panel door opens into a large reception room. . . ." At the time, the house contained "lovely" paneled wainscoting and four of the doors were said to have been imported from England. Shop-made nails, wooden pegs, and hand-sawed timber all bespoke the house's beginnings in what was then the Virginia wilderness. Garnett Williams also noted that the old underground spring and the "milk box" were of special interest. Seventeen steps led down to the spring which was still providing "excellent water" in 1937.[2]

Bellmont's history dated back to an early patent held by Henry Cary of Henrico County. In the spring of 1748, Cary wrote his will, mentioning his daughter, Judith: "Whereas, in consideration of a marriage heretofore had and solemnized between David Bell and my daughter Judith, I have put the said David Bell in the enjoyment and possession of three thousand acres of land situate lying and being upon Hatchers Creek in the county of Albemarle." Cary

Rosa Garnett (Agee) Williams, c. 1920s (ED AYRES COLLECTION)

During the late 1930s, Rosa Garnett (Agee) Williams wrote dozens of surveys about Buckingham County for the Virginia Historical Inventory, including the survey of Bellmont. Unlike her colleague, fieldworker Elizabeth McCraw, Garnett Williams of Dillwyn inconsistently signed her reports, using Rosa G. Williams, Mrs. Garnett Williams, and Garnett Agee Williams. "Garnett" was the daughter of Cornelius "Hamilton" Agee and Rosa Kate Claiborne. The Hamilton Agee family lived at Gravel Hill, not far from the Buckingham Collegiate Female Institute, and close to the old Claiborne home at Cold Comfort. Garnett married Fred Williams, the son of Samuel and Callie (Duncan) Williams. Fred and his brother-in-law, Hamilton "Hambone" Agee, owned and operated a store in Dillwyn. For many years Garnett was Treasurer for Brown's Chapel and lived into her nineties. She and Fred had one son and two grandchildren.

also bequeathed to the couple: fifteen slaves, along with "all the stock of hogs, cattle, horses, mares, utensils of husbandry and all other materials upon the said plantation at the time I so put him in possession thereof."[3]

By March of the following year, Henry Cary was dead and the process of proving his last will and distributing his property began. A complication in the bequest to Judith Cary required her husband to pay £300 to his brother-in-law, Archibald Cary, to settle her inheritance. This David Bell refused to do. Perhaps the Scotsman did not believe that this quarter farm in the western wilderness could possibly be worth £300. Perhaps, he had no ready cash or convenient way to raise it.[4] Ultimately, a compromise was reached between David Bell and Archibald Cary, which may explain the family tradition that Col. Cary "gave" the farm to his sister, Judith.[5] In 1752, Bell signed a quit claim deed for both the land and the slaves, resulting in the subsequent exchange between the siblings which included a transfer of land.[6]

Despite the fact that Henry Cary's will put the Bells "in enjoyment" of 3,000 acres in what was then southern Albemarle County, the couple and their growing family were far from taking pleasure in it. In October of 1755, David Bell and Judith, his wife, were still "of Chesterfield County," living at Warrick, when they deeded 1,000 acres in Albemarle County to Archibald Cary.[7]

Judith Cary, the eventual mistress of Bellmont, was born in Henrico County, Virginia on August 12, 1726. In about 1747, she wed David Bell and they began married life at Warrick, south of the James River near Richmond, in the part of Henrico that was to become Chesterfield County in 1749. There, Henry Cary had established a thriving plantation he called Ampthill and various non-agrarian industries, including a mill and ironworks.[8]

The Bells arrived in Albemarle at the Hatchers Creek farm sometime after 1755. By the spring of 1758, David Bell, Gentleman, and Judith, his wife, were "of Albemarle," living well at Bellmont, enjoying many goods imported from England, including four doors, while their home's more rustic components were created on site.[9]

This elegant life on the frontier was expensive. By the spring of 1758, the Bells had accumulated a crippling debt of £547 to a single source – London Merchants, represented by George Buckhannan and William Hamilton. As a result, David Bell was forced to sell 1,453 acres in Cumberland County, lying

Carved door at Bellmont (PHOTO BY FRANCES BENJAMIN JOHNSTON, LIBRARY OF CONGRESS)

on both sides of Randolphs Creek, which he had purchased from Isaac Bates in 1751. The sale required Judith Bell's consent. Since she could not "conveniently travail to the County Court of Albemarle," which was then located many difficult miles away at Scott's Landing on the James River, the court appointed three Gentlemen – Samuel Jordan, John Cobbs, and John Cannon – to witness Judith Bell's acceptance of the transaction.[10]

David and Judith Bell were not alone in their quickly accumulated debt. Lavish spending was even more prevalent in eastern Virginia, where Judith's brother, Archibald, suffered similar problems resulting from expensive tastes. Eventually, Ampthill, the Cary family seat and the mill at Warwick were sold at the auction block to satisfy Archibald Cary's enormous obligations.[11]

೮೦೦೮

In 1761, it was probably David Bell, Sr. who became the first Clerk of Court in Buckingham County.[12] He died intestate on March 28, 1770, leaving Judith to face the American Revolution as a mature widow. In 1773 and 1774, she was taxed at Bellmont also paying taxes for Benjamin Harrison, believed to be the husband of her daughter, Priscilla.[13] Following the Revolution, in October of 1783, Judith applied for a public claim and received £11.6.8 for her contribution to the cause – 1,420 lbs. of beef.[14]

According to a descendent, Rebecca Bell Branch, Judith was known as "Lady Bell," a nod to her great beauty and aristocratic carriage. The mother of as many as six adult children, her daughters, Judith Cary (Bell) Gist Scott and Elizabeth Cary (Bell) Bates, married and removed to Bourbon County, Kentucky. Their sister, Sarah (Bell) Langhorne Harrison eventually joined them.[15] Judith's son, Henry Bell, was a Vestryman and was made a Magistrate of Buckingham County in August of 1789.[16] Judith long outlived her husband, dying on April 16, 1798. Her son, David Bell, served as executor of her estate.[17]

Over the years, Bellmont's name continued to remember Col. David Bell, though it was increasingly written as "Belmont." According to Garnett Williams' historical survey, the farm was enjoyed by a series of Bell women, passing from Judith to her daughter, Mrs. Harrison, to her daughter, who married a Ligon.[18] By 1826, Theodorick C. Gannaway was the proprietor and Bellmont was no longer owned by a descendant of the Bell family. In 1838, Gannaway sold the land containing the Bell cemetery to family member, Rebecca Bell.[19]

Gannaway was a man of influence in Buckingham. He had served in the War of 1812 and, in the 1840s, he was appointed one of Buckingham's School Commissioners.[20] It was Gannaway's interest and involvement in higher education that made Bellmont the site of a momentous occasion in the county's history. In the winter of 1831, a small group of Buckingham's elite met at the house and planned the construction of Buckingham Female Collegiate Institute. A note written by Dr. J.W. Langhorne documented the event: "Met at Bellmont [the home of Theodorick Carter Gannaway] talked of the school, made a good start, looked at site, and discussed faculty. Should have building up by 1833, next year. Carrol made some sketches – very fair. Mr. Loving and Mr. Alley here to discuss plans."[21]

Following the Civil War, James M. Newman married Theodorick C. Gannaway's daughter, Patsy, and acted as overseer for Bellmont; his detailed farm books and other accounts survive today. These extraordinary primary resources became the basis for a book, *A Way Out of No Way*, in which Dianne Swann-Wright documented the lives of her enslaved ancestors who worked at Bellmont and two other Cary family plantations, Union Hill and Caryswood.[22]

Over the decades, Bellmont's dwelling house became one of the most well-documented structures in Buckingham County. During the 1930s, Buckingham historian Lulie Patteson wrote about "Beautiful Belmont" for *The Farmville Herald*. Waxing romantic, she began: "The rainbow hues of October spreading out on every side, bring out in vivid contrast the glossy green of the lone magnolia and its flanking boxwoods, which guard the front of lovely old Belmont, said to be the oldest frame house west of Richmond."[23]

Miss Patteson's closing was equally wistful, typical of her vivid style: "Funerals, 'wakes' as they were termed in parlance of past years and old customs, have been held in its walls, infancy has sent its first cries beneath its roof, and perchance other brides than Judith have dwelt happily within its rooms, but the old house whispers naught of the past, though we yearn for a glimpse of 'other days than ours.'"[24]

In 1934, Bellmont was included in the Historic American Buildings Survey (HABS). Detailed architectural drawings were made of the house, as well as

Frontier Elegance: Bellmont ~ 9

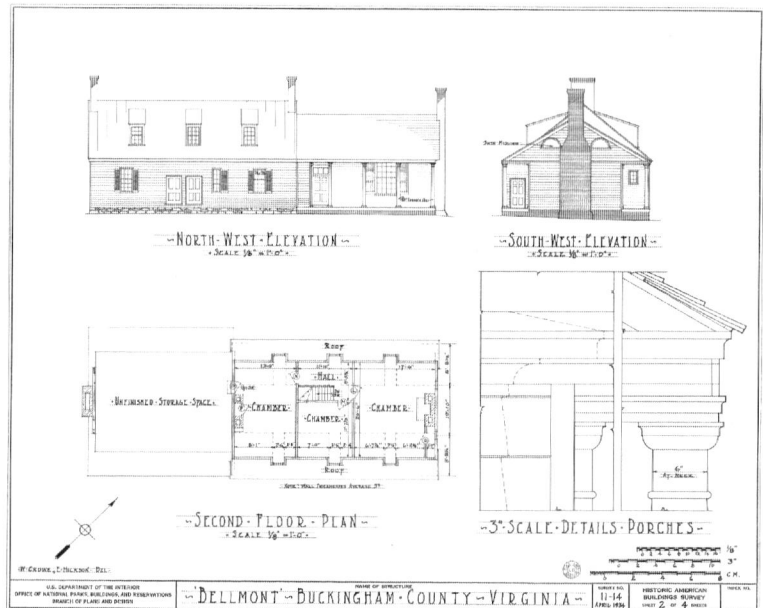

Bellmont (Historic American Buildings Survey, Library of Congress)

three large-format photographs. Judith (Cary) Bell's home has impressive company. The HABS collection, held at the Library of Congress, describes and depicts more than 38,600 structures, covering a wide variety of buildings from homes designed by Frank Lloyd Wright to obscure one-room schoolhouses in the American West. Rosny, a Bolling family property located in Buckingham County, is included.[25]

Bellmont was also documented in the Carnegie Survey of the Architecture of the Old South, photographed by Frances Benjamin Johnston (1864–1952). Seven beautiful images, taken in 1933, recorded Bellmont's surviving exteriors and interiors.[26]

In the late 20th century, when Dr. Margaret A. Pennington sketched Bellmont, the wing of the house had been removed, leaving only the main portion. Today, the house has been modernized and enlarged once more and is the residence of Rickie and Robyn Allen. The street name, Belmont Lane (running off of Route 667), remembers the Colonial home of David and Judith Bell and a deep vein of Buckingham history.[27]

Interior at Bellmont (PHOTO BY FRANCES BENJAMIN JOHNSTON, LIBRARY OF CONGRESS)

NOTES

1   Rosa G. Williams, "Bellmont," Virginia Historical Survey, 4 June 1937, Library of Virginia; Robert Alexander Lancaster, *Historic Virginia Homes and Churches* (New York, NY: Lippincott, 1915), 186–187; Margaret A. Pennington and Lorna S. Scott, *"The Courthouse Burned —," Book I* (Buckingham County, VA: Historic Buckingham, Inc., 2002), 165. The original spelling was likely Bellmont, after its proprietor, David Bell, though the plantation and its dwelling house are also known as Belmont. Newer architectural findings indicate that Bellmont may not be the oldest existing house in Buckingham County. During the 1965 restoration of Dixie, owned for generations by the Spencer family, a cornerstone dated 1741 was discovered in the dwelling's western section. Dixie, located just south of Buckingham Court House on Route 638, sits on land patented by Samuel Glover in 1737. Glover held multiple patents in what was originally Goochland, then Albemarle, and is today Buckingham County. See Genevieve Agee, "'Dixie' – 234 Years Old, *The Farmville Herald*, 4 June 1975, p. 12A; Samuel Glover, multiple patents, Virginia Land Office Patents and Grants Database, Library of Virginia.

2   Williams, "Bellmont."

3   Henry Cary will, 27 May 1748, proved 2 March 1749, Chesterfield County, Virginia, Will Book 1, p. 36; Chris Kraft, "Our Research: Henry Cary II," accessed September 2014, http://worldconnect.rootsweb.ancestry.com/cgi-bin/igm.cgi?op=GET&db=adgedge&id=I877. The use of the following slaves was also given to the Bells: Quash and his wife, Dinah; George and his wife, Belinda; Hector and his wife, Ruthman; Moll ("a young wench"); Joe and Frank ("two lads"); Criss ("a girl"); Sarah ("a negro wench"); and Ruthman's two children and her increase. Part of this bequest went to Cary's grandson, Henry Bell, who was born on June 17, 1745 in Chesterfield County. See Fairfax Harrison, *The Virginia Carys* (NY: The De Vinne Press, 1919), 172–173.

4   Tradition states that David Bell was born in Scotland. See Chris Kraft, "Our Research: David Bell," accessed September 2014, http://wc.rootsweb.ancestry.com/cgi-bin/igm.cgi?op=GET&db=adgedge&id=I875.

5   Pennington and Scott, *"The Courthouse Burned —," Book I*, p. 165.

6   Agnes Evans Gish, *Virginia Taverns, Ordinaries and Coffee Houses* (Westminster, MD: Willow Bend Books, 2005), 43, n 33.

7   A damaged copy of the deed dated October 18, 1755 survived in the Cary family papers. See Cary Family Papers, 1748–1772, Accession # 21434, Library of Virginia. The Cary family is widely documented. For a selected bibliography, see Chris Kraft, "Our Research: Henry Cary, II," ancestry.com, accessed September 2014, http://wc.rootsweb.ancestry.com/cgi-bin/igm.cgi?op=GET&db=adgedge&id=I877.

8   Harrison, *The Virginia Carys*, 85–90; Lancaster, *Historic Virginia Homes and Churches*, 106–110.

9   Williams, "Bellmont."

10   Ruth Sparacio and Sam Sparacio, *Albemarle County, Virginia Deed Book 1758–1761* (Arlington, VA: The Antient Press,1988), 49–50; Albemarle County Deed Book 2, pp. 168–170.

11   Gish, *Virginia Taverns, Ordinaries and Coffee Houses*, 33–35.

12   Jeanne Stinson, compiler, *Early Buckingham County, Virginia Legal Papers, Volume 1, 1765–1806* (Athens, GA: Iberian Publishing Co., 1993), 1.

13   Edythe Rucker Whitley, *Genealogical Records of Buckingham County, Virginia* (Baltimore, MD: Clearfield Co., 2000), 9.

14   Janice L Abercrombie and Richard Slatten, *Virginia Publick Claims, Buckingham* (Athens, GA: Iberian Publishing Company), 21.

15   Kraft, "Our Research: David Bell."

16   Whitley, *Genealogical Records of Buckingham County, Virginia*, 1; "A State of the Commission of the Peace for Buckingham County," *Calendar of Virginia State Papers and Other Manuscripts, August 11, 1792 to December 31, 1793* (Richmond, VA: A.R. Micou, 1886), 439–440.

17   Harrison, *The Virginia Carys*, 90; Robert Kirk Headley, *Genealogical Abstracts from 18th-Century Virginia Newspapers* (Baltimore, MD: Clearfield Co., 2007), 24; Whitley, *Genealogical Records of Buckingham County, Virginia*, 123. In 1795, David Bell, Jr. sold part or all of Bellmont to Thomas Levesay (1,000 acres) and to Thomas Moseley (400 acres). These sales were followed in 1799 by a sale of 6,000 acres to Brett Randolph. In 1812, Henry Cary Bell bought back some of the "Belmont tract," purchasing at least 176 acres from Moseley's estate. It was described as lying on Hatchers Creek, eighteen miles east of Buckingham Courthouse. See Roger G. Ward, *Buckingham County Virginia Records: Land Tax Summaries & Implied Deeds 1782-1814, Volume 1* (Athens, GA: Iberian Publishing Co., 1993), 30.

18   Williams, "Bellmont;" Roger G. Ward, *Buckingham County Virginia Records: Land Tax Summaries & Implied Deeds 1782-1814, Volume 2* (Athens, GA: Iberian Publishing Co., 1994), 211.

19   Ward, *Buckingham County Virginia Records: Land Tax Summaries & Implied Deeds 1782-1814, Volume 2*, pp. 30, 121.

20   *Journal of the House of Delegates of the Commonwealth of Virginia, 1844-1845* (Richmond, VA: 1844), 28; William Shepard, "Some Buckingham Soldiers in the War of 1812," *William and Mary Quarterly* (April 1930), 168–171.

21   William Shepard, "Buckingham Female Collegiate Institute," *William and Mary Quarterly* (April 1940), 171; Joanne L. Yeck, "A Noble Idea: Buckingham Female Collegiate Institute," *"At a Place Called Buckingham,"* (Kettering, OH: Slate River Press,

2011), 65–79. Dr. John Wesley Langhorne was a member of the supervising committee for the Institute. See National Register of Historic Places Inventory Nomination Form, accessed September 2014, http://www.dhr.virginia.gov/registers/Counties/Buckingham/014-0127_Buckingham_Female_Collegiate_Institute_Historic_District_1984_Final_Nomination.pdf. "Carrol" was Carrol Monroe Shepard, a builder, and son of Samuel Shepard, who played a key part in the forming of the Institute. See Shepard, "Buckingham Female Collegiate Institute," *William and Mary Quarterly* (April 1940), 171.

22 Dianne Swann-Wright, *A Way out of No Way* (Charlottesville, VA: University of Virginia Press, 2002).

23 Lulie Patteson, "Beautiful Belmont," *Felixville: A Forgotten Village in Cumberland County, Virginia and Other Sketches* (Farmville, VA: *The Farmville Herald*, 1967), 222–224.

24 Ibid., 223–224.

25 "Historic American Buildings Survey/Historic American Engineering Record/Historic American Landscapes Survey," Library of Congress, accessed September 2014, http://memory.loc.gov/ammem/collections/hh/. Since 1933, HABS has been administrated through cooperative agreements with the National Park Service, the Library of Congress, and the private sector. In Buckingham County, Rosny is typically spelled without an "e." The HABS record, however, reads "Rosney."

26 "Carnegie Survey of the Architecture of the South," Library of Congress, accessed September 2014, http://www.loc.gov/pictures/collection/csas/.

27 Pennington and Scott, *"The Courthouse Burned —," Book I*, p. 165.

In the early 19th century, the Magistrates of Buckingham County were responsible for collecting and distributing tax monies. Funds for the Poorhouse were collected by the Sheriff who was chosen from among the county's Magistrates (a.k.a. Gentleman Justices). In 1819, Phillip Duvall was Sheriff of Buckingham County. His deputy was Joel Ferguson. During 1819–1820, when Buckingham County's first Poorhouse was erected, planter George Chambers was compensated at least three times for his involvement in its construction. On November 20, 1819, Chambers was reimbursed $200.00 from the county coffers. On December 13th, he received an additional $850.00 from William H. Perkins and William Holman. In March of 1820, Perkins paid Chambers another $234.27.

Every scrap of paper relating to Buckingham County generated between the county's inception in 1761 and burning of the courthouse in 1869 is precious. Scant early 19th century reports generated by Buckingham's Overseers of the Poor and receipts concerning the erection of the county's first poorhouse are preserved in the Robert Alonzo Brock Collection housed at The Huntington Library in San Marino, California. In 2003, The Huntington Library and the Library of Virginia cooperated to microfilm the immense collection, making it widely available and more easily accessible to Virginians. (BUCKINGHAM COUNTY, VIRGINIA COURT RECORDS, ROBERT ALONZO BROCK COLLECTION, BR BOX 226, THE HUNTINGTON LIBRARY, SAN MARINO, CA)

Stewards of the Poor:
Buckingham County's Poorhouses

In Colonial days, the Anglican Church was responsible for charity within Virginia's parishes. Individuals provided for the needy and were reimbursed by their Churchwardens. Following the American Revolution, however, county governments were faced with assuming responsibility for the poor, widows, orphans, and the infirm. From feeding the hungry to burying the indigent, Buckingham County's government had a new problem to solve.

An act of the Virginia General Assembly, passed in 1791, formally laid out the duties of the county sheriffs and appointed boards known as the Overseers of the Poor. The sheriff, or an appointed collector of the poor rates (taxes), was ordered to collect funds annually on or by May 1st. Levies were paid in money or tobacco. Likewise, the Overseers were ordered to meet once a year on any day in September to discuss their ongoing responsibilities.[1]

A rare surviving example of the annual proceedings of Buckingham's Overseers of the Poor, dating from 1816, illuminates the county's care of the destitute. That year, Col. Robert Moseley served as President, joined by John Flood, William Bigley, Thomas Garnett, Stephen Chastain, Joseph L. Dillard, William Jones, John Johns, Jesse Holman, Robert Anderson, James Tapscott, and Miles Gipson, Jr. Their accounts indicate that the needy were still under the care of individual men rather than living collectively.[2]

The majority of the recipients listed were women and children, presumably including widows, fatherless children, and orphans. Stephen Chastain, for example, provided for seven women, three sets of children, and only one man. Col. Moseley, Gipson, Bigley, Dillard, Flood, Garnett, Jones, Johns, and Holman all submitted similar lists, enumerating their expenses for the poor to be reimbursed by the county treasury.[3]

Beyond the Overseers, charitable men and women of Buckingham supported the poor and were reimbursed from county coffers. For example, in 1816,

Nathan Ayres was paid $78.25 for the year-long care of one woman. Mary Beckham was paid $30.00 for "keeping" another woman.[4]

Then, in about 1819, Buckingham County decided to create a centralized place to care for the needy. The hope was that by providing them with shelter and an adequate farm, the "paupers" would in part care for themselves by contributing what labor they could towards their upkeep. Buckingham stands out as a forerunner in this new style of public charity. Neighboring Prince Edward County, for example, did not establish their poor farm until the autumn of 1826.[5]

During 1819–1820, George Chambers, a thirty-six-year-old planter living in Buckingham County's Slate River District, received over $1,100 for the construction of Buckingham's "poorhouses."[6] This was a sizeable investment on the part of the county at a time when many families lived in structures valued under $500.[7] It is probable that Chambers supervised the building of a cluster of shelters, commissioned by the county's Overseers of the Poor. He may have provided skilled labor from his own workforce of six adult male slaves.[8] Unlike 19th-century "workhouses" in England or urban "almshouses" in the United States, in rural Virginia a Poorhouse reflected the surroundings. They were typically "poor farms," equipped with multiple structures and supervised by a hired manager.[9]

The precise location of the Chambers-built structures is currently unknown, though the Herman Bōÿe map of Virginia (c.1827) shows Buckingham's Poorhouse sitting about three miles east of Maysville (Buckingham Court House), near Troublesome Creek, not far from today's intersection of Highways 20 and 15.[10] Its proximity to Maysville and the courthouse made it relatively convenient for the Overseers of the Poor and the Board of Supervisors to visit or inspect the facility in conjunction with a meeting at the county seat.

In 1829, Virginia passed a law requiring the Overseers of the Poor in all counties and cities to submit annual reports to the state Auditor of Public Accounts. The results revealed that many counties still did not support poorhouses. When the first submissions were reviewed, fifty-nine counties and two cities reported a functioning poorhouse; forty-three counties and one city lagged behind.[11]

Buckingham County complied with the new law and, on August 31, 1829, Miles Gipson, Agent for the Overseers of the Poor, submitted a summary of their activities during 1800–1829. Statistical in nature, it reported the following:

> Number of whites maintained at the public charge.
> Number of free blacks maintained at the public charge.
> Amount of poor rates levied annually for their support.
> The amount of donations for the use of the poor from individuals or otherwise.
> The number of poor maintained at poor or work houses. . . .
> The number boarded out or otherwise supported. . . .[12]

Interestingly, in Buckingham County, the number of whites supported steadily rose from fifty-one persons in 1809 to ninety persons in 1819. The number of free blacks was comparatively small and steady, ranging from one to three individuals. Over the same ten years, taxes collected rose significantly from $1,899.75 in 1809 to $3,709.20 in 1819.[13]

∽∾

The 1830 Federal census suggests that Miles Gipson was living at, or adjacent, the Poorhouse, acting as Steward or directly supervising the Steward. That year, his household was combined with the residents of the Poorhouse.[14] His wife was Nancy Saunders, daughter of Edward Saunders of Buckingham County. They were married on December 11, 1828 by the popular Methodist minister, Rev. John Ayres.[15]

Ten years later, Gipson may still have been in charge at the Poorhouse, however, his household was enumerated separately. The 1840 census offers not only basic statistics for the "paupers" but also gives a glimpse of the impact on the neighborhood. In the middle of sparsely populated, rural Buckingham County sat the Poorhouse, a comparatively densely populated farm, mixing able-bodied, though destitute, individuals with wards of the county. Women and children far outnumbered men. Three residents were labeled "blind and insane," one was "idiotic and insane," and one simply blind, but in his right mind. That year, five slaves worked for Miles Gipson and/or the Poorhouse.[16]

In 1835, Samuel Ford, President of the Overseers of the Poor, and Miles Gipson, Agent for Poor House Buckingham, signed a report summarizing five years of the county's support of the poor. As Agent, Miles Gipson may have been the assigned liaison between the Overseers while a Steward was hired to manage the day-to-day business at the Poorhouse.[17]

From the inception of Buckingham County's Poorhouse, there was likely a paid superintendent or manager, though these men were not always required to live "on site," as was the case with Thomas Christian. On October 11, 1841, Christian sought aid in his old age and declared his service during the American Revolution. One of Buckingham's oldest citizens, the eighty-one-year-old veteran recounted that he was born in the county and was drafted into the Militia, initially under Capt. Thomas Anderson and later under Capt. Charles Patteson. In the pension application, Miles Gipson attested to the fact that Christian had also served the county for several years as "The Steward of the Poorhouse." Gipson, speaking for the Overseers of the Poor, stated, "Christian never resided at the Poor House, but was permitted to reside in the neighborhood with his family." Now, at the end of his life, Thomas Christian was very poor and lame, himself in need of a little charity.[18]

By the mid-19th century, Rev. John Spencer became the Superintendent of the Poor, serving the county in this capacity for many, many years. In 1850, Spencer claimed only $500 in personal property, his residence likely provided by the county in exchange for his services. Along with a modest salary and whatever he was allotted for his ministry, Spencer supported a wife and eight children.[19]

Rev. John Spencer (1808–1889) was a Baptist minister and had married Elmina Frances Bagby on January 28, 1835. Following his ordination in 1841, he preached at "The Cedars" (Cedar Baptist Church) and, later, at Union Baptist and Wilderness Church, all of which were in the James River Association.[20] Despite self-doubt concerning his abilities and his lack of formal training, Spencer was a dynamic and original preacher who significantly influenced the county with the depth of his faith. During 1853–1854, he impressively converted 178 persons to the Baptist church. Complimenting his ministerial duties,

This report from the Overseers of the Poor in Buckingham County was written in 1835 and submitted to the state government in Richmond, complying with in an 1829 Act of the General Assembly of Virginia. (ROBERT VERNON COLLECTION, LIBRARY OF VIRGINIA)

Spencer would concern himself with the county's poor for over thirty years, taking a direct hand in their welfare, shaping their fate.[21]

In 1850, Spencer was responsible for thirty-five residents living at Buckingham's Poorhouse. That year, on the Federal Population Census, they were not enumerated in separate dwellings, giving the impression that there was one large building, though this was probably never the case. These cohabitating paupers were a mix of single persons, elderly individuals, whites, and free blacks. There were three families with small children. Of the three free blacks, one was very elderly, age 85; one was "idiotic;" and Sallie, from Cumberland County, was blind.[22] Sallie was not the only "roving" or "strolling" pauper living under Rev. Spencer's care. Two other elderly persons were born in Cumberland, and another was born in Powhatan County. Of course, they may have long resided in Buckingham, though paupers crossing county lines for better treatment or any aid at all was a common problem throughout Virginia.[23]

The residents of the Buckingham County Poorhouse were not simply poor; some, like Sallie, were dependent due to mental or physical health problems. Despite the fact that Western Lunatic Asylum had opened in Staunton, Virginia in 1828, the Buckingham County Poorhouse continued to receive "insane" citizens of the county.[24] One such insane pauper was a middle-aged woman who was living there with a man who was likely her husband or brother. In her case, this family member may have acted as her personal caretaker. Another middle-aged man and an elderly woman, age seventy, were also identified as "insane." They had no obvious caretakers.[25]

A report from J.M. Patterson, President of the Overseers of the Poor, to the Virginia Auditor of Public Accounts indicated that, during 1851, Buckingham County continued to assist many individuals not living at the Poorhouse. In addition to the thirty-six persons living on the county farm, twenty others received aid totaling $352.50. The Poorhouse farm produced corn, pork, oats, potatoes, and cotton for consumption and/or sale. Four of the paupers worked on the farm and, according to the report, "several of the females spin, knit, weave &c of those who receive assistance at other places, than Poor-House nearly all do some work."[26]

By 1860, John Spencer had been Superintendent of the Poorhouse for at least a decade. Still supporting a large family, Spencer's worldly goods had in-

Rev. John Spencer (MARY CAROLYN MITTON COLLECTION)

Rev. John Spencer (1808–1889) is buried in an unmarked grave at the Spencer family home, Dixie, located on Route 638 just south of Buckingham Court House. When Rev. Spencer purchased the farm in 1872, Dixie consisted of about 525 acres. He died there on November 1, 1889, age 81 years, 5 months, and 13 days. A brief biography of Spencer is included in George Braxton Taylor's Virginia Baptist Ministers *(4th series). According to Taylor: "For the most part, Mr. Spencer preached to weak, struggling churches. In the course of his ministry he was pastor of the Wilderness, Union and Cedar churches, in the James River Association, and before his career as a preacher was ended his son had succeeded him as pastor of at least one of these places. He did not attend the general meetings of the denomination, and was little known among his brethren of the ministry. He was instrumental in leading some 3,000 persons to Christ and he baptized nearly as many. He was married three times and was survived by his widow and six children. He was a subscriber to the* Religious Herald, *and used to say that it was the only paper he cared to read. He died November 1, 1889, paralysis being the cause of his death. 'His end was calm and peaceful, and loving hands laid him to rest in the joyful hope of the resurrection.'"*

creased in value to $4,500. S.P. Moseley's 1860 enumeration for the Poorhouse separated forty-one paupers into eight households. Currently, it is unclear whether there were actually eight separate structures, though it is probable that there was a "poor village," rather than a single large structure, at Troublesome Creek. Most of the groupings appear to be families. In one case, a thirty-five-year-old woman is enumerated with two elderly men; she may have contributed to her upkeep by acting as their caretaker.[27]

In 1870, the sixty-two-year-old John Spencer was still Superintendent of the Poorhouse. His household included his wife, Elmina (sixty-one, keeping house), and three of his sons: Robert H. Spencer (thirty-eight, a retail dry goods merchant), William O. Spencer (thirty-two, without occupation and identified as "insane"), and Samuel F. Spencer (twenty-four, a farmer). Nelson Spencer, a fifty-eight-year-old "mulatto," also worked at the Poorhouse. Living in a separate household with his wife, Edith, Nelson Spencer's primary occupation was given as farmer.[28]

That year, the "inmates" numbered only seventeen, living on 325 acres.[29] Once again, they were enumerated as though they were living in a single structure. Though the individual circumstances leading to destitution are unknown, in 1870, the census enumerator did not characterize anyone living at the Poorhouse as deaf, dumb, blind, insane, or idiotic. Five of the residents were black, most of them were elderly and some may have been former slaves. The majority of the residents, both black and white, could neither read nor write, which is not surprising. Public education in Virginia was just getting traction and the county was still full of self-supporting, but illiterate, individuals.[30]

෮෬

Beginning in the spring of 1869, reports of the Overseers of the Poor survive in Buckingham's Board of Supervisors Minute Books, providing small details of the county's welfare system. In November of 1870, John Spencer collected a salary of $175.00 for his work associated with the Poorhouse; Nelson Spencer also received wages of $60.00. That fall, accounts were presented to the Board of Supervisors and it was recorded that purchases for paupers totaled $550.00. Foodstuffs were appropriated; the Poorhouse was inspected; and, in December, new regulations for its operation were adopted. The following spring, Spencer received a clothing allotment for the poor and authorization to buy provisions.[31]

In 1875, after decades of public service, Spencer was succeeded as Superintendent of the Poor by James E. Jones, who failed to post bond the next year, and was followed swiftly by William S. Wise. In 1881, Wise was replaced by John J. Moss, a widower, who continued as Superintendent until at least 1887. A carpenter and a farmer, Moss also worked for the county building bridges.[32]

Year in and year out, paupers' accounts were presented at Buckingham Courthouse. Blankets, shoes and, occasionally, coffins were provided for the county's poor. Thirty-five barrels of corn and 800 lbs. of pork were required for the year of 1874. Two young cows were purchased, to provide milk or beef or both. Interestingly, in 1884, the Board of Supervisors passed a resolution refusing to pay the cost of making coffins and the burial expenses of any person except those that had been "approved and endorsed" by the Overseer of the Poor in the district where the individual died.[33]

In 1887, Rev. Spencer was still involved with the welfare of the poor and proposed turning the Poorhouse into a larger working farm, suggesting that the county purchase Wells Farm from Pattie B. Gantt. The price was $3,600, to be paid in five installments. Supervisors A.C. Garnett, Charles A. Scott, W.E. McCraw, and E.G. Cobbs, approved the purchase and, on July 11, 1887, the Buckingham Clerk of Court recorded the deed of conveyance from Mrs. Gantt to the county. The Wells Farm was about five miles from Buckingham Courthouse, located on Ripley's Creek, adjoining the land of George W. Patteson, Thomas S. Bocock, and others.[34] This considerably larger farm, containing about 750 acres, was established in the vicinity of Route 659 (Ranson's Road), at Ripley's Creek, near Walton's Fork.[35]

Concurrently, the old Poorhouse at Octavia was transferred to Ann Eliza Moss from her father, John J. Moss, who purchased the 400-acre farm from Buckingham County. The deed explained that the property repaid Moss' debt to his daughter for her years "of faithful service as his housekeeper" since the death of his wife. Her devotion was valued at $525.00.[36]

United States Postal Map, 1896 (LIBRARY OF CONGRESS)

Several maps over the decades located Buckingham County's poorhouses. The Herman Boye map (c.1827) indicates the first "Poor House" near Troublesome Creek. Charles E. Cassell's Civil War-era map of Buckingham and Appomattox counties shows the "Almshouse" at the same location. Over the years, Buckingham County tax records placed the "old Poor House" three miles east of Buckingham Courthouse at Octavia, which had a post office from 1895–1918. The tract was described as being on the New Canton Road (Highway 15), adjoining the lands of George Nixon. The cemetery once used for the Octavia poorhouse is located behind Buckingham County Preschool which sits on High School Rd (Rt. 690).

Today, the Carter G. Woodson Educational Complex (formerly the Middle-Elementary School Complex) sits near the site. The county's second Poorhouse was located northwest of Buckingham Courthouse near the Manteo post office.

During the early 20th century, the Poorhouse at Ripley's Creek continued to shelter the county's less fortunate individuals. From at least 1909–1920, William L. Patteson acted as Superintendent. He lived on the premises with his wife, Alice, and their children.[37] James Holman, a middle-aged black farmer, also worked at the county home; his wife, Mollie M. Holman, served as the cook.[38] Remains of a graveyard, containing a few pauper burials, marked only by field stones, are still visible off of Route 659. Spending public funds on tombstones would have been unthinkable.[39]

In 1910, one "Almshouse," housing ten paupers, operated in Buckingham County. Interestingly, the surrounding counties, with the exception of the more densely populated Albemarle, showed signs that a Poorhouse as a solution to public-supported charity was on the wane. That year, a report recorded the following number of county-supported paupers in Buckingham's neighboring counties: Albemarle (thirty-six), Nelson (seventeen), Appomattox (ten), Prince Edward (seven), Cumberland (two), and Fluvanna (eight). Powhatan County no longer supported an Almshouse.[40]

In 1920, the Buckingham Board of Supervisors decided to cease farming at the Poorhouse at Ripley's Creek. Their minutes state: "Motion by Mr. Guthrie, seconded by Mr. Word, that we will not attempt to farm the county farm as heretofore & we will sell all surplus stock as soon as the present crops are secured, motion carried by unanimous vote of the Board."[41] That year, just six paupers were living at the county home, four of whom appear on the Federal census. The taxpayers' burden was $143.76 per individual for six months. The overseer was paid $300 annually.[42] By 1922, the county was renting out part of the farm.[43]

Ten years later, as the Great Depression hit bottom, the Buckingham Board of Supervisors cut the monthly pauper allowance to $1.00 per person. Accounts from merchants providing provisions for the county home were to be reviewed quarterly. At this juncture, the Board of Supervisors was committed to giving the taxpayers some relief, pledging "economy in every possible way so long as consistent with good government."[44]

On March 14, 1939, Buckingham County's Poorhouse Farm was sold at public auction, ending a style of charity that had lasted nearly 120 years. The highest bidders for the property were Burruss Land and Lumber Company, which paid $1,000 for the timber, and V.E. Jones, who paid $1,515 for the remaining 450 acres, which included structures valued at $575.[45]

Across the decades, dozens of needy men, women, and children had found some relief from destitution under Buckingham County's organized charity. Several men had made a career of managing the Poorhouse, particularly Rev. John Spencer, who offered the comfort of faith as well as shelter and food. The early 19th-century notion of a Poorhouse, populated with virtually incarcerated "paupers" and "inmates," had slowly evolved to a county-operated farm of significant value, and finally gave way to more modern, less communal, forms of welfare.

NOTES

1   William Waller Hening, *Statutes at Large, Volume XIII* (Philadelphia, PA: Thomas Desilver, 1823), 262–264. For a concise social history of the treatment of Virginia's poor prior to the Civil War consult James D. Watkinson, "Rogues, Vagabonds, and Fit Objects the Treatment of the Poor in Antebellum Virginia," *Virginia Cavalcade*, Winter 2000, pp. 16–29.

2   "Proceedings of the overseers of the poor, 1816," Collection of Records of Virginia Courts, 1687–1898, County Courts Buckingham (only) Part VIII of VIII, Sheriff's Papers; Lists of Insolvent Lands; Taxes; Proceedings; Overseers of the Poor; Receipts; Misc. Records, Robert Alonzo Brock Collection, Box 226-A, Miscellaneous reels 4615 and 4616, Library of Virginia. This report includes the names of Buckingham citizens receiving aid. Each Overseer listed individuals he supported, with a dollar amount assigned to each recipient.

3   Ibid.

4   Ibid. In 1820, Mary Beckham was living in northern Buckingham County with another woman. One of them was age 26–44, the other was over 45. See Federal Population Census, Buckingham County, Virginia, 1820.

5   Melvin Patrick Ely, *Israel on the Appomattox* (New York, NY: Vintage Books, 2005), 190–191.

6   Collection of Records of Virginia Courts, 1687–1898, County Courts Buckingham (only) Part VIII of VIII, Library of Virginia. From 1850–1930, the names of paupers in Buckingham County can be found on the annual Federal Population Census. Other lists are preserved at the Library of Virginia in the files of the Auditor of Public Accounts. According to the Library, "Beginning in 1840 the reports (from Overseers of the Poor) become more detailed and by the 1850s the reports contain the names of the poor and often information on ages, physical condition, and morals. Years covered are 1800–1864, 1871–1881, 1884–1907, 1909." See "Local Government Expenses–Overseers of the Poor," Auditor of Public Accounts (1776–1928), Library of Virginia.

7   Buckingham County Personal Property Tax, 1815, Library of Virginia.

8   Federal Population Census, Buckingham County, Virginia, 1820.

9   Over the years, these managers also were referred to as stewards, overseers, or superintendents. They may or may not have lived at the Poorhouse.

10   Marianne M. McKee, "The Wood-Bōÿe County Maps of Virginia, *The Virginia Genealogical Society Newsletter* (May–June 1995), 1–2.

11   "Local Government Expenses–Overseers of the Poor." While the law directing Overseers of the Poor to report to the state Auditor of Public Accounts was not in force until 1829, the first reporting period was retroactive to January 1, 1800.

12   Ibid.

13   Ibid.

14   Federal Population Census, Buckingham County, Virginia, 1830. In 1819, Miles Gipson (a.k.a. Gibson) was Miles Gipson, Junior. His father, Miles Gipson, died at age 81 on April 3, 1822. Henceforth, Gipson dropped the Junior. See *Richmond Enquirer*, 15 April 1822, p. 3.

15   *Richmond Enquirer*, 20 December 1828, p. 3.

16   Federal Population Census, Buckingham County, Virginia, 1840. It is not known how long Miles Gipson served as Agent for the Overseers of the Poor or if he directly managed the Poorhouse. In 1816, he served as an Overseer of the Poor and may have for several years. Between 1821 and 1835, Gipson served as Agent for the Poorhouse and, in 1848, he or his estate sold 92 acres, described as "of Saunders," to the Poorhouse. His wife was Nancy (Saunders) Gipson. See Roger G. Ward, *Land Tax Summaries & Implied Deeds 1841–1870, Volume 3* (Athens, GA: Iberian Publishing Company, 1995), 110. Miles Gipson (a.k.a. Gibson) died on April 2, 1849; his will was recorded after Buckingham County's courthouse fire. See Buckingham County Will Book 1, p. 40; Rosa G. Williams, "The Will of Miles Gibson," Virginia Historical Inventory, 18 January 1938, Library of Virginia.

17   "Local Government Expenses–Overseers of the Poor Overseers."

18   Edythe Johns Rucker Whitley, *Genealogical Records of Buckingham County* (Baltimore, MD: Clearfield, 2000), 54.

19   Federal Population Census, Buckingham County, Virginia, 1850.

20   George Braxton Taylor, *Virginia Baptist Ministers, 4th Series* (Lynchburg, VA: J.P Bell Company, Inc., 1913), 55–56.

21   Randy Kidd and Jeanne Stinson, *Lost Marriages of Buckingham County Virginia* (Athens, GA: Iberian Publishing Company, 1992), 6; Charles Henry Spencer, editor, "The Diary of John Spencer" (Unpublished manuscript, transcribed 1943), Mary Carolyn Mitton Collection.

22   Federal Population Census, Buckingham County, Virginia, 1850.

23   Federal Population Census, Buckingham County, Virginia, 1850; Watkinson, "Rogues, Vagabonds, and Fit Objects the Treatment of the Poor in Antebellum Virginia," 20.

24   When Western Lunatic Asylum began admitting patients on July 24, 1828, its capacity was quickly overwhelmed. As a result, the Court of Directors limited admissions to patients "who were either dangerous to society from their violence, or those who were offensive to its moral sense by their indecency and to those cases of derangement where there is reasonable ground to hope that the afflicted may be restored." It is likely that the "insane" occupants of Buckingham County's Poorhouses were not in their right

mind but not dangerous to society. See "Western State Hospital," Virginia Department of Behavioral Health and Developmental Services, accessed September 2014, http://www.wsh.dbhds.virginia.gov/history.htm; "A Guide to the Records of Western State Hospital, 1825-2000," Library of Virginia, accessed September 2014, http://ead.lib.virginia.edu/vivaxtf/view?docId=lva/vi00937.xml.

25 Federal Population Census, Buckingham County, Virginia, 1850.

26 "Local Government Expenses–Overseers of the Poor Overseers."

27 Federal Population Census, Buckingham County, Virginia, 1860.

28 Federal Population Census, Buckingham County, Virginia, 1870.

29 Buckingham County Land Tax, 1871, Library of Virginia. The 1871 Buckingham County Land Tax locates the Poorhouse on the New Canton Road.

30 Federal Population Census, Buckingham County, Virginia, 1870.

31 Jeanne Stinson, *Buckingham County Virginia Board of Supervisors Minute Book 1870–1887* (Athens, GA: Iberian Publishing Co., 1994), 6–7. Similar reports of the Overseers of the Poor covering their work prior to 1869 were destroyed in the burning of the Buckingham County courthouse, wiping out records which would have illuminated the evolution of the county's care of the poor.

32 Ibid., 33, 36, 53, 60.

33 Ibid., 23, 59–60, 75.

34 Ibid., 89.

35 Buckingham County Deed Book 6, pp. 17–18. An 1886 deed conveyed Wells Farm from George and Kate Patteson to Pattie B. Gantt. The Buckingham County Land Tax records for 1889 indicate that the farm consisted of three parcels containing 125 ½ acres, 204 ¾ acres, and 398 acres. See Buckingham County Deed Book 5, pp. 352–353; Buckingham County Land Tax, 1889, Library of Virginia.

36 Buckingham County Deed Book 3, p. 216; Buckingham County Land Tax, 1889. In 1880, Eliza Moss was enumerated as housekeeper, living with her widowed father, John J. Moss, and her brother, William. In 1919, Ann Eliza Moss' property was still known as the "Old Poor House Farm." That year, she still owned 172 ½ acres. In 1920, a fraction of the farm, which included 40 acres and structures valued at $125.00, was purchased by Miss Mary Hocker and William Hocker of Clifton Forge, Virginia. In 1940, Mary Hocker, non-resident of Buckingham County, still owned the 40 acres. See Buckingham County Land Tax, 1919, Buckingham Courthouse; Buckingham County Land Tax, 1940, Buckingham Courthouse.

37 Federal Population Census, Buckingham County, Virginia, 1910, 1920; Board of Supervisors Minutes, Buckingham County, Virginia, 1909, p. 331, Buckingham Courthouse.

38   Federal Population Census, Buckingham County, Virginia, 1920.

39   Janice J. R. Hull, *Buckingham Burials, Volume II* (Westminster, MD: Willow Bend, 2002), 108.

40   *Paupers in Almshouses: 1910* (Washington, DC: Government Printing Office, 1915), 78. In 1910, the Federal government released statistics comparing Almshouses across the country. The report placed Buckingham County's Poorhouse at the Manteo post office, located in the western part of the county, near the James River. See Ibid.

41   Board of Supervisors Minute Book, Buckingham County, Virginia, 1920, p. 20, Buckingham Courthouse.

42   Ibid., p. 36.

43   Board of Supervisors Minute Book, Buckingham County, Virginia, 1922, p. 109, Buckingham Courthouse.

44   Board of Supervisors Minute Book, Buckingham County, 1932, p. 163, Buckingham Courthouse.

45   Board of Supervisors Minute Book, Buckingham County, 1939, p. 403, Buckingham Courthouse. In 1940, the address for Poor House Farm was at Howardsville. See Buckingham County Land Tax, 1940.

"Last Crossing of the Scottsville Ferry," 1907 (SCOTTSVILLE MUSEUM, SCOTTSVILLE, VA)

This photo of the Scottsville Ferry, attributed to local photographer William E. Burgess, captures the last days of ferry crossings at the Horseshoe Bend. Looking towards the Albemarle shore, the house at the top of the hill is Mount Walla, once owned by Peter Field Jefferson, son of Randolph Jefferson, and the President's nephew. In the lower right corner of the ferry stands the perpetually sociable Samuel R. Gault, who served as Scottsville's postmaster from 1883 to1939. Locally, Gault was known as "Mr. Scottsville."

    For over a century and a half, ferry travel across the James River connected the low lands of Snowden (Buckingham County) and Scott's Landing/Scottsville (Albemarle County). The new steel-girdered bridge, with its noisy plank road, was efficient, convenient, and modern, yet it lacked a certain charm associated with the ferry days. Virginia Moore in Scottsville on the James lamented the march of progress, writing: "No more hallooing George Thomas to bring his flatboat across to the other shore, shouts meaning, 'I'm here! Pick me up!' No more the splash of a pole plunged and replunged into the muddy James. Something was lost forever, but something was promised. And in a curious new way the bridge reaffirmed Scottsville's ancient connection with the river."

Ferrying across the James River

In 1907, the wood-planked bridge connecting Buckingham County and Scottsville was completed and the last ferry ran from the tip of Buckingham's Horseshoe Bend, heading northward across the James River. Marking the end of a distinctive style of transportation, the Scottsville Ferry was just one of many making a final run.

Established about 1745, the ferry originally ran from Daniel Scott's landing on the north bank to what would soon become Peter Jefferson's landing at Snowden on the south bank. Snowden's ferry house included an ordinary, offering food and ardent spirits. In the mid-18th century, ferries were the business of the Crown of England and the Virginia Assembly granted the permission to operate them and determined fares.

Beginning in February of 1745, Daniel Scott was allowed to run a boat from his land across the river to what was then still part of a vast Albemarle County.[1] Albemarle's new courthouse was located on Scott's land, making this ferry particularly vital. Fares were established at three pence for a man and three pence for a horse. Carriages and drivers were charged the same. Annually, Albemarle County paid Daniel Scott 1,000 lbs. of tobacco "for keeping a ferry at the courthouse." Eventually, Scott split this compensation with attorney William Battersby, who kept the landing on the southside.[2]

By 1750, Peter Jefferson owned the southside landing and the ordinary was leased to innkeeper, Richard Murray. Murray paid rent to Jefferson (and later to his estate) and pocketed the fares and proceeds from the ordinary.[3] The ferry thrived during the years when Albemarle County Courthouse was located at Scott's Landing. In 1761, traffic was likely reduced when Buckingham County was created and Albemarle's county seat was moved to Charlottesville. Yet, folks needed to cross the James River and the ferry landing at Snowden passed to the next owner, Peter Jefferson's younger son, Randolph Jefferson. Years later, the southside landing became the property of the Harris family, followed by

This image of the completed bridge at Scottsville was captured sometime between 1908 and 1925. (LARRY LAMB COLLECTION)

the Moon family, ultimately linking Buckingham and the bustling town of Scottsville.[4]

∞⌘

Operating any ferry came with risks, particularly when the James River flooded or when winter presented the hazard of ice floes. One heroic, yet devastating, story was recorded in *The Scottsville Register* on January 14, 1871.

> One of the most exciting and distressing sights we ever witnessed, was on Christmas morning, at the Scottsville Ferry landing. The ferryman, Mr. Peter V. Foland, assisted by young Willie Patteson, had started to carry two men across the river, cutting the ice as they went, and after getting within 75 yards of the other shore, they discovered, to their horror, that the ice thus cut loose was slowly moving upon them, and in a moments time came upon the boat, when they jumped out upon the ice and one of the men (Brightberry Toney) being more excited than the rest, ran upon the ice and broke through, drowning in a few minutes. Mr. Foland, Willie Patterson, and the remaining man

(although they had fallen into the water) succeeded in climbing upon a large piece of ice and remained upon it until the citizens on this side had carried a large number of planks from the shop of the J.R. & K. Co., (which fortunately was nearby) and laying them across each other, formed a walk to them, by which means they affected their escape from their perilous position.

It is our duty to add that our young friend, Mr. William S. Beal on this occasion, was most efficient, and deserves all praise. The boat on which the party attempted to cross the river and which was sunk by the ice, was found by Mr. John Butler, a few days since, one mile below town; but the body of the misfortunate (drowned) man has not been seen.[5]

༄༅༃

The ferry at Snowden was just one of many that came and went during the 18th and 19th centuries, carrying livestock, people, and goods across the James River, connecting Buckingham County to Amherst, Nelson, Albemarle, and Fluvanna counties on the other bank. As early as 1750, there was a ferry at Seven Islands on the south side of the river; there, the Cocke family of Bremo, Fluvanna County, received their mail.[6] Following Buckingham County's establishment in 1761, Joseph Cabell, who later served Buckingham in the House of Burgesses, was permitted a ferry in 1764. It ran from his land in Buckingham at Sion Hill across the James River (then known as the Fluvanna River) to his own land in Amherst County near Bowman's warehouse.[7] By 1769, Benjamin Howard, who resided on Rock Island Creek in Buckingham, was permitted a ferry from his land to the land of Neil Campbell, in the county of Albemarle. The fares remained three pence for man or horse.[8] In 1776, William Cannon, one of Buckingham's earliest residents and sheriffs, established a ferry on his land near the Buckingham/Cumberland line. Unsurprisingly, it was called Cannon's Ferry, and in 1793, on the bluff above it, New Canton would be incorporated.[9]

These were rope ferries, requiring a great deal of manpower to operate. Minnie Lee McGehee describes them in her article, "Fords, Ferries, Bridges and Signposts: Early Travel in Fluvanna":

Hatton Ferry, c. 1910
(EDNA NAPIER NEES COLLECTION, SCOTTSVILLE MUSEUM, SCOTTSVILLE, VA)

Edna Napier Nees provided this caption for the photo above to Scottsville Museum: "The Hatton Ferry, from the Buckingham Shore, ca. 1910; George A. Tapscott in front buggy; J.B. Tindall and Eugene Layne in rear buggy; Mrs. Sarah Frances Napier, mother of ferryman, Joe Napier, stands with her grandchildren/children of Joe Napier."

Standing at the ferry's edge, Sarah Frances Ripley Napier (1833–1920) is accompanied by her three grandchildren: Ethel "Minnie" Napier (b. 1904), William "Buster" Napier (b. 1906), and Monroe Napier (b. 1908/1909). When this photo was taken, Sarah's son and the father of the children, William Joseph Napier (1871–1947), was the ferryman at Hatton.

Over the years, George Allen Tapscott (1850–1935), pictured here, wore many hats including Civil War soldier, farmer, surveyor of Albemarle County, census enumerator, school teacher, merchant, corn miller, Freemason, and ferry master at Hatton. In short, Tapscott was the epitome of a multifaceted man of Buckingham County.

Beginning in 1906, Buckingham County native, James Benson Tindall (1877–1945), rented Brown's Store located on the Albemarle shore. Founded by James A. Brown, the crossing was known as Brown's, Brown's Store, and Brown's Landing. In September of 1914, J.B. Tindall purchased both the ferry and store from Brown's descendants. Tindall's business partner and neighbor, John "Eugene" Layne (1887–1960), was a Buckingham County native.

Upriver from the crossing was stretched a high cable from bank to bank between tall poles, about 20 feet above the water, with the cable several hundred feet upriver of the flat deck of the ferry. A rope (sometimes two ropes) connected the wooden platform or boat for passengers to the high up-river cable, and the ferryboat, caught at an angle by the current, crossed the river.[10]

The ferryman, who was on call twenty-four hours a day, seven days a week, collected the tolls for humans and freight. In addition to horses, he often ferried wagons, buggies, farm animals, lumber, and loads of various crops. As the 18th century progressed and Buckingham's population steadily grew, ferries dotted the county's long exposure on the James River. Many were public and sprang up during the 1790s when new river towns like New Canton and Wilson Cary Nicholas' Warren were incorporated. On December 11, 1789, the Virginia General Assembly permitted a ferry to operate from the lands of Wilson Cary Nicholas, in the county of Albemarle, across the James River (then the Fluvanna River), to the land of John Hardy, on the opposite shore, in the county of Buckingham. The price, at that time, for man or horse remained three-pence.[11] In 1791, John Horsley's ferry was established in conjunction with the founding of Diuguidsville at Bent Creek.[12]

The revised Virginia Code mentioned several ferries operating with landings in Buckingham. By 1819, the price to cross the river had risen to four pence for a man or a horse. The ferries included one from John Scott's to the lands of Randolph Jefferson (the original Scott's Ferry), one from Thomas Anderson's landing to Howard's landing, one from the land of John Cabell (Buckingham) to his own land on the opposite shore, one from the land of Joseph Cabell Megginson (Buckingham), who was Joseph Cabell's grandson, to his own land on the opposite shore. Additionally, John Nicholas operated a ferry across the Slate River, not far from where it entered the James River.[13] Other ferries were private, built and abandoned at the convenience of the planters who established them.

These ferries were a major improvement over the natural ford, which was viable in low water, but not so practical when the river rose in depth. Ferries were often unreliable and did not operate for various reasons: the river was

Hatton Ferry, 1942 (JEREMY WINFREY COLLECTION)
Buckingham County brothers, Joseph Hill Winfrey Sr. (in uniform) and Mathias Bolling Winfrey (in suit, with pipe) ride the Hatton Ferry.

Hatton Ferry, c. 1942 (ANNIE TAPSCOTT WINFREY COLLECTION, COURTESY JEREMY WINFREY)
In 1940, the Tindall family deeded the Hatton Ferry to the State of Virginia. At that time, Harvey Briddle (1891–1966) was the ferry operator. This poignant, lone ferryman may be Mr. Briddle, who, though lame and unable to swim, once saved the ferry during high water, following it downstream in a canoe.

too high, too low, flooded or frozen. When the ferries did function, however, they saved the traveler or merchant not only the wear and tear of fording the river, but also potentially miles of excess travel. While they were safe enough, the river itself could be dangerous, even deadly. Mrs. Louisa Cocke of Bremo in Fluvanna County wrote in her diary of one terrifying Sunday trip to Buckingham County's Trinity Presbyterian Church in New Canton. Sitting peacefully in her carriage, as the horses stepped onto the boat, the swift current pushed it, carriage, and passengers towards Richmond, seriously frightening, but not harming Mrs. Cocke.[14]

In addition to providing transportation, ferry landings often offered both travelers and locals small service centers. There might be an ordinary, providing lodging, food, and a very welcome tap room. Sometimes there was a post office. In 1800, a post office was established at New Canton. Local planters, including William Woodson and Thomas Pittman, served as postmasters in the early years. Beginning in 1870, a post office operated at Bolling's Landing. Postmasters there included John W. Brown, Thomas D. Kidd, Francis N. Maxey, Jr., and Richard H. Payne.[15]

Initially, Warren maintained a post office on both sides of the James River. Between 1827 and 1845, the post office at the Buckingham landing was dubbed Warren Ferry. Postmasters James Tapscott, Randolph Patteson, and James L. Wyndown kept the mail flowing there.[16] Later in the century, mail was collected only on the Albemarle bank. Buckingham memorialist, Emily Maxey Jenkins, remembered her grandfather crossing the river at Warren Ferry for over thirty years, picking up the mail in Albemarle and delivering it to Buckingham.

> I remember his many buggies and loved to ride in them with him. In the winter he heated a brick or bricks and placed [them] in the foot of the buggy. He picked the mail up at the little post office in Warren which was close to the Warren train station. He was a messenger of the sick, delivering items from neighbor to neighbor, and a general help to all on his route.[17]

Hatton Ferry, 1962 (PHOTO BY WIRT A. CHRISTIAN, LIBRARY OF VIRGINIA)

In 1962, Raymond D. Hackett served as Hatton Ferry's ferryman. In 1972, Hurricane Agnes damaged the ferry, threatening to bring service to an end; however, it was preserved. Today, Hatton Ferry still operates annually from April through October, the last poled ferry in the United States.

Hatton Ferry, 1962 (PHOTO BY WIRT A. CHRISTIAN, LIBRARY OF VIRGINIA)

Warren Ferry, 1962 (Photo by Wirt A. Christian, Library of Virginia)

In 1962, M. F. Martin served as the operator of Warren Ferry. In 1972, Hurricane Agnes permanently destroyed the historic ferry, ending an era of transportation at that place. People, animals, and vehicles had crossed the James River at Warren since 1789.

Warren Ferry, 1962 (Photo by Wirt A. Christian, Library of Virginia)

Hatton Ferry, situated between Scottsville and Warren, was a relative latecomer on the James River and, as a result, its history is the best documented of all the Buckingham County ferries. Ironically, after Albemarle merchant James A. Brown and the Gantt family cooperated to propose the ferry in 1870, Buckingham citizens living near the southside landing resisted the idea of ferry traffic across their property and took their complaint to the county Board of Supervisors.[18] Rather than fight, Brown switched his locale and established his ferry a couple of miles upstream, where it remains today. Originally known as Brown's, Brown's Store, or Brown's Landing, in the 1890s, the road to the river was referred to as Brown's Landing Road. Today, it is called Hatton Ferry Road.[19] Inexplicably, the crossing was ultimately renamed, Hatton Ferry, after Frank Hatton (1846–1894), who had no connection to central Virginia. An American politician and newspaperman, he served as Postmaster General in the cabinet of President Chester A. Arthur.[20]

As the decades progressed, bridges gradually replaced ferries and, in 1972, extreme flooding produced by Hurricane Agnes destroyed Warren Ferry. At the dawn of the 21st century, all but Hatton Ferry were gone. Now the last poled ferry in the United States, located just upstream from Scottsville, Hatton Ferry holds on by a tenuous thread maintained by ongoing private support. It remains a window into the past, though automobiles and tourists have replaced churchgoers and buggies. Annually, between April and October, the ferry is operational and continues to conjure a bygone era and a slower, perhaps more romantic, life on the river.

NOTES

1   William Waller Hening, *Statutes at Large, Volume V*, 364–365, accessed August 2014, http://vagenweb.org/hening/vol05-21.htm.

2   Albemarle County Order Book 1744–1748, 25 July 1745, p. 33.

3   John Harvie, Peter Jefferson Estate Account Book I, p. 36, The Huntington Library, San Marino, CA.

4   Joanne L. Yeck, *The Jefferson Brothers* (Kettering, OH: Slate River Press, 2012), 13–18. Eventually, Randolph Jefferson's son, Peter Field Jefferson, operated the ferry landing on the Scottsville side of the James River, followed by his grandson, Peter V. Foland, who would be the last owner of the Scottsville Ferry. See "Mount Walla," National Register of Historic Places, VLR 13 September 2000/NRHP 22 November 2000, accessed August 2014, http://www.dhr.virginia.gov/registers/Counties/Albemarle/298-0009%20-%20Mount%20Walla%20-%202000%20-%20Final%20Nomination.pdf.

5   "William 'Billy' Samuel Beal," Scottsville Museum, accessed August 2014, http://scottsvillemuseum.com/portraits/homeML07cdML01.html.

6   Minnie Lee McGehee, "Fords, Ferries, Bridges and Signposts: Early Travel in Fluvanna," *Fluvanna History* (Bremo Bluff, VA: Fluvanna Historical Society, 2009), 19.

7   Alexander Brown, *The Cabells and Their Kin* (Boston, MA: Houghton, Mifflin & Co., 1895), 142.

8   William Waller Hening, *Statutes at Large, Volume VIII*, 368-369, accessed August 2014, http://vagenweb.org/hening/vol08-18.htm.

9   McGehee, "Fords, Ferries, Bridges and Signposts," 19.

10 Ibid., 15–16.

11 William Waller Hening, *Statutes at Large, Volume XIII* (Philadelphia, PA: Thomas Desilver, 1823), 48.

12 Ibid., 273.

13 *The Revised Code of the Laws of Virginia, Volume II* (Richmond, VA: Thomas Ritchie, 1819), 249.

14 McGehee, "Fords, Ferries, Bridges and Signposts," 19.

15 U.S. Appointments of U. S. Postmasters, 1832–1971, ancestry.com; Jim Forte, "Postal History," accessed August 2014, http://www.postalhistory.com/postoffices.asp?task=display&state=VA&county=Buckingham.

16 Edith F. Axelson, *Virginia Postmasters and Post Offices 1789–1832* (Athens, GA: Iberian Publishing Company, 1991), 29–31.

17 Emily Maxey Jenkins, "The Warren Ferry," n.d., author's collection.

18 John Hammond Moore, "The Ferries of Albemarle," *The Magazine of Albemarle County History* (Albemarle County, VA: Albemarle County Historical Society, 1984), 12–19.

19 Land Contract, from Mrs. Sarah Allen to Mrs. Mahala Harris, Allen Family Papers, Mss1 AL546 c, Virginia Historical Society. The land contract mentions "a certain tract of land lying in the county of Buckingham in the state of Virginia, and described as lying immediately on the Brown's Landing road and adjoining the lands of Arthur Moseley and others." In 1892, Mahala Harris paid taxes on the 519 acre farm described as being on Brown's Landing Road.

20 "The Hatton Ferry," accessed August 2014, www.thehattonferry.org.

Buckingham Springs (RICHARD MORRIS COLLECTION)

"Going to the Springs" in Buckingham County

In the 19th century, "going to the springs" was an integral part of the life of Virginia planters. Virginians went to socialize. They went to heal what ailed them. Many of them journeyed west, to the mountains, escaping the summer heat. The lavish resorts in Bath County, Fauquier County, or Greenbrier County's White Sulphur Springs come to mind, complete with their scenic backdrops, expansive grounds, and wealthy clientele. There was a time, however, when Buckingham County had a White Sulphur Springs of its own and the local gentry visited regularly, seeking the same rest, repair, and society of the larger resorts.[1]

Natural springs were scattered throughout Buckingham County, though few developed health resorts. Garnett Williams, who surveyed several Buckingham County springs for the Virginia Historical Survey, wrote that Bolling Springs "is said to have been the only watering place for man or beast between New Canton and Buckingham [Court House] in early days. It is also said that an acre of land was given to the public to be used for camping over night or anything that the public might need it for."[2]

One farm, called Pleasant Springs and located just south of Sprouses Corner, was named for the numerous springs not far from the dwelling house. Indian Springs, located just north of Gold Hill on Highway 15, was named for the many, long-abandoned, purported Indian trails running through the property. Mrs. Williams' survey for the site of Indian Springs commented on the impressive number of "very large springs on the place." In 1937, one was still in use.[3]

Additionally, Physic Springs was once a well-known health resort; the waters there were particularly renowned to cure diseases of the skin.[4] In 1839, Garland Brown, J.G. Brown, Elijah G. Hanes, and Samuel Taylor incorporated the Physic Springs Company expressly "for the purpose of improving and carrying on a house or houses of entertainment for visitors and invalids who may resort" there.[5]

Even into the 20th century, new springs were announced in Buckingham County, most notably Buckingham Lithia Springs, located near New Canton. In 1904, *The Times-Dispatch* announced plans for a new health resort in the northeastern corner of the county:

LITHIA SPRINGS.
Company Secures Them and Will Establish Health Resort.
NEW CANTON, VA. Dec. 28. – The old lithia springs on the place of Mr. Reuben Boatwright, great-grandfather of President F.W. Boatwright, L.L.D. of Richmond College, have been procured by a number of capitalists and business men, who formed the Buckingham Lithia Springs Company. They are now rapidly shipping this fine water to various parts of the United States, while the grounds are being prepared and laid off for hotels, cottages and sanitariums to supply the many demands for accommodations from people suffering with all forms of stomach, liver and kidney troubles.

In 1777 Mr. Reuben Boatwright found these bold streams bubbling from rock basins in the side of large hills filled with minerals, and for one hundred and twenty-seven years they have been supplying their healing waters to suffering humanity. These waters have been analyzed and are endorsed and prescribed by physicians and used by sufferers throughout the country.[6]

The announcement was hopeful, but the company failed to attract the necessary investors and a large resort was never built on the Boatwright property.[7]

෴

The biggest, best-known, and longest lasting of the spas was Buckingham Springs, located in the southeastern part of the county. In 1834, Samuel Morris purchased 360 acres, known as Green Springs, from the estate of his mother. In addition to farm land, the property included outcroppings of granite and four natural springs, two of which were sulphur springs, containing lithia water with significant amounts of lithium salts such as lithium carbonate or lithium chloride.[8]

Natural lithia springs are relatively rare, while the potential range of healthful benefits has long been believed to be very broad, making the waters valuable and sought-after. In the 19th century, physicians recommended lithia water for an astounding variety of ailments including depression, rheumatism, eczema, and gout.[9] Buckingham Lithia Springs, at New Canton, advertised in Richmond's *The Times-Dispatch* unabashedly announcing that its water cured: "Dyspepsia, Rheumatism and skin disease, Kidney and Bladder Trouble, Beautifies the Complexion. Chronic cases desired."[10] While *The Farmville Herald* noted that Dr. N.C. Sheppard of Richmond, Virginia, "has great faith in the sulphur water [of Buckingham County] and not only comes up to drink it, but has it shipped to him to Richmond." Over the decades, testimonials of positive results similar to these, rather than scientific studies, drove the consumption of lithium-rich waters.[11]

During 1834–1836, the enterprising Samuel Morris created a resort at what became known as Buckingham Springs. The resort was an immediate success, in part due to satisfied customers who experienced the curative powers of the sulphur water and, in part, due to Samuel's genial personality. According to his descendant, Richard Morris, III, "He was a happy, sociable man who genuinely liked to please his guests."[12]

Samuel Morris initially built a long hotel and cottages, which accommodated families, while enhancing the access to the two sulphur springs. One he developed for drinking and the other he designed for bathing.[13] According to Buckingham County historian, Lulie Patteson, one spring was paved with stone, sporting a "pretentious pavilion." She went on to note that "the springs were enclosed within [an] immense stone basin, cut by Samuel Hardwich, a Frenchman, from rock material taken from Willis Mountain."[14]

Buckingham Springs attracted an array of Virginia gentry, including Col. William Bolling (1777–1849) of Bolling Hall in Goochland County who kept a diary in 1840. Among notations of everyday events, he wrote of visiting Buckingham Springs. His daughter, Jane, may have spent extended time there, though her malady is not mentioned. Bolling does, however, disclose the ailments of others. In September of 1840, David B. Harris and his brother,

Frederick, were at the Springs, "where the latter had gone in consequence of a spinal affliction received no benefit – still unable to walk." On the contrary, Bolling found his dear Jane in "good health."[15]

Many of the patrons at the Springs were from the immediate environs. During Bolling's stay, Mrs. Cabell, who suffered from asthma, was there. Mrs. Eppes of Millbrook visited for the day. On Sunday, the Bollings and Cockes attended services at nearby St. Peter's Church, about three miles from the Springs. The following day, Col. Bolling was surprised to greet his old friend, Henry E. Watkins. Having heard that Bolling was there, Watkins dropped in and spent the evening. Such was the easygoing life of the gentleman farmer.[16]

Bolling related the social nature of the resort, with its constant political talk. Vocal members of the Whig and Locofoco Party made for lively, if temporary, companions. Watkins introduced Bolling to Dr. Jones of Mecklenburg County, who was "a thorough Loco, but otherwise a free, intelligent and agreeable acquaintance. Mr. Thweat & lady of Prince Edward [were] also among our new acquaintances."[17]

That fall, one cabin at the Springs was called the "Tippecanoe House" and may have attracted only Whigs in the heated atmosphere of the 1840 election between William Henry Harrison, a Whig and military victor over the Shawnee in 1811 at the river of Tippecanoe, and incumbent, President Martin Van Buren.[18]

Stone Bachelor's Quarters at Buckingham Springs (RICHARD MORRIS COLLECTION)

On Friday, September 11, 1840, Bolling described his arrival at Buckingham Springs:

> Left [Col. Robert] Hubard, passing thro' Curdsville, a little village at the head of the navigation of Willis's Creek, now called Willis's River, a good brick manufacturing mill, one or two dry goods stores and groceries and a large [tobacco] factory – over roughest road I almost ever traveled of fine road, we arrived at the Springs 12 miles from Hubard's to dinner, where I did not find a gentleman that [I] had ever seen before. Quartered in the Tippecanoe House, 2 or 300 yards from the Hotel where we met with Mrs. & Gen'l. Cocke, whose company lended much to the pleasure of the place, she being there with a grandson of the General's, Frank Cabell's son, an interesting little boy but afflicted with Epileptic Fits.[19]

After a four-day visit to Buckingham Springs, Col. Bolling sang the praises of its healing waters. "[T]he use of the water having seen of magnificent benefit to my wife. They are composed of sulphur, epsom salts and magnesia. They are weak in comparison of the trans-mountain Springs but evidently passed medicinal qualities removing bile, and operating also on the kidneys."[20]

About the time of Bolling's visit, Samuel Morris decided to expand his resort and on July 30, 1841, ran the following advertisement in the *Richmond Whig*:

> The liberal patronage, which the subscriber received during the last season, has induced him at great expense, to make considerable additions to the buildings, and other accommodations at these justly famous mineral springs. He will be prepared to receive visitors on or before the 1st day of July 1841.
>
> The Buckingham White Sulphur Springs are situated within a mile from the town of Curdsville, in the county of Buckingham, and 70 miles from Richmond, 45 miles from Lynchburg, 12 miles from Farmville, and 10 miles from Buckingham C. H. The situation is healthy; and, though in a retired and elevated situation, the traveler seeking health or pleasure is conducted to the Springs over good roads,

through a well cultivated country. The subscriber is well prepared to accommodate from 350 to 400 visitors. His buildings are commodious and convenient; and, in their location and construction, special reference has been made to the comfort and pleasure of visitors. A most attentive Hotel-keeper has been procured; also, an active and excellent Bar-keeper, from one of the cities. With George Walker at the head of the Band, it is unnecessary for the subscriber to say, that visitors will be entertained with the best of music. But the medical character of the waters form the chief virtue of the Springs. There are four Springs, the two principals of which have been carefully submitted to chemical analysis D. P. Gardner, M.D., late of London, and now professor, filling with distinguished ability the chair of Chemistry at Hampden-Sydney College. The following is from a letter from Dr. Gardner to me: "You ask my opinion of the properties of those Mineral Springs. They are to be considered saline, autaird, and sulphurous waters; and, on comparing their contents with that of the celebrated White Sulphur Springs, I find the solid and gaseous ingredients almost identical."[21]

Morris felt "at liberty" to refer readers to several notable gentleman for testimonials including Col. Bolling of Goochland, Mr. Whitlock of Petersburg, the Hon. E.W. Hubard, Messrs. Samuel C. Anderson and Henry E. Watkins of Prince Edward, and Judge Wilson of Cumberland. While naming the local "rich and famous," Morris revealed that many of his patrons came from a distance to experience the healing waters.[22]

During 1840–1841, the so-called "Morris House" was built across the private road from the original hotel to accommodate overflow. According to family tradition, and oft repeated over the years, the timbers for the Morris House came from a cocoonery for a failed silk business which had been established on Willis Mountain by Samuel's father, Nathaniel Morris.[23]

In 1936, Elizabeth McCraw described the building for the Virginia Historical Inventory:

> The three story frame building is large and roomy, containing 17 rooms and a double "veranda" on the front. A broad hall extends the

length of the house on the first floor. . . . A broad one flight stairway leads from the back of this hall to the second floor. Across the entire front of the second floor is a large room known as "the ball room." . . . The floors in the house are of wide plank. . . . The outside kitchen of years ago, has been torn down. The "office", built of native stone, is yet in the yard, but in a poor state of repair. To the side of the house, is a high box wood hedge.[24]

Additionally, Samuel built an eight-room structure of local stone, located to the side of the house, up the hill toward the sulphur springs; it accommodated visiting bachelors. Above the springs sat a row of family cottages. Other amusements included a racetrack, barroom, and possibly a gambling house.[25] In the 19th century, Virginians loved horse racing and, according to Morris family history, Samuel Morris was especially fond of the sport.[26]

Feeding the many patrons at Buckingham Springs was an enormous task. A large brick kitchen sat in the yard.[27] Lulie Patteson wrote of the kitchen and the very valuable, enslaved cook who arranged the meals there:

> The table menus must have been of the highest order for $1800 was paid for the head cook "Agnes" and of course there were many other slaves. . . . In reference to the cook, it should also be said that the kitchen was a large brick building with two 8-foot high fireplaces and a large brick oven since there were as many as seven hundred guests here in a season, the food supply was no small item, doubtless "Agnes" sent forth many a beaten biscuit, many a platter.[28]

In August of 1850, a meeting took place at Buckingham Springs to discuss the fate of Buckingham Female Collegiate Institute, the county's renowned women's college. The gathering, described in a letter from William B. Shepard to J.H. Evans of New Orleans, attested to the impressive capacity of the kitchen:

> When I was at Buckingham White Sulphur Springs last week at a meeting of friends of the Institute, Mr. Gannaway discussed his expectation of enlarging the attendance. Speaking to the assembled guests

at dinner, I begged all the gentlemen present to send their daughters to the Institute. Several gentlemen gave me money and Col. Page promised to solicit in Richmond and gave me fifty dollars to place in the hands of the business manager. There were four hundred persons at dinner at the White Sulphur and I have many promises of assistance.[29]

In November of 1850, Samuel Morris died, dividing his land equally among his ten children.[30] A decade later, the main hotel was destroyed by fire; following the Civil War, it was never rebuilt.[31]

Not all the visitors found cures. In at least one case, death came at Buckingham White Sulphur Springs. Col. Henry Gantt of Albemarle County died there in October of 1884. The precise cause of his death is unknown; however, he was seriously wounded in the face at the Battle of Gettysburg and, over the years, regularly experienced facial hemorrhages. These unresolved complications of the decades-old wound likely led to his sudden death.[32]

Despite the reduced accommodations, patrons continued to come long distances to visit the Springs, as reported in *The Farmville Herald* on September 7, 1896:

> The once famous "White Sulphur Springs" of Buckingham are again becoming much patronized by health-seekers. Visitors are there from Texas, Philadelphia, Petersburg, &c., and all are strong in their praises of the efficacy of the waters, and the management of the hostess, Mrs. John Morris. Situated as these springs are, away from the maddening ultra-fashionable summer resorts, still within easy reach of railroad, they afford an opportunity to the great middle-class to enjoy the benefits of superb mineral waters at a minimum cost. A large party assembled at "The Springs" on Saturday last to welcome Miss Price, of Philadelphia, and Miss Hancock, of Howardsville, guests of Miss Virginia Gilliam. Some 60 or 70 young men and maidens were there, bringing their own eatables and having a jolly good time.[33]

Writing about Buckingham Springs, Lulie Patteson mentioned that many prominent weddings took place there and that slaves were often married in the hall beneath the ballroom. In her typical romantic style, she also envisioned dancers filling the once luminous ballroom, warmed by two generous fires:

> The ballroom boasts of two fireplaces, and is an immense room compared with other rooms of its time. To sit quietly in this room alone, is to invoke visions of the long ago. Belles and beauxs in a courtly grace, long crowded from much of our worry and haste; throng through its doors. There are happy smiles, and whispered compliments as the dance begins. The phantom music throbs through the air and one can almost hear the tread of the dancers in the autumn wind, that sighs softly around the house. Ere long, a door opens somewhere; the dancers fade away; away back to the lonely country graveyards; the music is still, and the autumn wind is just a wind again.[34]

There were indeed glorious dances held at the Springs, as recorded in the August 15, 1896 issue of *The Farmville Herald*. The dapper couples were mentioned by name and the dresses of the young ladies described. Miss Nettie D. Morton, for example, appeared on the arm of William Pettit Venable, wearing a pink silk waist with pearl passamenterie trimming. There was yellow crepon trimmed in black lace. Pink, white, pearl grey, and blue organdies swished across the ballroom floor, trailing ribbons of nile green and black velvet.[35]

Brilliant Dance

Buckingham Springs, Va. August 15, 1896

A delightful dance was given Tuesday evening at Buckingham Springs in honor of a few young ladies who are visiting in Farmville. The event was one of the most enjoyable of the season. Many Japanese lanterns were suspended from the large trees in front of the house which presented quite a pleasing scene.

At 1 o'clock a.m. everybody retired to the dining hall where delicious refreshments consisting of cake, cream, ices and fruits were served in old Virginia style. The music was executed with exactness by Messrs. W. E. England and Asa Jenkins, both of Farmville. . . .[36]

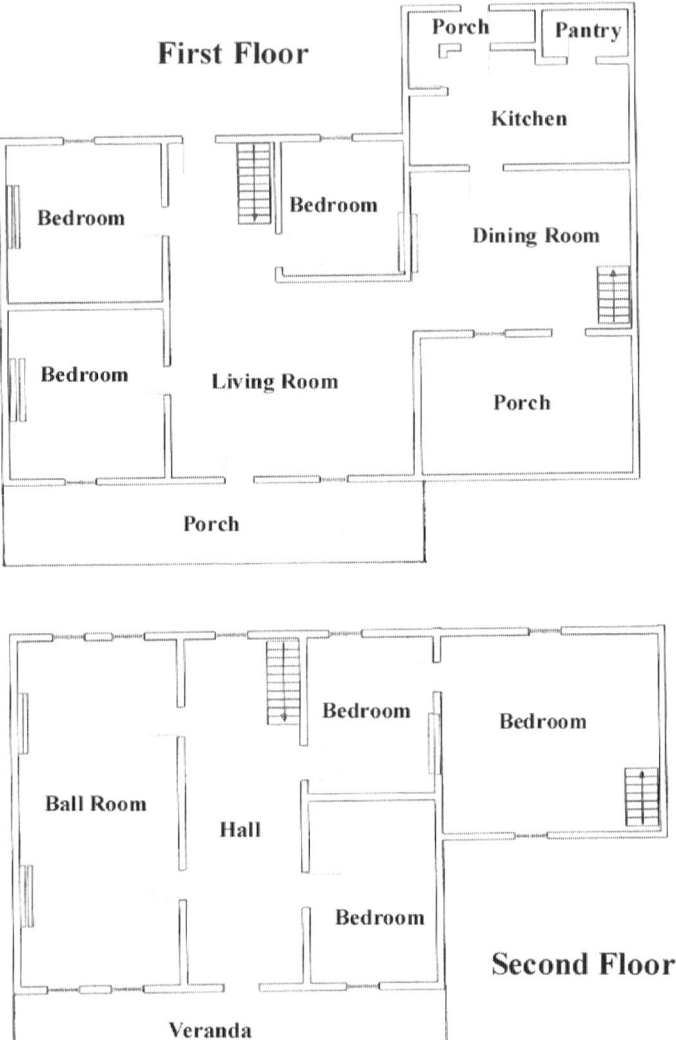

Buckingham Springs floor plan (Richard Morris Collection)

Buckingham Springs Layout
Third Floor and Attic

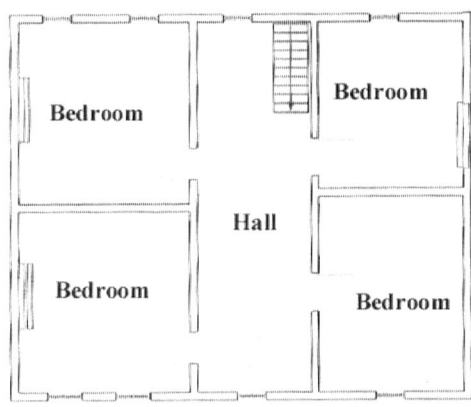

Third Floor

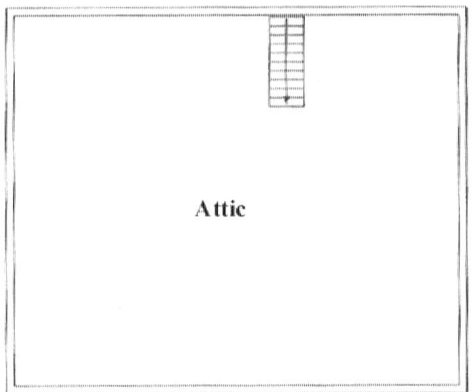

Attic

Buckingham Springs floor plan (RICHARD MORRIS COLLECTION)

Buckingham Lithia Water

In 1905–1906, the Newport News Bottling Company advertised "Buckingham Lithia Water" in the city's Daily Press. On October 29, 1905, the company enthusiastically announced production. The source was described as "Spring No. 1." Its exact location was not disclosed.

Buckingham Lithia Water
From the mineral hills in the eastern part of Buckingham county flow three springs, giving forth water the equal of any in the world. For more than 125 years people from all the surrounding country have been want to go to the springs when suffering from disorders of the stomach, liver and kidneys, always getting relief. The property passed into new hands, who wished to know what the virtues were, so had the water analyzed. The analysis exceeded all expectations and steps were at once taken to give this water to suffering humanity. This was ten months ago and almost without an exception every physician and person who has drank this water recommends it. The price of this water is 30c half gallon at all drug stores, but to let every person become acquainted with its virtues it will be sold for six months at five gallons for 75c.

These demijohns are filled at the springs by taking the water from beneath the surface, corking and sealing on the ground, and every seal has written on its face the name of the proprietor in his own handwriting. There can be no substitution or change in the water nor taste from old barrels or straining rags. The sediment sometimes seen in the water is purely mineral and does not hurt it. Just strain it off.

With this we introduce the public of Newport News, Buckingham Lithia Water from Spring No. 1. Sold by Newport News Bottling Co.

Testimonials, rather than scientific results proving cures, were the sales tools of anyone peddling spring water. On February 11, 1906, the Daily Press ran this advertisement:

DYSPEPSIA

"I had suffered for years with nervous dyspepsia and chronic constipation until after drinking Buckingham Lithia Water, in six weeks I discontinued medicines and gained 12 pounds and felt better than I had for several years."

BUCKINGHAM LITHA WATER
UNSURPASED IN RESULTS.   5 Gallons. 75c.

Newport News Bottling Co.
Bell Phone, 333   Citizens. 433

3200 Huntington Avenue.

༂༠༼༃

Traffic to the Springs lasted into the 20th century, though the glory days when the resort accommodated hundreds of persons was now a dim memory. It had been a long decline beginning with the death in 1850 of its genial host, Samuel Morris, to the burning of the hotel, to the vicissitudes of the Civil War, and the protracted economic depression in the region. Fashions changed and modern medicine offered scientifically proven alternatives to "healing waters."

The restful nature of the place, however, remained constant. On August 10, 1900, the editor of *The Farmville Herald* wrote about his recent visit to Buckingham Springs, which, at that time was owned by Wiley Bledsoe Morris, grandson of Samuel Morris, the resort's founder:

> My first resting place on the return trip was at Buckingham Springs, a place about which I have been hearing all of my life but which I never saw until last Friday, and I am glad to have been there. The large hotel and many cottages of other days which in their day gave welcome, said shelter, and rest, and comfort to 800 guests at once, are no longer there, but a massive and typical country mansion embowered in a yard of shade trees, evergreens and flowers, remains, and nearby that health-giving sulphur spring, from which so many tired ones have drunk and been made well again. As I dipped and drank, and rested, I wondered that any Southside Virginian should want to go to the Greenbrier White or the Montgomery White, when in easy touch sparkles, and bubbles, and flows the Buckingham White, just as pure, more palatable and just as remedial. And here I know is a feature not to be found at either of the other Whites, or any other summer resort in the land. In well-high hand-pull of that spring is a glorious watermelon patch, so that the pleasure seeker and seeker after health can indeed and in truth get them "fresh off of de vine." The habit of the owner is to go to that patch early "of mornings" and fill that spring chock full of choice melons, so that if by ten a.m. the gods were in search of food fit for them they might find it right there. The only

regret about the experience I had there and in that hospitable home, where a Virginia matron presides and provides as they only can, is that like all of earth it came to an end.[37]

Indeed, during the early years of the 20th century, proprietor Wiley Morris, who had inherited a percentage of the property in 1887, still welcomed visitors.[38] In the fall of 1901, he was expecting a hunting party. Patrons continued to be mentioned in the Society Section of Richmond's *The Times–Dispatch*.[39] The summer months brought campers; the gathering was a cornucopia of the old names of the tri-county area:

> Mr. E. L. Morris, wife and children, and C.B. Cunningham, wife and children, are spending a pleasant time camping in the front yard at Buckingham Springs, enjoying the fine sulphur water. Between 30 and 40 were at dinner on Sunday and enjoyed an old fashioned Brunswick stew, fried chicken and sweet cider. Among those at dinner were Dr. W. J. Gills, wife and son; Dr. W.E. Anderson, J.D. Watkins, J. W. Garnett, R.G. Cowan, Hugh Gilliam, Oscar Morris, George Carter, J.W. Overton, Leon Gills; Misses Virginia Smith, Lizzie Smith, Ruth Garnett, Annie Garnett, Rosa Garnett.[40]

※

In the mid-1980s, Gene and Bonnie Figy restored the Morris House, dreamed of creating an authentic 19th century-style retreat, and entertained their first guests in 1986. The old country inn was transformed into a bed and breakfast, as well as a restaurant. Their friendly brochure stated: "Guests are welcome for just overnight, but encouraged to stay longer and be taken back in time and away from the hustle and bustle of today's world."[41] In 1991, however, the Figys put the property on the market and it was purchased by Philip Fenaux.

Today, the Morris House still stands. Nearby, numerous Morrises rest in the ancient family cemetery.[42] For decades, the elite met and the weak sought strength at Buckingham Springs. Late night balls delighted the local youth and the great brick kitchen served thousands of guests. Years ago, Lulie Patteson, who never tired of envisioning Buckingham County's yesteryear, summed up a ghostly vision of the place:

> Buckingham Springs, or the shadow of it, lies just two miles southwest of Curdsville, and though once the pride of that section, few people today visit or even know of its one time glory. But to those who do visit, there is a fascination that draws one again and again. The great paved court, now grass grown, the boxwoods that have heard the whispered words of many a courtship . . . moonlit summer evenings, the romantic situation of the whole place, draws irresistibly one who loves the scenes of the past.[43]

NOTES

1 For more about health spas throughout Virginia, see "Taking the Waters: 19th Century Medical Springs of Virginia," University of Virginia, accessed September 2014, http://exhibits.hsl.virginia.edu/springs/introessay/; Charlene M. Boyer Lewis, *Ladies and Gentlemen on Display: Planter Society at the Virginia Springs, 1790-1860* (Charlottesville, VA: University of Virginia Press, 2001).

2 Rosa G. Williams, "Bolling Springs," Virginia Historical Inventory, 20 January 1938, Library of Virginia.

3 Elizabeth McCraw, "Pleasant Springs," Virginia Historical Inventory, 1 October 1937, Library of Virginia; Rosa G. Williams, "Site of 'Indian Springs'," Virginia Historical Inventory, 6 April 1937, Library of Virginia.

4 Rosa G. Williams, "Physic Springs Site," Virginia Historical Inventory, 25 June 1937, Library of Virginia.

5 *Acts of the General Assembly of the Commonwealth of Virginia* (Richmond, VA: Samuel Shepherd, Printer to the Commonwealth, 1839), 114. The Browns, Haneses, and Taylors were neighbors at Physic Springs. It was also the home of Elijah G. Hanes' Humanity Hall Academy.

6 "Lithia Springs," *Times Dispatch*, 29 December 1904, p. 5.

7 Ruby Loving, letter to author, 19 February 2014. In the summer of 1905, the Buckingham Lithia Springs Company announced that they were now open for boarders. These visitors were likely accommodated in small numbers. See Advertisement, *Times-Dispatch*, 25 June 1905, p. 9.

8 Samuel Morris, born on October 20, 1785 in Buckingham County, Virginia, volunteered as a private in the War of 1812 and eventually rose to the rank of Captain in the Buckingham County Militia. See Richard S. Morris, III, compiler, "Buckingham Springs: Information and Pictures of Buckingham Springs" (September 2001), 2, 71–72.

9 Lithia Springs, Georgia, with its Sweetwater Park Hotel, was one of the most famous sources of lithia water. See "Chronicles Of Lithia Spring," accessed August 2014, http://lithiaspringshistory.com/id42.htm.

10 Advertisement, *Times-Dispatch*, 25 June 1905, p. 9.

11 Robert G. Flippen, *Historical Notes on Buckingham 1900–1909* (Farmville, VA: Southside Virginia Historical Press, 2001), 186.

12 Morris, "Buckingham Springs: Information and Pictures of Buckingham Springs," 2.

13 Ibid., 65.

14   Ibid., 25. In the 1980s, Professor Jim Jordan and students from Longwood College investigated the site around the mouth of one of the springs, exposing an area approximately 68 feet around the spring which might have held a pavilion-like structure. Additionally, there were large rocks (potential seating) near the spring and what might have been stepping stones leading to it. See Tana Knott, "Springing to Light," *The Farmville Herald*, in Richard S. Morris, "Buckingham Springs," 40–41.

15   Colonel William Bolling Diary 1838-1842, 6–7 September 1840, accessed August 2014, http://lefeberleaguecity.ieasysite.com/ColonelWilliamBollingDiary's1838-1842.pdf.

16   Bolling Diary, 11–15 September 1840.

17   Ibid. According to the *Encyclopedia Britannica*, "Locofoco Party, in U.S. history, radical wing of the Democratic Party, organized in New York City in 1835. Made up primarily of workingmen and reformers, the Locofocos were opposed to state banks, monopolies, paper money, tariffs, and generally any financial policies that seemed to them antidemocratic and conducive to special privilege. The Locofocos received their name (which was later derisively applied by political opponents to all Democrats) when party regulars in New York turned off the gas lights to oust the radicals from a Tammany Hall nominating meeting. The radicals responded by lighting candles with the new self-igniting friction matches known as locofocos, and proceeded to nominate their own slate." See *Encyclopedia Britannica*, "Locofoco Party," accessed August 2014, http://www.britannica.com/EBchecked/topic/345859/Locofoco-Party.

18   "Tippecanoe and Tyler Too" was the popular and influential campaign song during the 1840 United States presidential election which promoted the Whig Party's "Log Cabin Campaign." William Henry Harrison (the "hero of Tippecanoe") and John Tyler were praised in contrast to President Martin Van Buren, a Democrat.

19   Bolling Diary, 11 September 1840.

20   Ibid., 15 September 1840.

21   "Buckingham White Sulphur Springs," *Richmond Whig*, 30 July 1841, p. 3. In 1849, some of the improvements at Green Springs were destroyed by fire. See Roger G. Ward, *Land Tax Summaries & Implied Deeds, 1841–1870, Volume 3* (Athens, GA: Iberian Publishing Company, 1995), 196.

22   "Buckingham White Sulphur Springs," *Richmond Whig*, 30 July 1841, p. 3.

23   Morris, 2, 25, 72; Parke Morris Wills, "Buckingham White Sulphur Springs," *Today and Yesterday in the Heart of Virginia* (Farmville, VA: The Farmville Herald, 1935), 279.

24   Elizabeth McCraw, "The Morris House," Virginia Historical Inventory, 25 May 1936, Library of Virginia.

25 Mrs. R. J. Wojnicki, "Buckingham Springs, Once Famous Resort, Now a Tranquil Dwelling," 20 March 1956, in Richard S. Morris, "Buckingham Springs," 30; Lulie Patteson, "Springs in Buckingham Gave Help to Health Seekers," n.d., clipping files, The Housewright Museum, Buckingham, Virginia.

26 Morris, 72.

27 Ibid., 2.

28 Morris, 26.

29 William Shepard, "Buckingham Female Collegiate Institute," *William and Mary Quarterly* (July 1940), 350–351.

30 Morris, 65. By 1870, a large extended Morris family lived adjacent each other on the property, including the families of Robert James Morris, Samuel Morris, Jr., and Elizabeth (Morris) Booker. See Federal Population Census, Buckingham County, VA, 1870.

31 Ibid., 66.

32 Richard Ludlam Nicholas, "Colonel Henry Gantt and the Gantt Family of Albemarle County Virginia (2003), 23, Manuscript CS71.G227 2003, Virginia Historical Society; Henry Gantt, Obituary, *The Sun* (Baltimore, MD), 21 October 1884, p. 4.

33 Robert G. Flippen, *Historical Notes on Buckingham 1890–1899* (Farmville, VA: Southside Virginia Historical Press, 1996), 109.

34 Morris, 25, 72.

35 Flippen, *Historical Notes on Buckingham 1890–1899*, 105. Passamenterie refers to trimming, such as braids, gimp, tassels, or cords.

36 Ibid.

37 "In Buckingham," *The Farmville Herald*, 10 August 1900, p. 3.

38 Morris, 66.

39 "Sheppards Shots," *The Farmville Herald*, 11 October 1901, p. 3; Advertisement, *Times-Dispatch*, 25 June 1905, p. 9.

40 "Buckingham Springs," *The Farmville Herald*, 27 August 1909, p. 1.

41 Morris, 31–32, 34–41, 52.

42 Janice J. R. Hull, *Buckingham Burials, Volume 1* (Alexandria, VA: Hearthside Press, 1997), 363–365.

43 Morris, 26.

Buckingham Hotel, 1933 (Photo by Frances Benjamin Johnston, Library of Congress)

Hospitality and Entertainment: Buckingham Hotel

In 1969, the "Buckingham Court House Preservation Zone" was added to the National Register of Historic Places. It encompassed much of what was once called Maysville. The application begins by describing the village as follows:

> Stretched out along a ridge between Bryant Creek and Slate River, Buckingham Court House survives as a well preserved Piedmont courthouse community with a population of approximately two hundred eighteen people. The village extends for a little more than a half mile on either side of Route 60 with the courthouse square located near the center. . . . On the west side of the courthouse is a one-story twentieth century office building, and on the east is the one-story late-nineteenth century clerk's office with later additions. Behind is the former jail house.[1]

Structures listed as part of the historic zone include: the Confederate monument, the former Buckingham Tavern, the former Buckingham Inn, the Leitch House, the Presbyterian manse, the Masonic Hall, Rose Terrace, and Maysville Presbyterian Church. The application goes on to note, "It is interesting that nearly every building in Buckingham is covered with the slate shingles for which the county has become so famous."[2]

A significant structure goes unnamed. Razed not long before, in about 1960, the Buckingham Hotel (a.k.a. The Moseley House) served the courthouse neighborhood for many years.[3] Built circa 1800, the hotel sat diagonally across Route 60 from the courthouse. In the early 20th century, it was believed to be the oldest house in the village.[4] In 1937, Elizabeth McCraw described the then ancient hotel for the Virginia Historical Inventory:

This rambling old house on a corner in the village of Buckingham, Virginia, has both a front and a side entrance. The front entrance is through a porch, that extends almost the entire length of the house. This modern porch replaced a much smaller one that was originally here. Through a new door one enters the large front room or hall. The winding stairway, with spool-like newels, leads from this room and is very noticeable and old fashioned looking. To the right of this room is the parlor with [its] large fireplace, deep wainscoting and small windows.

The side entrance is through double doors into a rough looking hall. The wood pegs and shop-made nails used in the construction of the house are plainly seen in this hallway. The HL hinges and six panel doors are points of interest, as well as the low ceiling and high mantels.[5]

Buckingham historian Lulie Patteson noted that the building was "part log structure and weather boarded over."[6] This log section may have been quite old, dating back to the era of the establishment of Buckingham's courthouse in 1761, long before Maysville was incorporated in 1818.

Though original deeds to the property were lost in the Buckingham courthouse fire of 1869, Elizabeth McCraw's description of the materials used and design of the hotel also supports an early date of construction. She states that the original builder is unknown, but McCraw believed that by about 1830, Patrick Henry Hickok was the proprietor of the place. Indeed, in 1834, Patrick H. Hickok first paid taxes on a lot in Maysville which he purchased from Hezekiah Lipscomb.[7] The lot likely included at least a log structure and it may have been Hickok who elaborated it into a house which eventually included "twelve rooms, wide flooring boards, and eighteen inch paneling on some of the walls. There was also an unusual hanging chimney."[8]

By 1850, this house across the road from the courthouse was filled with Hickoks: P.H. Hickok (fifty-two, born Amherst County), Elizabeth (thirty-one, born Buckingham County), Mary (eighteen), Robert (sixteen), Louisa (fourteen), John (four), and Alice (three), and there were at least two other Hickok children, Charles Henry (b. 1845) and Pattie Lewis (b. 1857).[9]

In 1937, Nannie Pratt (Moseley) Spencer remembered that her great grandfather, Patrick Henry Hickok, operated a hotel. In 1850, the census states that P. H. Hickok and his son, Robert, both worked as merchants. If they operated a store out of the house, this might explain the two entrances. Living in the immediate neighborhood of Maysville were competing merchants, a shoemaker, a saddler, a tanner, two tailors, a lawyer, etc.[10] The census does not indicate that Hickok's home doubled as a hotel or boarding house. If Mr. Hickok did operate a hotel in addition to a store, there was stiff competition from the long established Maysville Hotel, built by Maysville founder, Thomas May.[11]

In 1861, two of the Hickok sons, Charles Henry and John James went off to war with the company known as the Buckingham Leaches. Historian Lyon

John James Hickok (1846–1907) grew up at the Buckingham Hotel and, in 1861, survived the Battle of Rich Mountain. (COURTESY LYON G. TYLER, MEN OF MARK PUBLISHING COMPANY)

Gardiner Tyler described the price the family and Buckingham quickly paid at the battle of Rich Mountain:

> [John James Hickok's] father, Patrick Henry Hickok, was a farmer and merchant, a man of inflexible honesty and high ideals, who had married Miss Elizabeth M. Pittman. In his boyhood John James Hickok was of slender physique. His home was in a village. From his earliest years he was exceptionally fond of music and of reading. He attended school with regularity until he was about fourteen. The breaking out of the Civil War interfered with further attendance at school. His former teacher, and six of his school mates were killed in the battle at Rich Mountain, in 1861; and of these six schoolmates, one was his only brother, Charles Henry Hickok.[12]

At the end of the war, tradition holds that Mrs. Hickok served General Robert E. Lee coffee from her porch as he passed through Buckingham on his way home from Appomattox in 1865.[13] Following the surrender, John James Hickok left Maysville to establish himself in Cumberland County, where he was a partner in a country store at Cumberland Court House.[14] By the summer of 1870, Anna, Virginia, Pattie, and Nannie Hickok occupied the house; Anna headed the household.[15] Later that year, Confederate veteran Capt. Samuel Perkins Moseley married Pattie Lewis Hickok and there was once again a man in the household.[16]

Capt. Moseley was among the first to enlist in the Buckingham Leaches and was with the Hickok boys at the Battle of Rich Mountain in July of 1861. He served during the entire war, joining the Richmond Howitzers after the Buckingham Leaches disbanded and fighting with General Jackson in many battles. Moseley's war wounds rendered his left arm useless, making "hotel-keeper" a viable occupation.[17]

It is possible that Sam Moseley actually established the Buckingham Hotel and his warm personality made for a genial and popular innkeeper. His light-hearted qualities carried him not only through the hardships of the war, but also through the difficulties of the Reconstruction years. A talented banjo player, one of Sam's most notable performances was in 1908 when he played at the unveiling of the Confederate Monument at Buckingham Court House.[18]

In 1880, the Buckingham Hotel was a blended household of Hickoks and Moseleys. Sam Moseley headed the household and acted as hotelkeeper. Pattie, his wife, was the busy mother of four young children: Rosa Clinton, John Hickok, Charles Henry, and William Washburn who had just been born in April. Another daughter, Nannie Pratt Moseley, was born in 1883. Pattie's spinster sisters, Alice and Louisa, taught school and remained at home. Catherine Woodson, the family servant, lived in.[19]

By 1900, Pattie Moseley operated the hotel, living with four of her five children and her unmarried sister, Alice. At that time, Sam Moseley was boarding in Maysville with an attorney, John F. Rogers, and living adjacent his first cousin, Langdon C. Moseley.[20] The reason for Sam's displacement from the Buckingham Hotel is currently unknown.

This detail from the 1908 photo of the Confederate Veterans Reunion at Buckingham Courthouse is believed to be Capt. Samuel Perkins Moseley, who played his banjo at the festivities. (SCOTTSVILLE MUSEUM, SCOTTSVILLE, VA)

In 1909, Pattie died and was buried in the cemetery at Maysville Presbyterian Church. Located across the street from the Buckingham Hotel, the church played an important part in the lives of the Moseley family. Sam Moseley was baptized there on July 13, 1834, the infant of William Perkins and Nancy (Trent) Moseley, though he was not received into the church until October 29, 1910. His wife and daughters were part of the congregation as well. Pattie joined on September 6, 1884, as did her daughter, Rosa. Both were baptized the following day.[21]

Capt. Samuel Perkins Moseley died in Staunton, Virginia on March 14, 1912. His body was brought home to Buckingham and was buried with his wife, Pattie, in the Maysville Presbyterian Church cemetery.[22] A lengthy obituary praised Sam as one of Buckingham County's most colorful citizens:

> On Thursday, March 14, 1912, Capt. Samuel Perkins Moseley, Confederate soldier and veteran, passed away after a comparatively brief period of ill health. Captain Moseley was born at "Wheatland," Buckingham county, Va., July 28, 1833. His father was Dr. William Perkins Moseley, a prominent citizen and physician of the county. His mother, before her marriage, was Miss Nancy Trent. He received a fair education at "The Academy," a private school erected and patronized solely by the neighborring [sic] planters of those wealthy ante-bellum days.
>
> He was of a bright, cheerful, sunny disposition, always looking on the bright side of life and everything in it; fond of out-door sports and music, with a quick sense of humor and deeply imbued with the highest and most exalted respect for women. These qualities, all of which existed in him to a very marked degree, helped throughout a long life to render him a remarkable man in many respects, as well as to carry him through the hardships of the war, "reconstruction" days and subsequent trials in a manner which was often a marvel to all those who knew him best.
>
> When the war between the states broke out he enlisted for the whole war, and fought bravely to the bitter end. He belonged to

Company E, Twenty-first Regiment Virginia Infantry, Gordon's division, Army of Northern Virginia, of which he was captain. He was severely wounded in the left arm, which, stiff and inactive, ever afterwards served as a reminder of those stormy days of civil strife. He was taken prisoner, too, after being wounded, but his sunny temperament won him friends even in a Northern hospital, and a kind nurse hid a ten-dollar gold piece within the leaves of a hymn book for him as he was leaving.

During the war he was in many strange and fearful as well as humorous situations, about which a most splendid memory enabled him to give exact and minute accounts almost to the day of his death.

When the war ended he went to work with the same good [cheer] with which he always did everything. He was deputy sheriff of the county for years.

In 1870 he married Miss Patty Hickok. She died in 1909.

He leaves four children, Mrs. Frank Spencer, of Buckingham, Va.; Miss Rosa Moseley, of the same place; Mr. Willie W. Moseley, who is in business in Lynchburg, and Mr. Charlie Moseley of Richmond.

His kindly manners, cheerful disposition and a wonderful talent for playing the banjo won him many friends, and there was probably no one for miles around more generally liked or well known.

He was a member of the Maysville Presbyterian church, and was buried in the cemetery belonging to it on Sunday afternoon, March 17, 1912.[23]

Buckingham County's Confederate Monument

On June 30, 1908, William B. Megginson posed in his "wheeled chair" next to the newly erected Confederate Monument. (COURTESY HISTORIC BUCKINGHAM)

UNVEIL STATUE TO BUCKINGHAM DEAD

BUCKINGHAM, VA., July 1.—The Confederate Monument just erected here was unveiled yesterday at the same time that the cornerstone was laid. The double ceremony was very impressive and was attended by a large crowd, including a great number of veterans.

Mr. William B. Megginson, an aged veteran, who has been bedridden for many years, was placed in his wheeled chair and rolled to the base of the monument and he pulled the string that threw aside the veil, and displayed to sight the beautiful monument.

A great cheer went up from the crowd when the veil was removed. The inscription on the monument reads: "To commemorate the devotion and heroism of the Confederate soldiers of Buckingham county, who valued principle more than life, and fought for a cause they knew to be just."

Judge Duke's speech was a gem, and when he referred to Lee as a godlike man he was cheered long and loud. He was introduced by Colonel [R.T. Hubard], who also made a neat little speech, in which he mentioned the bravery and patriotism of the late Captain Carter Irving, who was captain of the Lee Guard, and who first said he hoped a monument would be erected to the memory of the brave boys of Buckingham, who laid down their lives. One man out of every five of Captain Irving's company fell at the battle of Rich Mountain.

There was a splendid dinner served on the grounds, which the old soldiers seemed to enjoy. A band of young girls dressed in red, white, and blue sang Dixie and a number of the war songs of long ago. Captain Sam P. Moseley was on hand with his banjo and played and sang.

When the day was well-nigh spent in happy reunion and rejoicing there were calls made for a speech from Hon. E.W. Hubard, who responded briefly.

The Times-Dispatch (Richmond, Virginia), 2 July 1908

It is unclear how long the Buckingham Hotel was known by that name and when locals started calling it "The Moseley House." The two names may have coexisted for a long time. Lulie Patteson believed that it was known as the Buckingham Hotel until 1890.[24] The *Appomattox and Buckingham Times*, however, reported the following in 1903, still calling it the Buckingham Hotel:

Entertainment at Buckingham Hotel

A small, but delightful, entertainment was given at the Buckingham Hotel last night (July 22); by Mrs. P. L. Moseley, in honor of her son, Mr. Willie Moseley, of Lynchburg, who is at home on a visit, and also to celebrate the birthday of her daughters, Misses Rosa and Nannie Moseley.

The ladies present were: Mrs. P. L. Moseley, Mrs. Tom Rice, Mrs. Ashlie Grigg, and Misses Alice Hickok, Rosa Moseley, Nannie Moseley, Mary Housewright, Alice Spencer, Annie Taliaferro, of Richmond, Edna Spencer and Annie Irvine. The gentlemen present were Messers. Jim Spencer, Garnett Smith, Willie Moseley, Cland Robertson, of Lynchburg, Dick Grigg, and Dr. Lightfoot Morriss.

The young people played a number of games, among them one called, "A Penny for your Thoughts," in which two prizes were given. The first prize was received by Miss Edna Spencer, and the second by Mr. Garnett Smith.

Refreshments were served at half-past ten, and at twelve o'clock the thoroughly enjoyable evening ended with an old-fashioned, yet ever amusing, "donkey" game, in which each one, blindfolded, tried to pin the donkey's tail on. The prize was won by Miss Alice Spencer, who pinned it nearer right than any of the others.

The young people of Buckingham Courthouse have lately been enjoying a number of small entertainments, given at different houses in the village. Old-fashioned games are the chief amusement at these entertainments, and there is no end to the fun that is had in playing them. We are all quite lively and gay "in the good old summer time." July 23, 1903.[25]

Hospitality and Entertainment: Buckingham Hotel ~ 77

In 1903, Caroline Matilda "Callie" Housewright (1830–1906) attended the Tacky Party at The Moseley House (a.k.a. Buckingham Hotel). (Mary Carolyn Mitton Collection)

A veritable who's who of Buckingham Court House, evenings like these frequently brightened the village square. In August, the *Appomattox and Buckingham Times* followed this news with another story featuring the Buckingham Hotel. This time, however, it was referred to as the Moseley Hotel:

Tacky Party at Moseley Hotel

On Thursday night, August 20, a big "tacky party" was given at the Moseley Hotel to the young people of the Courthouse, who attended in costumes that would be rather difficult to describe. The only thing that can be stated about these costumes is that, for variety and color, they were quite wonderful.

The ladies present were: Mrs. P. L. Moseley, Mrs. Ashlie Grigg, Mrs. John Snoddy, Mrs. Jas. Noble, Mrs. Jennie Fisher, Mrs. Ned Miles, Mrs. Tom Rice; Misses Rosa and Nannie Moseley, Edna Spencer, Annie Irvine, Fleda Rice, and Florence Taylor (of Lynchburg); Alice Hickok, Callie Housewright, Bettie Moseley, Maria, Mary, and Trent Pratt, Lorna Hubard, Ellis Miles, Rosa Garnett, Annie Housewright, Marie Whitehouse (of Norfolk), and Mary Pearson.

The gentlemen present were: Messrs. John and Addie Spencer, Ashlie Grigg, John Snoddy, Tom and Dan Rice, Philip Nicholas, and William Pierce, of Arvonia; John Housewright, of Lynchburg; Stratton Pearson, Jim Spencer, Beverley Moss, Moses Smith, Phil, Leon, and Dick Grigg, Sidney Puryear, Leroy Harley (of South Carolina), Robert Rice, of Lynchburg, and Dr. Lightfoot Morriss.

The evening was passed with music, dancing, and games. Refreshments – apples, pop-corn, peanuts, and "all-day suckers" – were served, after which the prizes, consisting of a head of cabbage hollowed out and filled with "old maids," a red bandana, and a sunflower, were presented by Mr. Ashlie Grigg – to Miss Fleda Rice, Mr. Leon Grigg, and Mr. Jim Spencer, who were decided by three chosen judges to be the "tackiest" among the extremely "tacky" crowd.

The young folks had no end of fun and all hope to attend another "tacky party" in the near future.   August 21, 1903.[26]

৪০০৪

Nannie Pratt Moseley married Frank Spencer and became an exceptionally active member of Maysville Presbyterian Church and, in 1963, was awarded an "Honorary Lifetime Membership" in the organization of Presbyterian Women. She was known for her friendliness and kindness, traits she shared with her father.

The Last Man Hanged in Buckingham County

All manner of activities at Buckingham Courthouse could be viewed from the Buckingham Hotel, including public hangings. In middle age, Nannie Pratt (Moseley) Spencer still vividly remembered a hanging she witnessed in 1893. Only ten years old, she watched from the upstairs window of her home, "The Moseley House." She remembered seeing the doomed man, riding to his death, perched astride his casket.

In 1904, she witnessed another hanging. Nannie sewed the black hood for the jailor, Frank Spencer. His son, Frank Spencer, Jr., knotted the hangman's noose; he and Nannie would soon marry. She kept a souvenir piece of the hemp rope which is now preserved by her great-granddaughter, Tina Maxey Powers.

Soon all executions were made the responsibility of the state and the hanging of John Henry Banks turned out to be Buckingham County's last. On October 1, 1904, Richmond's *The Times-Dispatch* covered the story:

HANGING IN BUCKINGHAM
John Henry Banks Pays Penalty
for John Brown's Murder

GRAVEL HILL, BUCKINGHAM, VA, September 30. – John Henry Banks, a negro, was hung to-day at Buckingham Courthouse at 10 o'clock for the murder of "Old Uncle John Brown," a very worthy colored man in July last.

Banks walked up on the scaffold with a firm step, with Deputy Sheriffs Lewis Williams and Charles McCraw on either side. The noose and black cap were adjusted by Sheriff William Williams, who opened the trap.

In twenty minutes Dr. G. L. Morris pronounced Banks dead. The body will be shipped to Richmond to the Medical College.

The Spencers lived at his family's boardinghouse in Maysville known as Spencer's Tavern or Spencer's Boarding House, located on the same side of the highway as the courthouse within easy walking distance of The Moseley House. In May of 1910, Sue Spencer's boarders included Edmund W. Hubard, Commonwealth Attorney; a seventy-year-old widow, Nannie W. Gilliam; the seventy-seven-year-old Miss Annie Scruggs; and five African Americans who worked as servants: Fred Hillard and Matilda Davis with her children, Bessie, Jim, and Harvey Davis.[27] Ultimately, The Moseley House fell into disrepair and was demolished, bringing an end to its long service across from the courthouse. Today, three of Frank and Nannie (Moseley) Spencer's grandchildren, Spencer Adams, Pattie Bailey, and Nancy Maxey, continue to live in the courthouse area, keeping alive the memories of the venerable old hotel.

NOTES

1   "Buckingham Courthouse Preservation Zone," National Register of Historic Places Inventory Nomination Form, VLR (9 September 1969) and NRHP (17 November 1969), Section 7.

2   Ibid. The Nomination Form identifies the Leitch House as the Leach House. See *"The Courthouse Burned—," Book I* (Buckingham, VA: Historic Buckingham, Inc., 2002), 17. Rose Terrace, a.k.a. Rose Cottage, was the home of the Moseley and Grigg families, among others. See Elizabeth McCraw, "Rose Cottage," 5 June 1936, Virginia Historical Inventory, Library of Virginia.

3   Lulie Patteson, "Buckingham Hotel," *Today and Yesterday in the Heart of Virginia* (Farmville, VA: *The Farmville Herald*, 1935), 276. Dates vary as to the demolition of the Buckingham Hotel. According to Lorna S. Scott, the building was condemned as a hazard and torn down in 1958. See Pennington and Scott, *"The Courthouse Burned—," Book I*, p. 4.

4   The Davidson House, which sits diagonally across from Buckingham Courthouse, has a wall dated 1740, suggesting that at least part of the structure considerably predates 1800. See Pennington and Scott, *"The Courthouse Burned—," Book I*, p. 7.

5   Elizabeth McCraw, "The Moseley House," 20 August 1937, Virginia Historical Inventory, Library of Virginia.

6   Patteson, "Buckingham Hotel," *Today and Yesterday*, 276.

7   Roger G. Ward, *Land Tax Summaries & Implied Deeds, 1815–1840, Volume 2* (Athens, GA: Iberian Publishing Co., 1994), 165. In 1814, Hezekiah Lipscomb purchased 273 acres on the Buckingham Road which was previously charged to John Glover. See Roger G. Ward, *Land Tax Summaries & Implied Deeds, 1782–1814, Volume 1* (Athens, GA: Iberian Publishing Co., 1993), 187. In 1819, Lipscomb purchased a lot in Maysville from John McReynolds, who purchased it from Daniel Guerrant in 1818. Earlier that year, Guerrant purchased the lot from William Lewis, who may have bought the lot when Maysville was laid out. See *Ward, Land Tax Summaries & Implied Deeds, 1815–1840, Volume 2*, pp. 145, 212, 215, 229.

8   Scott and Pennington, *"The Courthouse Burned—," Book I*, p. 4.

9   Federal Population Census, Buckingham County, Virginia, 1850; Federal Population Census, Buckingham County, Virginia, 1900. Daughter Mary was born in Nelson County, while daughter Louisa was born in Buckingham County, indicating that Patrick Henry Hickok settled in Buckingham sometime between 1832 and 1836. In 1840, Capt. P.H. Hickok was enumerated, in Buckingham County, with three young boys and three young girls, but with no apparent wife. The gap in age between Mr. and Mrs. Hickok, as well as the gap in the ages of the children, strongly suggests that Elizabeth was the second Mrs. Hickok.

10   Federal Population Census, Buckingham County, Virginia, 1850.

11   "The Maysville Hotel," Virginia Department of Historic Resources PFI Information Sheet, 5.

12   Lyon Gardiner Tyler, "James Henry Hickok," *Men of Mark in Virginia, Ideals of American Life; A Collection of Biographies of the Leading Men in the State, Volume 5* (Washington, D.C.: Men of Mark Publishing Company, 1909), 204–207. The teacher of the Hickoks, Lt. John Granville Sharpe Boyd, graduate of Randolph-Macon College, Class of 1845 (A.B.) and 1848 (A.M.), died at the Battle of Rich Mountain on July 11, 1861. On November 11, 1861, his "tragical and untimely end" coupled with his "dauntless courage and self-sacrificing heroism" was noted in the Buckingham County court records. Boyd was buried in Mount Iser Cemetery, Randolph County, West Virginia. See "The Battle of Rich Mountain," *The Times-Picayune*, 21 July 1861. J. G. S. Boyd left a widow, Mary S. Boyd, and at least one child, John Granville Sharpe Boyd, Jr. See Federal Population Census, Buckingham County, Virginia, 1860.

13   Elizabeth McCraw, "The Moseley House," 20 August 1937, Virginia Historical Inventory, Library of Virginia.

14   Tyler, "James Henry Hickok," *Men of Mark in Virginia, Volume 5*, p. 204.

15   Federal Population Census, Buckingham County, Virginia, 1870.

16   Samuel Perkins Moseley, Obituary, Mary (Pratt) Spencer Papers, n.d., Mary Carolyn Mitton Collection.

17   Eugene A. Maloney, *A History of Buckingham County* (Buckingham County, VA: Historic Buckingham, 2014), 109; Mary Carolyn Mitton, emails to author, January 2013.

18   *Richmond Times Dispatch*, 2 July 1908, p. 2.

19   Federal Population Census, Buckingham County, Virginia, 1880.

20   Federal Population Census, Buckingham County, Virginia, 1900.

21   Carl Coleman Rosen, Sr., *History of Maysville Presbyterian Church, Buckingham Court House, Virginia, 1824–1996* (Buckingham, VA: Maysville Presbyterian Church, 1997), 27, 30, 44, 203.

22   Coleman, *History of Maysville Presbyterian Church*, 203. Willie Moseley (1880–1937) and Rosa C. Moseley (1872–1935) are buried with their parents in the cemetery at Maysville Presbyterian Church. Misses Alice and Lou Hickok rest nearby. See Janice J. R. Hull, *Buckingham Burials, Volume I* (Alexandria, VA: Hearthside Press, 1997), 351–360.

23   Samuel Perkins Moseley, Obituary, Mary Carolyn Mitton Collection.

24   Patteson, "Buckingham Hotel," *Today and Yesterday*, 276.

25 *Appomattox and Buckingham Times*, 29 July 1903.
26 *Appomattox and Buckingham Times*, 26 August 1903.
27 Federal Population Census, Buckingham County, Virginia, 1910.

Work For a Quarter of a Million Men

"WE are giving opportunity of employment to one-quarter of a million of the unemployed, especially the young men who have dependents, to go into the forestry and flood-prevention work. This great group of men have entered upon their work on a purely voluntary basis, with no military training and we are conserving not only our national resources but our human resources.

FRANKLIN D. ROOSEVELT

President Roosevelt Signing Reforestation Work Bill

Happy Days: Authorized Weekly Newspaper of the Civilian Conservation Corps, Vol. 1, No. 1, 20 May 1933 (JOANNE YECK COLLECTION)

Spirit and Industry:
Buckingham County and the
Civilian Conservation Corps

From the very first days of President Franklin D. Roosevelt's administration, he advocated jobs, not relief, as a solution to America's deepening economic depression. In March of 1933, the Emergency Work Act cleared both houses of Congress; the result was the formation of the Civilian Conservation Corps (CCC). In May of 1933, the first CCC Camp in the country, appropriately dubbed Camp Roosevelt, opened in Shenandoah County, Virginia, near Massanutten Mountain in the George Washington National Forest.[1] By July 1st, there were 275,000 enrollees in 1,300 camps across the country; it was the fastest peacetime mobilization in American history.[2]

Each CCC camp consisted of a company of approximately 200 enrollees, aged eighteen to twenty-five, and was administered by a company commander who was either a regular army or a reserve officer. The enrollment term was six months, with an opportunity to reenlist. The men, unmarried and U.S. citizens, were provided with denim work clothes, a uniform/suit, and shoes. They were fed three square meals a day and paid $30.00 per month – $25.00 automatically went home to their families and $5.00 constituted their spending money, benefitting local merchants.[3] On July 17, 1933, Buckingham County joined the rapidly expanding program, opening Camp P-56, Company 1367 at the foot of Willis Mountain. Commonly called Camp Buckingham, it operated until December of 1937, employing dozens and dozens of young men with meaningful work.[4]

The terrain at Willis Mountain would have required the blasting of significant rock to erect typically large barracks to house the men. Instead, fifty-two small structures, measuring 14 x 18 feet, were constructed in parallel rows, each housing four men. The Mess Hall served three hearty meals a day, including a

Camp Buckingham, c. 1933–1934 (Courtesy Richmond Times-Dispatch)

Beginning in May of 1933, CCC Camps organized with lightning speed. By June, thirty-two camps in Maryland and Virginia provided 6,400 much-needed jobs. Many camps were built on private land, including those in Buckingham, neighboring Albemarle County near Crozet, Cumberland County near Farmville, and Fluvanna County near Fork Union. In Virginia alone, there were eventually 101 camps putting thousands of young American men to work in soil conservation, forestry, and engineering projects. Founded on July 17, 1933, Camp Buckingham's initial company was made up of White enrollees, pictured here in the District's "Official Annual." These annual publications included a general history of the CCC as well as histories and rosters for the companies in the District. The small barracks were an unusual feature of the camp in Buckingham County.

On June 7, 1934, Camp Buckingham was reconstituted as an African-American facility. The in-house newspaper, dubbed "Camp Chatter," covered camp news as well as national stories. (Center for Research Libraries Collection, Library of Virginia)

variety of styles of beef, ham, chicken, fish, and pork, with supplies coming from Fort Monroe and local farmers. The Recreation Hall included both a traveling and permanent library. Other buildings in the compound included a kitchen, a hospital and ward, a school, offices, latrine, bathhouse, blacksmith, and garages.[5]

The legislation that created the CCC stipulated that there was to be no discrimination towards enrollees based on race, color, or creed. Some camps were integrated and minority enrollment reflected percentages in the national population.[6] Camp Buckingham was established with White enrollees. Then, on June 7, 1934, as the camp neared its first anniversary, it was reconstituted as an exclusively African American camp. The men who worked there came from Virginia, Maryland, and the District of Columbia. Staff members in key positions were retained from the first company until July 1, 1935.⁷ Initially, Capt. Robert F. Berry, Jr., who had commanded the first group of men enrolled at Camp Buckingham, remained in charge; he was followed by Capt. John G. Whittman who was transferred from a CCC Camp in Pennsylvania.⁸

On July 13, 1935, the *Richmond Times-Dispatch* reported that the people of Buckingham County wanted the camp to enroll more local men. When the company was reconstituted in 1934, there were 196 men enrolled.⁹ A year later, the enrollment had severely declined and this notice appeared in the *Richmond Times-Dispatch*:

> BUCKINGHAM, July 12 – There are only 100 Negro men left at the CCC camp at Willis Mountain. Buckingham people hope that these will soon be replaced by a full quota of 200 with men to be chosen from among Buckingham men in need of work to support their families. A request for this has been forwarded to the War Department by the board of supervisors of the county.¹⁰

Camp Buckingham remained an African-American camp. Official reports sent to the national administration indicate that enrollment fluctuated and that men continued to come from outside of Buckingham County. Periodic camp investigations reveal a clean, orderly, and fairly well-equipped company and preserve statistics about camp life, as well as medical reports and menus. It is surviving fragments of Camp Buckingham's in-camp newspaper, *Camp Chatter*, however, which give personality to camp life.

The August 7, 1935 issue proclaimed itself to be "A paper for people who think." *Camp Chatter* covered world news as well as camp activities and sports. One issue included an article about the death of national celebrities Wiley Post and Will Rogers running alongside a story about a former slave, Anne Young of Amelia County, Virginia, who died at the age of 101.¹¹

The Associate Editor of *Camp Chatter*, S. Matthew Henderson, wrote of his efforts to bring African American-literature to the camp library, suggesting volumes by W.S. DuBois, Booker T. Washington, Paul Laurence Dunbar, and Buckingham County-born Carter G. Woodson.¹² In a subsequent district annual, the resultant collection was dubbed "splendid."¹³

NEGRO BOOKS

No library is complete without some Negro books. Taking under consideration the fact that this is a colored camp the reason is all the [more] obvious that there should be works by Negro Authors. Recently I borrowed a copy of the works of "Paul Lawrence Dunbar" and was pleased to find that he also thought we should have books of our race. Such books as the following:

Works of:

    W.S. DuBois   George Carver

    Countee Cullen   Paul Robeson

    Carter G. Woodson   Booker T. Washington

    Paul L. Dunbar

Biographies of:

    Frederick Douglas

    Roland Hayes

    ----- would be a creditable addition to any library.

                                                S.M. HENDERSON

The August 7, 1935 issue of Camp Buckingham's *Camp Chatter* highlighted the camp library, encouraging the men to read African-American history and literature. Editor Sam Henderson suggested titles, including the work of Buckingham-born Dr. Carter G. Woodson.

Carter G. Woodson, 1915 (Courtesy of Scurlock Studio Records, Archives Center, National Museum of American History, Smithsonian Institution)

Protestant church services were held weekly at the camp and a priest visited monthly. Trucks were provided for the men who preferred to attend church services in town. In one editorial, Associate Editor Matthew Henderson bemoaned the loss of Chaplin Vaiden, who had served the camp for several months and was reassigned to another district. Henderson wrote, "During the time he was with us he created a marvelous Friendship and understanding among the boys. This friendship was further extended when the 'Gospel Four' quartet accompanied him to his church in the Blue Ridge Mountains."[14] The Gospel Four was one of two quartets at Camp Buckingham. The men also formed an orchestra, taking programs to churches and neighboring schools as well as performing on radio broadcasts.

The Recreation Hall provided a meeting place for groups, including the Leaders Club, Dramatic Club, Debate Club, and Fireside Music. Vocational-educational programs offered the men of the CCC significant opportunities to improve themselves. Illiterate men enrolled and frequently left reading and writing. At Camp Buckingham, educators included an advisor, company officers, members of the technical staff, and WPA teachers. Elementary and high school coursework, as well as vocational training, was available at the camp. Men could take correspondence courses and the Forestry Department also frequently offered lectures.[15]

In addition to basic classes in English, Geography, History, Mathematics, and Penmanship, the men at Camp Buckingham studied first aid, barbering, cooking and baking, drawing, electricity, general construction, shoe repair, and woodworking. Motor mechanics was particularly popular.[16] Some enrollees were already skilled men, from stone masons, to piano tuners, to musicians. As Matthew Henderson noted in *Camp Chatter*, "In every community it takes different types of people who are useful to make a good place in which to live."[17]

Women were allowed to visit the camp, per national regulations, and *Camp Chatter* acknowledged many visitors. On Wednesday, August 21, 1935, for example, Miss Dorthy (sic) Stokes of Farmville gave a whist party in honor of the camp members. It was followed by a dance.[18] Throughout the summer, *Camp Chatter* noted that vacationers stopped to see the camp:

Most of these people come from the large cities to spend their vacations in the land of their birth. We are pleased to say that when visitors pay us a call the men of the company are so polite and well mannered that many sigh when they take leave of us. This splendid record of politeness that is awarded our men anywhere they go is just a preview of the smooth inner workings of our camp. With this in view we broadcast our motto: "If we please you tell others, if not tell us."[19]

These group photos of Camp Buckingham's African-American enrollees were taken c.1935 and printed in the District's "Official Annual." (COURTESY MELISSA BLAKE PALMORE, JAMES BLAKE COLLECTION, LIBRARY OF CONGRESS)

In the summer of 1935, plans were underway for a basketball court.[20] The camp's winning baseball team played local teams including Bedford City, Green Bay, Fort Harrison, Buckingham, Appomattox, Fork Union, and Farmville.[21] Additionally, there was boxing, horseshoes, and volleyball. Pool tables and other indoor games were provided in the Recreation Hall.[22] On weekends, it was common for the men of Camp Buckingham to climb Willis Mountain and enjoy the view, looking south to Farmville.

From time to time, accidents happened, including deaths. In the fall of 1934, a CCC truck from Camp Buckingham was returning to Willis Mountain when an accident occurred on the Howardsville Road, six miles west of Buckingham Court House. It was about midnight and twenty-one men were returning from a Glee Club concert when the driver miscalculated a sharp curve in the road. One man reported that the driver was blinded by the headlights of an oncoming car. William Jones, a twenty-five-year-old enrollee from Baltimore, was killed and seventeen others in the truck were injured. The injured were taken to Southside Hospital in Farmville, where ten were admitted. According to the *Richmond Times-Dispatch*, Doc "Hanna" of Buckingham and Ryland Harris, address unknown, were seriously injured.[23]

Life at the camp was not without internal tension. In February of 1935, two members of Camp Buckingham engaged in a knife fight. Charles Bray stabbed James L. Dent, who died from the wounds. Bray was charged with murder.[24]

Contagious diseases were also a problem, magnified by the men living together in close quarters. In the summer of 1935, Virginia was plagued with Infantile Paralysis (Polio) and Rocky Mountain Spotted Fever. The CCC camp at West Point was quarantined for measles and Buckingham County reported cases of Spotted Fever.[25]

It didn't take long for the work done by the men of Camp Buckingham to pay off. By the fall of 1935, the citizens of the county and of the region were enjoying the fruits of the young men's labors, particularly the road they built to the summit of Willis Mountain. The *Richmond Times-Dispatch* reported:

> On September 19 there will be a conference of representatives of the Episcopal churches in Appomattox, Buckingham and Cumberland of which the Rev. R.S. Wickers Jr. is rector[. The] meeting will be held

on the topmost peak of Willis Mountain and Bishop A. M. Thompson of Portsmouth will be present and take part in the services.

A road to the top has been built by the CCC boys who are in camp at the foot of the mountain.[26]

At the summit, the men built a tourist lodge or "rock cabin."[27] Within two years, thousands of tourists had used the CCC-built road to visit the top of Willis Mountain. Oddly, the guest book they signed was destroyed and the incident was reported in the *Richmond Times-Dispatch*: "H.P. Baker superintendent of the CCC camp at Willis Mountain had kept a registration book at the kitchen on the top of the mountain for tourists to register. There were 5,000 names signed in it, with people from a majority of the States, and some from abroad. A few days ago some vandal destroyed the book."[28]

In addition to creating hundreds of miles of fire lanes and dozens of miles of truck trails, the men of Camp Buckingham connected a telephone system, created toolboxes for fire wardens, built vehicular bridges and lookout towers. A system of roads was built to the top of Spears Mountain, 1,500 feet above sea level.[29]

ಬಲ

On April 17, 1936, the 3rd anniversary of the Federal program, President Roosevelt addressed the members of the CCC over the NBC radio network:

> To the million and a half young men and war veterans who have been, or are today, enrolled in the Civilian Conservation Corps Camps, I extend greetings on this third anniversary of the establishment of the first CCC Camp.
>
> Idle through no fault of your own, you were enrolled from city and rural homes and offered an opportunity to engage in healthful, outdoor work on forest, park and soil conservation projects of definite practical value to all the people of the nation. The promptness with which you seized the opportunity to engage in honest work, the willingness with which you have performed your daily tasks and the fine spirit you have shown in winning the respect of the communities in which your camps

have been located, merits the admiration of the entire country. You, and the men who have guided and supervised your efforts, have cause to be proud of the record the CCC has made in the development of sturdy manhood and in the initiation and prosecution of a conservation program of unprecedented proportions.

Since the Corps began some 1,150,000 of you have been graduated, improved in health, self-disciplined, alert and eager for the opportunity to make good in any kind of honest employment. Our records show that the results achieved in the protection and improvement of our timbered domain, in the arrest of soil wastage, in the development of needed recreational areas, in wild life conservation and in flood control have been as impressive as the results achieved in the rehabilitation of youth. Through your spirit and industry it has been demonstrated that young men can be put to work in our forests, parks, and fields on projects which benefit both the nation's youth and conservation generally.[30]

The following July, an article ran in the *Richmond Times-Dispatch*, celebrating Camp Buckingham's 3rd anniversary:

Buckingham Camp, P-56, Company 1367 CCC, will celebrate its third birthday on July 17th.

During the first year of the camp 333 miles of lanes were cleared through forests in the county to enable trucks laden with men and firefighting apparatus to reach fires. These lanes have proved of practical uses in reaching and extinguishing forest fires. It has now been decided also to construct good narrow roads or truck trails from 14 to 16 feet wide and build strong bridges across streams. The roads as far as practical will be built on ridges with grades held at a minimum and each end connected with a public road or highway.

The first project accomplished by the force from the camp was the construction of a road one mile in length leading from U.S. Route 15 to the summit of Willis Mountain and the erection of a watchtower on the highest peak of the mountain, where a watchman of the State

Forest Service is on duty during the spring and fall. From this altitude the watchman can see over the entire county and can locate accurately the location of any fire.

Tourists by the thousand visit Willis Mountain. A parking lot in the open space on top of the mountain and a widening of the road up its side became necessary. A kitchen 20 feet square of stone with a concrete floor and covered with slate will be ready for use by tourists and picnickers in the next 60 days.

The workers from the camp have built 75 miles of permanent roads in this county, including one in the heavily wooded section around Spear's Mountain in the extreme western section. A road also has been built up to the summit of Spear's Mountain, 1,500 feet above sea level, with a 30-foot watchtower.[31]

The hard work of Camp Buckingham and neighboring CCC camps was changing the Virginia landscape. By the autumn of 1937, the impact was significant and the *Richmond Times-Dispatch* applauded the change:

> About 50,000 acres of land in mid-Southside Virginia, much of it within 60 miles of Richmond, soon will be added to the State's elysian fields for huntsmen, fisherman and outdoor lovers. . . .
>
> Although the scheme has been under consideration for some time, it isn't generally known how highly the acreage, virtually useless for farm purposes, has been developed for pleasurable and useful ends by CCC workers under FSA direction.
>
> There are a half dozen lakes, some completed and some in course of construction, in the three land project areas which are to be taken over by the State and which lie in the Appomattox, Buckingham, Cumberland and Prince Edward Counties.[32]

The article went on to commend the Cumberland forest project (15,000 acres) and the Appomattox-Buckingham project, including the Appomattox Surrender grounds (30,000 acres).[33] The Cumberland County project had two lakes, one of which covered fifty acres and, by 1937, the CCC enrollees in

WPA Life Histories

Among the WPA Life Histories collected in Buckingham County at the end of the 1930s, three oral histories written by John W. Garrett included stories of Buckingham youth who joined the CCC. All of them were sent to camps outside of Buckingham County; however, the $25.00/month sent home to their families circulated in the local economy.

Twenty-year-old William R. Massey was living near Dillwyn when he enrolled in the CCC and was sent to the camp in Chesterfield County. Massey, whose opportunities were limited by a sixth grade education, studied to be an electrician.

One eighteen-year-old Buckingham resident named Aeinis Moore, whose father was a tenant farmer, was accepted at Appomattox County's Camp Lee-Grant. Moore went into the CCC with a second grade education, unable to read. While enrolled, he studied to be a car mechanic; the money he sent home to his family in Buckingham went towards a new truck for his father.

Seventeen-year-old Buckingham County native Herman W. Gunter begged his parents to "sign for him" to enroll in Chesterfield's camp where a friend worked, and had written to Herman extolling the great opportunities and friendly atmosphere of the CCC. A "ruddy country lad," Herman disdained school, preferring to hunt squirrel, turkey, and possum. While living at home, Herman was earning ten cents per hour shoveling dirt at a Buckingham gold mine, often working at hard labor for as long as ten hours a day. Once in the CCC, Herman still only made $1.00 a day but with it came three square meals a day, clothing, education, comradery, and, typically, a forty-hour work week.

Herman Gunter studied to be an electrician. He dutifully wrote to his mother, explaining that, after doing some K.P. duty, he was learning self-discipline and respect for order:

> The boss is a good old scout, but he means what he says. I think I'll be in on time from now on. Like my work fine and my electric work is a corker, coming home Xmas. Got a new suit en every thing. I'll tell you the C.C. Camp is a swell place for a boy to learn. Glad you and Pa sign me up. Will tell you all about it when I come home. We have good eats en everything. You ought to see how much I have gained.

Complete oral histories by these men are available in the WPA Life Histories Collection at the Library of Virginia.

Authorized Weekly Newspaper of the Civilian Conservation Corps

Appomattox and Buckingham had already completed one lake, "heavily stocked with game fish."[34] Photos of dam building promised new fish and game preserves and outdoor "playgrounds." Holliday Creek Dam was in process and was expected to soon flood 117 acres, impounding 500,000,000 gallons of water.[35]

Most of the work done by Camp Buckingham focused on building roads and bridges; however, in the spring of 1937, the men found themselves doing very different and demanding work. Stiff winds and dry conditions left large areas of Virginia vulnerable to forest fires. In early April, five separate fires were reported in Buckingham County. One at Spears Mountain raged over 1,000 acres. Across the state and across the nation, the men of the CCC were praised for their fire-fighting efforts.[36]

೮೦೦ಬ

Camp Buckingham closed in December of 1937. Reasons for this decision are not currently known; however, as the decade progressed, camps nationwide were not refunded. The camp buildings were quickly demolished. In the 1940s and 1950s, the Gene Dixon family purchased the land, including Peaceful Valley. Gene Dixon, Sr. moved the CCC-built picnic shelter down from Willis Mountain, relocating it at Peaceful Valley where it has continued to serve many church picnics, reunions, and weddings over the decades.[37]

In the mid-1990s, Jim Blake, son of James Edward Blake who was one of Camp Buckingham's first enrollees, initiated a request for a historic marker dedicated to the CCC Camp. In 1997, his efforts resulted in Historic Resources Marker Number F 63. It reads:

> *On this site in July 1933, CCC Camp P~56 Company 1367, opened with an enrollment of 192 Virginia men. The camp, which was organized as one of President Franklin Delano Roosevelt's New Deal employment programs, consisted of 52 small barracks, a large dining hall, two garages, and many other buildings. While at this camp, the men constructed 275 miles of forest roads, several bridges, three lookout towers, and numerous recreation buildings. The CCC also provided opportunities for the young men to further their*

education. In December 1937 "the camp" closed and all the buildings soon were demolished.[38]

When the marker was erected, William "Buck" Bailey remembered his experiences as an early enrollee at Camp Buckingham. "We cleared areas, built roads. Most of the roads in this county were constructed by the Corps.... And, we fought fires." According to Bailey, some of those fires were sparked by moonshiners' stills. Bailey's family lived in Buckingham and, evenings, he could walk home to the family farm near Salem Church. Ultimately, Bailey worked at five different CCC camps across the state. When he emerged from the program at the mandatory age of twenty-five, he was prepared to work for the highway department.[39]

༄༅

As a result of the 101 camps across Virginia, the state gained the foundation of its park system, including Appomattox–Buckingham's Holliday Lake State Park. The CCC also built cabins and recreational facilities in six state parks – Douthat, Fairy Stone, Hungry Mother, Seashore (now First Landing), Staunton River, and Westmoreland – as well as the Great Lodge at Douthat State Park. They helped create Skyline Drive.[40]

It has been over eighty years since the establishment of CCC Camp P-56, Company 1367 and Buckingham County continues to enjoy the fruits of the hard labor of many young men. While not as showy as Skyline Drive or the Great Lodge at Douthat State Park, much of the legacy of Camp Buckingham has long been integrated into everyday life in the county. Routinely, locals and visitors drive on country roads first laid down by the men of the CCC. A few scattered structures and an altered landscape are scant reminders of the spirit and industry employed by these young men during America's Great Depression. The opportunities the CCC offered its men, however, were possibly even more lasting, inextricably changing the lives of many . . . for the better.

NOTES

1   "Camp Roosevelt: America's First CCC Camp, 1933-1942," *Civilian Conservation Corps Legacy*, accessed August 2014, http://www.ccclegacy.org/Camp_Roosevelt_68B9.php. Most of the records concerning the CCC are housed at the National Archives in Washington, D.C. See "Records of the Civilian Conservation Corps," National Archives, accessed August 2014, http://www.archives.gov/research/guide-fed-records/groups/035.html. The National Personnel Records Center in St. Louis, Missouri maintains the enrollee papers for the Civilian Conservation Corps (CCC). See "Civilian Conservation Corps (CCC), Enrollee Records," National Archives, accessed August 2014, http://www.archives.gov/st-louis/archival-programs/civilian-personnel-archival/ccc-holdings-access.html. For more about the formation of the CCC camps nationwide see John A. Salmond, *The Civilian Conservation Corps, 1933-1942: A New Deal Case Study*, accessed September 2014, http://www.nps.gov/history/history/online_books/ccc/salmond/index.htm; "Civilian Conservation Corps Legacy," accessed September 2014, http://ccclegacy.org/; "The Civilian Conservation Corps," *American Experience*, accessed September 2014, http://www.pbs.org/wgbh/americanexperience/films/ccc/.

2   Milton Harr, *C. C. C. Camps in West Virginia: 1933-1942* (Quarrier Press, Kindle Edition, 2013), Kindle locations 48–54.

3   Harr, *C. C. C. Camps in West Virginia: 1933-1942*, Kindle Locations 70–73. According to Harr, "Originally, enrollees were to be between the ages of 18 and 25 and from families on relief, but in 1935 the age requirement was raised to 28 and in 1937 the age limits were changed to 17 to 23 years and the relief requirement dropped." See Ibid. There were also "Veterans Camps," to provide jobs for older men who had served in the Spanish-American War and World War I. See Connie M. Heddleston, *Georgia's Civilian Conservation Corps* (Chicago, IL: Arcadia Publishing, 2009), 67–82. In 1999, Greg Eanes privately published "Virginia Civilian Conservation Corps Camps" which included histories of Camp John J. Pershing (Crewe, Virginia) and Camp Gallion (Green Bay, Virginia).

4   "CCC Camps Virginia," *Civilian Conservation Corps Legacy*, accessed September 2014, http://ccclegacy.org/CCC_Camps_Virginia.html. In early 1934, the camp was identified as "Willis Mountain Camp." See Camp Report, Camp P-56, Dillwyn, Virginia, 27 February 1934, James Blake Collection.

5   Camp Report, Camp P-56, Dillwyn, Virginia, 27 February 1934; Inventory of Serviceable Excess Property at Camp P-56, 21 February 1938, James Blake Collection.

6   Olen Cole, Jr., *The African-American Experience in the Civilian Conservation Corps* (Gainesville, FL: University Press of Florida, 1999), 1–18. By February of 1935, eighteen of the sixty-five CCC camps in Virginia had been designated as "Negro camps," housing the state's quota of 5,000 men. See *Richmond Times-Dispatch*, 9 February 1935, p. 2. In July of 1935, integrated CCC camps were disbanded at the national level when CCC

Director Robert Fechner issued a directive ordering the "complete segregation of colored and white enrollees." See "African Americans in the Civilian Conservation Corps," *New Deal Network*, accessed August 2014, http://newdeal.feri.org/aaccc/.

7   "The 1367th CCC Company, Camp P-56, Dillwyn," pp. 188–189, James Blake Collection; Camp Report: Camp P-56, Co. 1367, Dillwyn, Virginia, 4 December 1935, James Blake Collection.

8   Camp Report, 4 December 1935.

9   Ibid.

10   *Richmond Times-Dispatch*, 13 July 1934, p. 7. As of February of 1934, fifty-seven local men had been enrolled since the camp's inception, indicating that the majority of men were not from Buckingham County. See Camp Report, Camp P-56, Dillwyn, Virginia, 27 February 1934, James Blake Collection. This was a common issue, not particular to Buckingham County. Douthat State Park was one of six Virginia recreational parks created by the State Commission on Conservation and Development. In Covington, only 16 of 202 men working at Camp Carson in Douthat State Park were local enrollees. The vast majority came from other parts of Virginia and Maryland. See "Douthat Park CCC Company Enrolls 202," *Richmond Times-Dispatch*, 2 November 1934, p. 8.

11   "World News," *Camp Chatter*, 21 August 1935, p. 5.

12   "Negro Books," *Camp Chatter*, 7 August 1935, p. 4. In 1940, forty-two-year-old Matthew Henderson was living in Fluvanna County and working as a farm laborer. The census also recorded that, on April 1, 1935, he was living in Buckingham County. See Federal Population Census, Fluvanna County, Virginia, 1940.

13   "The 1367th CCC Company, Camp P-56, Dillwyn," pp. 188–189.

14   "Editorials," *Camp Chatter*, 7 August 1935, p. 2.

15   Camp Report, 27 February 1934; "The 1367th CCC Company, Camp P-56, Dillwyn," pp. 188–189. According to Milton Harr, "Many camps recruited 'Local Experienced Men' or 'L. E. M.' to supervise the work crews and assist the technical staff. These 'L. E. M.' were usually older men with certain skills and experience in various crafts such as carpentry, stone work or woodcraft." See Harr, *C. C. C. Camps in West Virginia: 1933-1942*, Kindle Locations 116-122.

16   "The 1367th CCC Company, Camp P-56, Dillwyn," pp. 188–189; "Camp News," *Camp Chatter*, n.d; Emergency Conservation Work Camps, Camp No. P-56, Virginia, 3 December 1934, James Blake Collection.

17   S.M. Henderson, "Camp News," *Camp Chatter*, n.d.

18   "Activities," *Camp Chatter*, 21 August 1935, p. 3.

19   "Camp News," *Camp Chatter*, n.d.

20   "Camp News," *Camp Chatter*, n.d.

21 "Athletics," *Camp Chatter*, n.d.

22 Camp Report, Camp P-56, Co. 1367, Dillwyn, Virginia, 23 March 1937, James Blake Collection.

23 "One Is Killed, 17 Injured In Truck Wreck. CCC Vehicle Overturns in Buckingham; 2 Men Are Seriously Injured," *Richmond Times-Dispatch*, 2 November 1934, p. 8. According to a camp report, E.J. (Earl J.) Haden was the contracted physician at the camp at the time of the accident and may be the doctor mention in the news article. See Camp Report: Camp P-56, Co. 1367, Dillwyn, Virginia, 27 February 1934 and 4 December 1935, James Blake Collection.

24 "Negro Held on Murder Charge," *Richmond Times-Dispatch*, 5 February 1935, p. 3.

25 "Paralysis Up, Spotted Fever Hits Virginia: Summer 'Tick" Disease Kills Child, 6 Cases," *The Washington Post*, 28 July 1935, p. 10.

26 "Mountain Top Chosen For Episcopal Meeting," *Richmond Times-Dispatch*, 16 September 1935, p. 5.

27 "The 1367th CCC Company, Camp P-56, Dillwyn," pp. 188–189.

28 "C.C.C. Registration Book Destroyed by Vandals," *Richmond Times-Dispatch*, 24 July 1937, p. 3.

29 "The 1367th CCC Company, Camp P-56, Dillwyn," pp. 188–189.

30 *James F. Justin Civilian Conservation Corps Museum*, accessed August 2014, http://www.justinmuseum.com/famjustin/cccfdr1.html; "Third Anniversary of C.C.C.," accessed August 2014, http://www.pbs.org/wgbh/americanexperience/features/primary-resources/fdr-anniversary/; "The New Deal Network," accessed August 2014, http://newdeal.feri.org/.

31 "CCC Camp in Buckingham To Celebrate 3rd Birthday," *Richmond Times-Dispatch*, 2 July 1936, p. 2.

32 "Recreational Areas Near City Soon to Be Made Available," *Richmond Times-Dispatch*, 28 November 1937, p. 10.

33 Ibid.

34 Ibid.

35 "For Fun Outdoors," *Richmond Times-Dispatch*, 28 November 1937, p. 10.

36 "Warning Issued On Menace of Forest Fires," *Richmond Times-Dispatch*, 4 April 1937, p. 5. The men of the CCC continued to come to Buckingham County's aid even after Camp Buckingham closed in 1937. In March of 1939, similar conditions resulted in 244 separate fires across Virginia. On March 25th, 200 acres in Buckingham burned within five hours. Across the James River, at Howardsville, crews from the CCC Camp near White Hall in Albemarle County joined county forest wardens to fight a blaze

there. For days, fires continued to ignite. State Forester F.C. Pederson called the situation "very critical" because of massive amounts of dry vegetation. On March 27th, Pederson visited a fire near Dillwyn where 100 men from CCC camps in Amherst and Cumberland counties were fighting the year's largest reported fire, covering 1,200 acres. It was brought under control by 7 p.m. that evening. See "Winds and Dry Weather Blamed for Hundreds of Forest Fires Throughout Virginia," *Richmond Times-Dispatch*, 25 March 1939, p. 7; "Predicted Rain May Halt Fires Burning Throughout Virginia," *Richmond Times-Dispatch*, 27 March 1939, p. 3.

37 Margaret Thomas, emails to the author, February 2013.

38 Virginia Historical Highway Markers, Virginia Department of Historic Resources, accessed August 2014, http://www.dhr.virginia.gov/hiway_markers/hwmarker_info.htm.

39 Tana Knott, "Depression-Era Camp Raised Lasting Legacy," *The Farmville Herald*, 18 July 1997, pp. 1–2; Kathryn Orth, "Marker would honor workers' labors, Buckingham man remembers Conservation Corps," *Richmond Times-Dispatch*, 11 March 1996. Today, in Buckingham County, Bailey Road (Route 792) runs not far from Salem Church Road (Route 634).

40 "C.C. CAMP IS A SWELL PLACE FOR A BOY TO LEARN," Library of Virginia, accessed August 2014, http://www.lva.virginia.gov/exhibits/newdeal/ccc_camp.htm.

MAYSVLLE GALLERY

Frances Benjamin Johnston (1864–1952). (LIBRARY OF CONGRESS)

Frances Benjamin Johnston

In the 1880s, Frances Benjamin Johnston studied art in Paris, returning home to Washington, D.C., where she learned photography. Nationally recognized as a professional photographer and businesswoman, her pictures straddled the art and commercial worlds, resulting in a sixty-year career blending news and documentary work with portraiture and images of contemporary architecture, gardens, and landscapes.

At the height of the Great Depression, Johnston traveled thousands of miles by car, creating over 7,100 images for the Carnegie Survey of the Architecture of the South. The goal was to record both vernacular and "high style" structures. In 1933, Maysville, also known as Buckingham Court House, served as one of Johnston's subjects. She also documented Buckingham County's Bellmont, built by the Bell family c. 1770.

In the 1940s, she moved to New Orleans where she died in 1952.

Unidentified house, Buckingham, Buckingham County, Virginia. (PHOTO BY FRANCES BENJAMIN JOHNSTON, 1933. LIBRARY OF CONGRESS)

Left to right:

1. Buckingham Hotel (a.k.a. The Moseley House) sat directly across from Buckingham Courthouse and was demolished c.1960.

2. In 2014, the next house was still standing and is currently a private rental residence. Long owned by the Spencer/Moseley family, for many years it was the Boy Scout House.

3. The two smaller white houses on the right probably provided residences for the hotel's African-American staff. Significantly, a fence separates the two structures on the left and the two on the right. Mid-20th century, the small white house on the right was torn down. In 2014, the remaining house was a private rental residence.

Maysville

Incorporated in 1818, the founding of Maysville attempted to re-establish a village at Buckingham Courthouse after the failure of Greensville, incorporated in 1792. This time, the village was successful. By 1835, according to Joseph Martin's *Gazetteer of Virginia*, Maysville had a population of 300 residents. In addition to the county buildings, there were about fifty dwelling houses, one Free Church and Maysville Presbyterian Church, The Fairchild School (a female academy) and two elementary schools for boys, four mercantile stores, an apothecary shop, and three taverns. Tradesmen and craftsmen included a tanner, two saddlers, two boot and shoe manufactures, a silversmith and watchmaker, a milliner and mantua maker, two wagon makers, two cabinetmakers, three tailors, a tin plate worker, and a miller. Professionals included five resident attorneys and three physicians. Mail was delivered five times each week. County courts were held monthly on the 2nd Monday, quarterly in March, May, August, and November. Judge Daniel held his circuit Superior Court of Law and Chancery on the 10th of August and September.

Nearly 100 years later, photographer Frances Benjamin Johnston (1864–1952) documented Maysville for the Carnegie Survey of the Architecture of the South.

Unidentified house, Buckingham, Buckingham County, Virginia. (PHOTO BY FRANCES BENJAMIN JOHNSTON, 1933. LIBRARY OF CONGRESS)

The Davidson House

This structure went unidentified by Frances Benjamin Johnston, as did most of her photographs taken in Maysville. The goal of the Carnegie Survey of the Architecture of the South was to document vernacular architecture, not to record history.

Commonly known as the Davidson House, it sits diagonally across from Buckingham Courthouse and has had many owners and purposes over the years, including a store, a bank, a lawyer's office, a bar, a tea room, and a private residence. It may, at least in part, be one of the oldest structures in Buckingham County. One wall is dated 1740.

It is named for Thomas J. Davidson, who owned the house when Frances Benjamin Johnston made her picture. A bachelor, Davidson was a merchant. In 1935, Frank H. Spencer purchased the house, living there with his wife, Nannie, and his family; they also operated a general store.

In 1937, Elizabeth McCraw surveyed the house for the Virginia Historical Inventory, writing: "The house has two entrances on the front; one being a very large single door with two glass panels in the upper half. The other is a double door also partly of glass. Over each door is a half moon shaped plastered arch. ... The room to the left on the first floor, has a large fireplace over which is a low carved mantel. [A] cased-in winding stairway leads from this room to the second floor. This room is said to have been the counting room for the store years ago."

Old Colonial Home for Tourist, Buckingham, Buckingham County, Virginia. (PHOTO BY FRANCES BENJAMIN JOHNSTON, 1933. LIBRARY OF CONGRESS)

Dr. Tucker's House

In 1933, Dr. Tucker's House (built c.1820) advertised itself as: "Old Colonial Home For Tourist – Sandwiches-Meals-Rooms-Baths." While far from Colonial, the home was legitimately historic. Originally built to warehouse tobacco, it was also used by the county Treasurer's Office, by the Masons for meetings, and possibly as a bank. Over the years, Mrs. W. E. Pratt, as well as Mrs. Pittman Tucker, took in boarders or lodgers. Four doctors have been associated with the property: Dr. Whitcomb Eliphalet Pratt, Dr. Price "Perkins" Glover, Dr. Garland "Lightfoot" Morris, and Dr. Edward Pittman "Pitt" Tucker, who purchased the house in 1917, practiced in Buckingham for thirty-three years, and died at his home in 1939. One obituary for Dr. Tucker read, "While for years he was not altogether a physically vigorous man, he gave himself unreservedly to his profession, even rough roads, heat and cold, darkness and fatigue never holding him back from his ministry to the people of the county which he served."

Dr. Tucker's House is included in the Buckingham Court House District, Virginia Landmarks Register and National Register of Historic Places. Its rare Jeffersonian accordion (peak and valley) roof can be seen in Frances Benjamin Johnston's photograph. The expansive front porch, lined with cushioned cane chairs, is a testament to the Tuckers' hospitality. In 1933, watching the world go by on Highway 60 was an entertaining pastime for locals as well as visitors.

Unidentified house, Buckingham, Buckingham County, Virginia. (PHOTO BY FRANCES BENJAMIN JOHNSTON, 1933. LIBRARY OF CONGRESS)

Rose Terrace is included in the Buckingham Court House District (VIRGINIA LANDMARKS REGISTER AND NATIONAL REGISTER OF HISTORIC PLACES), *which notes the building's fine Flemish bond brickwork. Today, the expansive, inviting veranda and balconies which attracted Frances Benjamin Johnston's eye are closed in.*

Rose Terrace

Originally called Rose Cottage, in the late 1930s this house was renamed Rose Terrace to distinguish it from the Rose Cottage located just outside Maysville. Rose Terrace sits at the extreme west end of Buckingham Court House on the north side of Highway 60.

In 1936, Elizabeth McCraw described Rose Terrace's lovely entry for the Virginia Historical Inventory: "A flagstone walk leads to the entrance door. This heavy six panel door with a fan shaped transom, leads into the front hall, which is more like a room than a hall." The interior included a welcoming parlor, with a cornice of plaster and "a matching decoration in the ceiling in the shape of a diamond." The eight-room house included a "splendid basement of three rooms," as well as a "unique stairway" from the main floor to the basement. Mrs. McCraw also described the back of the house, photographed by Frances Benjamin Johnston: "A Dutch door opens from the kitchen to the 'veranda' which is under the back porch, and floored with brick. A brick walk leads to the office building in the side yard."

The original section of the house was erected sometime between 1776 and 1800. Dr. William Perkins Moseley (1794–1863) purchased the property in 1820 and elaborated it to accommodate his large family. In 1833, Dr. Moseley became an elder at Maysville Presbyterian Church, where he served until his death.

In 1936, Elizabeth McCraw's informants included Florence LaSalle (Moseley) Pratt (1855–1951). Her husband, Dr. Whitcomb Eliphalet Pratt (1849–1901), was the grandson of Alexander Trent Moseley (1786–1873), who was born in the house. Mrs. McCraw also interviewed Margaret G. (Mrs. Philip Ashley) Grigg (1869–1960), the owner and resident of Rose Terrace when the photo was made.

Well house, Buckingham, Buckingham County, Virginia. (PHOTO BY FRANCES BENJAMIN JOHNSTON, 1933. LIBRARY OF CONGRESS)

Note the Buckingham slate roof atop the well house at Rose Terrace.

The Well House at Rose Terrace

In 1936, when Elizabeth McCraw surveyed the property for the Virginia Historical Inventory, she not only described the architectural details of the residence but also mentioned the pleasant yard, writing: "The back and side yards deserve mention for the variety of roses and the many beautiful trees, such as tulip, poplar, South Carolina Poplar, Osage Orange, holly, magnolia, ash and mimosa. A young tree is coming out from a stump of an ailanthus, which was brought from England and planted here in 1848."

The well house has been maintained and still stands in the yard.

Unidentified house, Buckingham, Buckingham County, Virginia. (PHOTO BY FRANCES BENJAMIN JOHNSTON, 1933. LIBRARY OF CONGRESS)

During the 1930s, Maysville Hotel was known as The Pearson Hotel.

Maysville Hotel

In 1933, when Frances Benjamin Johnston photographed the historic "Maysville Hotel," it had been known as The Pearson Hotel for nearly two decades. John E. Pearson and his wife, Alma, were the hotel keepers. John Pearson died in 1923, leaving Alma the sole proprietor.

The hotel, which still sits across the street to the west of Buckingham Courthouse, was built c.1815. The original proprietor and town founder, Thomas May, operated it until his death in 1837. His obituary in the *Richmond Enquirer* noted: "Thomas May, proprietor of the Manor at our Court-house – an honest, worthy man, of kind and social feelings, his lady having deceased about three years before him. He has left an amiable family of sons and daughters to mourn their great bereavement."

In 1814, and from 1825–1827 and 1829–1831, Thomas May held Ordinary Licenses and operated a tavern at the hotel. Prior to May's death, his "Tavern" (which included the hotel grounds and a contiguous farm of 700–800 acres) was offered for sale. Commissioners, including Buckingham County leaders, Charles Yancey and Thomas Moseley Bondurant, were appointed in March of 1837 to auction the property. An announcement in the *Richmond Enquirer* described the hotel and its amenities:

> . . . the land and Tavern referred to in said act of Assembly, it being the well known and very valuable establishment, formerly and so long kept by Thomas May, Esq. The Tavern buildings are of brick, very large and commodious, and slate roofed, with a lot of ten acres of land, on which are also very large and roomy stables, recently built, perhaps large enough to receive one hundred and fifty horses, with an upper story large enough to store a winter's forage; also a kitchen, with a well of excellent water near the door, an office, meat and ice houses, with an ice pond convenient, carriage, servant's and other houses, thus rendering this one of the most complete and convenient houses in the interior.

Covered connecting passageway, Buckingham, Buckingham County, Virginia. (Photo by Frances Benjamin Johnston, 1933. Library of Congress)

This archway connects the Maysville Hotel and an adjoining apartment.

In the summer of 1860, Alexander Trent Moseley was the "landlord" of the hotel. His lodgers included a lofer (sic), law student, saddler, clerk, and lawyer. The hotel changed hands several times between Moseley and the Pearsons in the early 20th century. For at least ten years, 1863–1873, Capt. John Clark Turner, planter and entrepreneur, owned the property. When Buckingham's courthouse burned in 1869, initial meetings to cope with the disaster where held at Turner's "Brick Tavern."

In the 21st century, the hotel was transformed once again into a bed and breakfast appropriately named Maysville Manor. In addition to lodgers, proprietor Nancy Maxey hosts weddings and other special events throughout the year.

Unidentified outbuildings, Buckingham, Buckingham County, Virginia. (PHOTO BY FRANCES BENJAMIN JOHNSTON, 1933. LIBRARY OF CONGRESS)

Outbuildings, Maysville Hotel, no longer standing.

Unidentified outbuildings, Buckingham, Buckingham County, Virginia. (PHOTO BY FRANCES BENJAMIN JOHNSTON, 1933. LIBRARY OF CONGRESS)

Outbuildings, Maysville Hotel, no longer standing.

PART TWO

PEOPLE OF BUCKINGHAM COUNTY

Humanity Hall, 2010 (Joanne L. Yeck Collection)

Elijah G. Hanes and Humanity Hall Academy

In the days before public schools in Virginia, many private schools came and went in Buckingham County. In the 18th and early 19th century, the gentry conducted so-called plantation schools, like the one at Seven Islands, home of Col. John Nicholas. There, select young gentlemen boarded, learning their Latin and Greek. Some were bored and played pranks. Some went on to college. Many were satisfied, as were their parents, to have their rough country edges smoothed off by a learned professor.[1] At the other end of the spectrum were the so-called field schools, where teachers were paid by the day and children from local farms attended when they could. Farm work, inclement weather, or an outbreak of whooping cough often took precedence over attending school.[2]

Across the 19th century, numerous institutes, seminaries, and academies for boys and girls operated in Buckingham County. As early as 1820, there was a schoolhouse at Red Oak, near Whispering Creek, on the property of Peter Stratton. It accommodated about a dozen children.[3] Beginning in the mid-1820s, John Fairchild and his wife were the Principals at their seminary, commonly known as The Fairchild School or Buckingham High School for Young Ladies. Located at Maysville, it flourished for about twenty years until a fire destroyed the building in the mid-1840s.[4] The Moseley and Bondurant families established Slate River School, which operated in the 1830s.[5] The crown jewel for young ladies was Virginia's first college for women, Buckingham Female Collegiate Institute, located on the Richmond–Lynchburg stage road, not far from Alpha.[6] Likewise, one of the finest educational opportunities for young gentlemen in central Virginia was also in Buckingham County at Humanity Hall Academy.

Founded by Elijah Garland Hanes, the original location for Humanity Hall Academy was not far from the eventual site of the Buckingham Female Collegiate Institute, near the Buckingham–Cumberland County line east of Nuckols.[7] Born about 1796, Elijah G. Hanes came to Buckingham from

Hanover County to teach school. While boarding at the Brown home, Physic Springs, Hanes got to know his bride-to-be, Mary Jarman Brown.[8] In 1824, they married and in about 1826 they settled on 300 acres along Randolph's Creek, conveyed to Elijah by his father-in-law, Garland Brown. There, Hanes established Humanity Hall Academy.[9]

The school's name may have remembered another Humanity Hall Academy in Hanover County. Rev. Robert Ryland, who later became President of Richmond College, prepared at Hanover's Humanity Hall, where he studied Latin and Greek under Rev. Peter Nelson from 1820 to 1823.[10] Did Elijah Hanes also study there before he came to Buckingham County? Whatever the source of his Academy's name, it is notable. Elijah Hanes did not name his school after himself or after a place, such as Slate River School, but after a philosophy of study... with an emphasis on humanity. This unusual orientation will be supported in the anecdotes of his pupils, the reputation of the school, and of its master.

By the early 1830s, Hanes was well-established and regularly advertised his academy in the Richmond newspapers, proclaiming its healthful location, the strength of his curriculum, and the gentleness of his approach:

> **HUMANITY HALL ACADEMY** – The subscriber, grateful for the very liberal patronage he has received, during the present and many preceding years, respectfully informs his friends and the public generally, that the exercises of his school for the ensuing year, will commence on the 15th January, and be continued until the 15th November, making a term of ten months, without vacation. The utility of this course has been tested by experience, and must be obvious to every reflecting mind. In this Seminary, will be taught every thing necessary to prepare young men for College, or fit them for the ordinary avocations of life.–Tuition, Board, Washing, Lodging, &c., will be furnished at the very reduced price of $85 the term, $35 in advance, and the balance ($50,) at the end of the term. Those who engage for a shorter time than ten months, will pay $10 per month. Humanity Hall is situated in the lower end of Buckingham, near Physic Springs, in a remarkably healthy, retired and peaceful neighbourhood, entirely remote from the haunts of vice and dissipation. The discipline of this school is mild and parental, and the best testimony I can give of its character, is a reference to the many young men who have, in part, been educated at it or under my care. – Address, Physic Springs, Buckingham.
>
> ELIJAH G. HANES[11]

Hanes repeatedly informed the readers of the Richmond newspapers that his seminary taught Greek, Latin, English, geography, arithmetic, as well as natural and moral philosophy. He reassured parents of potential students that their souls, as well as their minds, were safe with him: "Those disposed to confine their children or wards in my care, may rest satisfied, that the same attention will be paid to their morals and welfare, as to my own children. Personal attention will be paid to their reading the Scriptures and other moral and religious books on the Sabbath."[12]

Over the years, Hanes invited prospective parents to contact successful alumni: "Those disposed to become interested in this School are referred to Robert Hubard, Esq., member of the Legislature, and to all others, who for a period of more than twenty years, may have been at any time concerned in this School, whether they be parents, guardians or pupils."[13] He also referred readers of his advertisements to Rev. William A. Smith, Doctor of Divinity, and President of Randolph-Macon College.[14] He often pointed out the school's proximity to the prestigious Buckingham Female Collegiate Institute. Indeed, Humanity Hall Academy had a broad and solid reputation.

HUMANITY HALL ACADEMY.

THE exercises of this school will be resumed on Monday, the 16th January, and will close on the 16th Nov. 1843, making a term of ten months—no vacation. The terms for Tuition, Board, Washing, Lodging, &c. will be $130 the term, payable on the 16th November, but a deduction of 20 per cent. per annum will be made on all sums paid previous to that day. In this Seminary will be taught every study necessary to prepare young men for College, or fit them for the ordinary business of life. Those disposed to become interested in this School are referred to Robert Hubard, Esq., member of the Legislature, and to all others, who for a period of more than twenty years, may have been, at any time concerned in this School, whether they be parents, guardians or pupils.

ELIJAH G. HANES.

P. S. Address, Physic Springs, Buckingham co., Va.

de 7 d1tcwt15J

☞Enquirer and Richmond Christian Advocate will copy until 15th January.

Humanity Hall Academy advertisement, 1843 (Courtesy Richmond Whig)

Hanes' own family steadily increased in size and the Hanes children were growing up in an intellectually rich and physically healthy environment. Six lived to adulthood, including Garland Brown and James C. Hanes, who would follow in their father's footsteps as school teachers. Their mother, Mary, however, was only thirty-two when she died in 1840.[15] She was buried in front of the house, in what long served as an orchard.[16]

> *Here lies the body of Mary J. Hanes*
> *Second daughter of Capt. G. Brown and wife of Elijah G. Hanes*
> *In sure and steadfast hope to rise*
> *And claim her mansion in the skye*
> *A christian here her flesh laid down*
> *The Cross exchanging for a Crown*
> *2nd Jan'y A.D. 1840*
> Aetatis 32[17]

In time, the Hanes property was sold out of the family, though they retained the cemetery. In 1937, Garnett Williams described what remained:

> Although the Hanes family preserved one acre for the cemetery, the present owners have cultivated over every grave except one, this one of Mary J. Hanes. That tomb stands in perfect condition today, although it has stood there for nearly a hundred years. The grave is walled up of brick about two feet with an oval shape concrete top. The head stone is unusually large and is of marble. The foot stone is a smaller marble slab. The grave is completely surrounded by growing corn. I have been told there were many graves there at one time.[18]

Following Mary's death, with the help of nine slaves above the age of ten, Elijah Hanes managed the farm, the house, and the school, complete with sixteen boarding scholars and his own children. In 1840, a total of thirty-eight pupils attended the Academy.[19]

At the school, Hanes was assisted by William B. Shepard, A.M. In 1846, he described his assistant: "Mr. Shepard is a Virginian, and a graduate of Hampden

Sydney College, and admirably fitted by experience and education, for the station he will occupy in this Academy."[20]

With his own small children to rear, Elijah Hanes needed a helpmate and found one in Judith Leake Ayres.[21] In 1847, Hanes purchased 1,050 acres on Joshua's and Turpins Creek, near Chambers' Mills, about ten miles north of Buckingham Courthouse, paying $10,000 for the farm.[22] He announced the new location of Humanity Hall Academy in the *Richmond Enquirer*:

> The subscriber having purchased a Farm, the late residence of Ambrose Ford, Esq., a few miles East of Buckingham Court House, will commence a School at that place on the third Monday in January, 1848, for the instruction of boys in the most useful branches of English and Classical Literature. He will take a few Boarders at the very moderate price of 100 dollars each, for a term of ten months – that sum embracing all the charges for Board, Washing, Lodging, and the Tuition fee.
>
> The subscriber's long experience and great success in training the minds and shaping the morals of youth, he deems a sufficient pledge for the most faithful performance of every duty connected with his profession.[23]

Humanity Hall, 18th century mantel restored (COURTESY MARTHA STOKES)

The farm, previously owned and developed by the Holman family, included a handsome manor house.[24] This tract, which became known as Humanity Hall, lay just across Slate River from Edgehill, the home of Hanes' wife, Judith Leake Ayres. In this lovely rural setting, graced with terraced gardens and abundant shade trees, the Haneses were surrounded by Judith's nieces and nephews and Elijah's grandchildren.

Elijah Hanes was conservative in his politics and was affiliated with the Whig party.[25] A Methodist, Hanes helped establish a chapel located almost a mile northeast of Humanity Hall called Stony Point. In 1853, he served as both Class Leader and Steward. His wife, Judith, and his children, including Garland B. and James C. Hanes, joined him in worship there.[26] Later, in 1859, Hanes Chapel replaced Stony Point. Erected in Elijah's honor, it was constructed about a half mile east of the Academy. Still in use today, the oldest grave there dates from 1841.[27]

In 1850, Elijah G. Hanes celebrated thirty-five successful and satisfying years of teaching, describing the new location of his school as "midway between Buckingham Court House and the Female Collegiate Institute."[28] By 1854, Hanes had expanded his facilities and could accommodate twenty boarders. Overflow was welcome at Apple Hill, the home of his neighbor, Selah Holbrook.

Hanes Chapel (JOANNE L. YECK COLLECTION)

That year, his son, Garland B. Hanes, was advertised as his Assistant.[29] In addition to the academic building and the student dormitory, Elijah Hanes had a separate office and library.[30]

In the summer of 1854, an anonymous Humanity Hall Academy alumnus wrote to the editors of the *Richmond Whig* extolling the talents of the Hanes family and the virtues of Humanity Hall Academy.

FOURTH OF JULY AT HUMANITY HALL ACADEMY, BUCKINGHAM.

Messrs Editors: – Together with a very large audience I had the pleasure to-day of witnessing the exceedingly interesting exercises at this venerable institution of learning. I say *venerable*, because its universally esteemed Principal (Col. E.G. Hanes) has been at its head largely upwards of thirty years. The exercises commenced with the examination of the Students, conducted principally by the Rev. John C. Blackwell, President of the [Buckingham Female Collegiate] Institute, and the result was in every way highly credible both to themselves and teacher.

After the examination was completed the Declaration of Independence was read–that document which "spoke an empire into birth and its own existence into immortality." Then followed an intellectual feast such as we seldom meet with on 4th of July occasions. I allude to the address of Mr. Garland B. Hanes, [son of the Principal, and a recent graduate of Randolph Macon College] before the students who had previously invited him to do so. . . .

At the conclusion of his address the large company adjourned to a beautiful lunch, and returned to witness the concluding exercises of the evening, which consisted of various speeches and essays from the students – original by the young men and extracts by the boys – all exceedingly entertaining and complimentary to themselves. The little boy, whose subject was "Pulchritudine Nitida," will long be remembered with a merry laugh. But enough. I can't enter into details. The worthy Principal gave notice that we might expect "a few more of the same sort," this day twelve months. God speed to my old *Alma Mater*.

ALUMNUS

Examiner and *Herald*, copy.[31]

Cyrus McCormick's reaper, 1846 (COURTESY, *THE CULTIVATOR*)

Selah Holbrook:
Humanity Hall Academy's Talented Neighbor

APPLE HILL FOR SALE. — The subscriber offers for sale his Farm in Buckingham county, containing 318 Acres, about one half in original Timber of superior quality for building purposes, adapted to the culture of tobacco, a healthy location and near the Slate River Navigation, and adjoining Col. Hanes' Acadamy (sic), having the advantage of taking boarders for the same and a good location for a Physician. The improvements are a new Two Story Dwelling house, large and well finished, with all other necessary out houses, an office in the yard, a superior Apple Orchard and first rate Spring of excellent water. The price and terms of payment will be accommodating. For further particulars address,

SELAH HOLBROOK
Chambers Mills, Buckingham County, Va.

In 1856, Selah Holbrook considered selling his farm, Apple Hill, nestled in the neighborhood of Chambers Mills, adjacent Humanity Hall Academy. There Holbrook farmed and worked as a carriage maker. The farm with its sweet water and superior apples did not sell and Holbrook remained in Buckingham County into the 1860s. Years before, Selah Holbrook had made a significant contribution to Cyrus McCormick's famous reaper. An article, published in the *Pacific Rural Press* on May 16, 1885, related the story of their partnership:

> At length, in 1841 . . . [McCormick] made the acquaintance of a man named Selah Holbrook, a Vermonter, who had immigrated to Virginia, and erected an old-fashioned tilt-hammer, with blacksmith shop attached, near Fort Republic, in Rockingham county. Mr. Holbrook was perhaps [at] that time the most skilled workman both in iron and steel in the State. McCormick went to the shop and home of Holbrook, where he remained for over a week, instructing and assisting him in making the first successful sickle that was ever made for a harvesting machine. In those days it required a great deal of labor to make a sickle, for the steel from which the sickle was made came in large, heavy, flat bars, and had to be forged into shape with tilt-hammers and sledges. In the fourth trial Mr. Holbrook succeeded in securing the desired shape and temper.
>
> The hammer, anvil and block that was used by Mr. Holbrook during his engagement with McCormick were preserved by his son, John H. Holbrook, until the year 1870, when all, save the anvil block, were carried away in the disastrous flood of that year, the most destructive ever known in the valley of the Shenandoah. . . . This anvil block is all that is now left of the once widely known shop of Mr. Holbrook, in which an important part of the first McCormick reaper was made; and while the name of Holbrook is hardly ever mentioned, in fact almost forgotten, it is extremely doubtful, but for the aid he gave the inventor, that the great McCormick reaper might possibly have been second or third, and not first among the laborsaving machines of the world.

HUMANITY HALL ACADEMY.
Buckingham County, Va. Nov. 5th 1857

Dear Sir,

The following Report exhibits the progress and deportment of your son Lewis, during the past quarter.

PROGRESS IN STUDY.		Times.	Demerits.
Geography,	Absent from Recitation without excuse,		
English Grammar,	" " Prayers " "		
Arithmetic,	" " Premises " "		
History, Modern,	Late at Recitation, " "		
" Ancient,	Failure to prepare Recitation, without excuse,		
Spelling, 6	Disorder in Room, " "		
Chemistry,	" " Recitation Room, " "		
Natural Philosophy,	Profanity,		
	Gambling,		
Latin, 5	Keeping Fire Arms,		
Greek,	Failure on Composition,	1	15
Mathematics, 6	" " Declamation,	2	15
Declamation, 0	EXPLANATION.—Nos. 1, 2 and 3 = 3rd grade.		
Composition, 0	" 4, 5 and 6 = 2nd "		
	" 7, 8 and 9 = 1st "		

When the demerits of any Student, at any time during five months, shall have reached one hundred and fifty, he will be positively and immediately sent home.

Very Respectfully,

E. G. HANES, Principal.

Had Lewis remained and prepared himself for an examination, it is probable he would have a higher grade on his studies.

Lewis Ayres, Progress and Deportment Report, 1857, Humanity Hall Academy
(GENE LIGHTFOOT COLLECTION)

In late summer of 1856, another letter appeared in the *Richmond Whig* praising the academy's annual commencement exercises. The author, "Viator" of Dinwiddie County, Virginia found the entire event delightful and his rambling recitation of the day reveals not only the mid-19th century pace of Buckingham County, but also at least one Virginian's enthusiasm for the virtues of a gentlemanly education:

HUMANITY HALL ACADEMY, BUCKINGHAM, VA.

I have just returned from a visit to the annual exhibition of this institution. What I saw and heard induces me to ask the use of your columns to direct public attention to this old and eminently useful institution of learning....

The exercises of this interesting occasion were varied, and consisted of declamations and original orations by the students of the academy, together with several literary addresses. After prayer by Rev. Mr. Cheatham, Wm. B. Shepard, Esq., a young lawyer of promise and note in Buckingham, was introduced to the audience and addressed a few practical *extempore* remarks to the young men. His remarks abounded in sound views, wholesome advice and liberal encouragement....

At this hour, Wm. M. Cabel, Esq., a distinguished gentleman from Nelson, was engaged to address the young men of the Academy; but a few days before the appointed time he notified them that important professional engagements would prevent his attendance. They then applied to Mr. Garland B. Hanes, the elder brother associated in the board of instruction, at this place, to occupy the hour assigned to Mr. Cabel in their programme of exercises.... It is due to Mr. Hanes to state, in this connection, that he had just returned from his bridal tour, in the spring region of Virginia. I can very well imagine that, in this state of beatitude and freedom from care of the school-room and the scholars' sanctum, to say nothing of his absorption in this new care of his life–a wife.... But, nevertheless, when the hour arrived, he took the stand and discharged the duty in a manner so masterly, that I, at least, did not regret–and I opine few did–the circumstance which afforded us such a delightful literary repast. Time will not allow an extended notice of this interesting address. His subject was "the scholar's mission." He was clear in thought, chaste and classical in style, felicitous in expression and manner. I predict for him a brilliant and useful course. He deserves it, and will attain it.[32]

The author went on to discuss the address of Garland's younger brother, James C. Hanes, who spoke of "the christian scholar" and claimed "that Humanity Hall Academy is one of the first institutions of learning of this grade in our country. It is one of the oldest, if not the very oldest in Virginia. It has been in continued operation, since January, 1815, under the management of its present Principal. Col. Hanes."[33]

"Viator" concluded by exalting Col. Hanes as a "pioneer and veteran in the cause of learning" and commending "his educated and talented sons following in his illustrious wake!"[34] And follow they did. In 1850, at the age of nineteen, Garland B. Hanes was teaching in Cumberland County. By 1854, he had graduated from Randolph-Macon College, earning his Bachelor of Arts, followed by a Master of Arts degree in 1857.[35] James C. Hanes also studied at Randolph-Macon earning his Bachelor's degree in 1855 and his Master of Arts degree in 1858.[36] Their father, Elijah G. Hanes, died in1858, leaving the future of Humanity Hall Academy to his sons. Richmond's *The Daily Dispatch* announced his death:

AFFAIRS OF BUCKINGHAM

Col. Hayne (sic), Principal of Humanity Hall Academy in this county, died suddenly on last Saturday. He was in good health at morning prayers, but before noon was a corpse. Apoplexy was the disease causing his death. The Academy will be continued by his son who is [in] every way qualified for the charge.[37]

Garland rose to the task of Principal and James was his Associate. In the winter of 1859, they advertised, with a sorrowful note, in the *Richmond Whig*:

HUMANITY HALL ACADEMY.
BUCKINGHAM COUNTY, VA.

Garland B. Hanes, A.M., Principal.

James C. Hanes, A.M., Associate.

The exercises of this School will be resumed on the 12th of January, 1860, and continue until the 30th of June following.

In the government of the school, we shall endeavor to be guided by the principles practiced so long and successfully as a teacher by our lamented father.

The long standing and permanency of this institution, its healthful and retired location, we trust, will continue to recommend it to the favorable consideration of the public.

TERMS (from 12 Jan. To 30th June)

Board, with every necessary, except lights.....$66.00

Tuition..$27.50

Primary English $20.00

One-third in advance, the balance at the close of the session.

Gravel Hill P.O.[38]

By 1861, Garland B. Hanes, now thirty years old, was joined by P. Fletcher Ford, A.M., who had been trained at Humanity Hall and was a recent Honor Graduate of Randolph-Macon College, as his Associate Principal. That winter, their broadside advertised the Spring Term, beginning February 4, 1861, stating the familiar refrains: "This Institution is located in a retired and healthy section of Buckingham County, six miles west of the Female Collegiate Institute. Its successful operation for many years bespeaks the favorable consideration of the public."[39]

Hanes and Ford explained, "The Course of Instruction is thorough and systematic." It included English, Mathematics, Latin, Greek, and French. "The discipline is firm," they warned. "The strictest attention is paid to the cultivation and preservation of proper habits." Board and tuition was priced at $170 per session of ten months, $70 of which was to be paid in advance. The balance was due at the end of the term.[40]

Within two months, the Civil War was under way. Garland Hanes helped lead the Buckingham Institute Guards (Company F, 20th Regiment, Virginia Infantry) as captain of Company F.[41] James C. Hanes enlisted in the 2nd Regiment of the Virginia Artillery, organized in February of 1862. He was captain of Company K.[42] Fletcher Ford joined the fight, as well, dying at Gettysburg.[43] In their absence, the Academy carried on. Some responsibility may have fallen to Garland's wife, Mary Elizabeth, who was educated at the Buckingham Female Collegiate Institute, teaching French and Music there until her marriage. She was the daughter of Dr. John C. Blackwell, Methodist minister and educator, who was concurrently struggling to keep the Institute in operation.[44] In 1862, Garland Hanes was wounded and ultimately discharged, surviving the war.[45]

Following the war, during May, June, and July of 1868, Garland B. Hanes advertised a "new" Humanity Hall Academy announcing that his highly-educated wife, Mary Elizabeth (Blackwell) Hanes, and her sister, Josephine, would join him as teachers.

HUMANITY HALL ACADEMY,
Buckingham County VA.

First-Class School For Girls

This Institution, being known to the public as a School for boys, under the management of the subscriber's father, Col. Elijah G. Hanes, deceased, will be opened as for girls exclusively, on the 1ST DAY OF SEPTEMBER, 1868, by the following experienced teachers:

Garland B. Hanes, A.M.,
Mrs. Mary Lizzie Hanes,
Miss Josephine Blackwell.

Both ladies are graduates of the Buckingham Female Collegiate Institute.

Our purpose is to establish permanently a FIRST-CLASS SCHOOL FOR GIRLS, combining every educational advantage with the comforts of home. The course of instruction will embrace Modern and Ancient Languages, Mathematics and Music, and every other branch usually taught in Female Schools or Colleges.

Only ten (10) boarders will be received, who will board with and be treated as members of the principal's family; and will be required to give the strictest attention to the cultivation of their minds and manners, not only in the school-room, but in their private apartments, and in the social and family circles. Our object is to CULTIVATE and EDUCATE.

TERMS: $250 per session of ten months, one-half in advance without exception; the balance at the expiration of the first five months. Pupils boarding in the neighborhood will be charged from $40 to $70, payable as above. No extra charges.

At the beginning and end of the session of ten months a comfortable carriage for pupils (attended personally by the principal) and a conveyance for their baggage, will be furnished from and to New Canton, on the James river and Kanawha canal, free of any expense. Apply before 1st August to

GARLAND B. HANES, A.M.,
Principal.

GRAVEL HILL P.O., BUCKINGHAM COUNTY, VA.[46]

Similar advertisements did not follow in the *Richmond Whig* indicating the female academy may have been short lived; however, statistics collected by the Virginia Department of Education stated that Josephine Blackwell was teaching at Humanity Hall Academy in 1872.[47]

By 1870, Garland B. Hanes was practicing law in Buckingham County, where he also served as Commonwealth Attorney. That year, there were numerous Hanes children living in the Humanity Hall dwelling house, but no indication that students boarded on the grounds.

Garland died on December 18, 1879, leaving Mary Elizabeth Hanes to head a large household, which now included her father, Dr. John C. Blackwell; her mother, Mary; her sister, Josephine; and a brother, Joel. Mary Elizabeth's own children remaining at home numbered eight; two of them, young Mary and Lizzie, were teachers. Her brother-in-law, James C. Hanes, who lived nearby, served as the Superintendent of Public Schools in Buckingham County.

Dr. John C. Blackwell (JOANNE L. YECK COLLECTION)

Fond memories of Humanity Hall Academy lingered in Buckingham and beyond for many years. Like James Hilton's fictional Mr. Chips, Elijah G. Hanes shaped generations of boys, maintaining and promoting the genteel values of 19th-century Virginia planters.

In the 1930s, Buckingham historian Lulie Patteson described the popular educator in an article for *The Farmville Herald*. She wrote, "Col. Hanes, the master of this school for the greater part of his life, was a born teacher, we may judge from the stories which are told of his wise, beneficent rule in the classroom in an age when stern precept was imprinted on the pupil's mind, if not on his heart, by physical means, more often than otherwise."[48]

Miss Patteson relates a story of Col. Hanes' kindness in the classroom. During class one day, a boy named George was suffering from hiccups. Naturally, George was embarrassed and, as his condition progressed, class was increasingly disrupted. Suddenly, Col. Hanes demanded, "George, what's that you've been SAYING about me?" George, who was devoted to his professor, adamantly denied, through continuing hiccups, that he had ever made a disparaging remark about Col. Hanes. Then Hanes escalated his demand. "Now think George, haven't you been telling your home people something on me?" George, both shocked and startled, was now speechless. A hush fell in the classroom and a sly smile appeared on Hanes' face. "Hiccoughs gone, George?" Problem solved and the boys' esteem for their beloved instructor was restored.[49]

One former student, Malcolm Hart Crump, committed his recollections of Humanity Hall Academy to paper. During the Civil War, Malcolm, his siblings, and their mother, Mary Quinn Crump, were refugees from Culpeper County, Virginia, who found safety and shelter in Buckingham County. Malcolm was first enrolled at the Buckingham Female Collegiate Institute, then was more appropriately placed at Humanity Hall Academy. Looking back on his youth, he remembered his year in Buckingham and the Academy's beautiful setting about three miles from where he was living at the Nuckols farm on the Slate River. On his way to school, he passed Miller's Shop, the Flood home, John Rolfe Eldridge's mill, and Hanes Chapel, the lovely spot in the woods which served the local Methodist Episcopal congregation.[50]

Malcolm was ten years old when he attended the Academy in September of 1864. Maj. Garland B. Hanes had returned from the war and Malcolm readily recalled his classmates, who included some of Elijah Hanes' grandsons and other boys too young to serve the Confederacy. At that time, enrollment being low with so many young men occupied with the war, the Academy opened its doors to some of the neighborhood girls, which included two Saunders sisters. Mary Elizabeth (Blackwell) Hanes acted as their instructress.

The oldest of these was undoubtedly Mary Elizabeth "Betty" Saunders, age sixteen, whose family lived adjacent Humanity Hall on Turpins Creek. Malcolm Hart Crump did not find Betty as beautiful as Martha West, who had sparked his fancy while he was having lessons at the Institute. No matter. Within a few years, Betty would marry John T.L. Woodson, a youthful CSA veteran and schoolteacher, and settle down just across the creek from Humanity Hall. The other Saunders' sister in Malcolm Hart Crump's class was Emma Thompson Saunders who eventually taught school in Cumberland County and carried forward the long-held ideals of Humanity Hall Academy into post-war Virginia.[51]

Emma Saunders was just one of many young people trained at Humanity Hall Academy who were inspired to carry on its teachings. Through their lives as teachers and as future parents, the humane approach of Elijah G. Hanes, his sons, and his extended family influenced the coming generations in Buckingham County and beyond.

NOTES

1   Joanne L. Yeck, *The Jefferson Brothers* (Kettering, OH: Slate River Press, 2012), 84–85; "Seven Islands School," *Richmond Whig*, 7 August 1866.

2   Virginia journalist and humorist Dr. George W. Bagby began his education in field schools in Buckingham and Cumberland counties. See Joseph Leonard King, Jr., *Dr. George William Bagby: A Study of Virginian Literature 1850-1880* (New York, NY: Columbia University Press, 1927), 6.

3   William Shepard, "Buckingham Female Collegiate Institute," *William and Mary Quarterly* (April 1940), 168.

4   "The Buckingham High School For Young Ladies," *Richmond Enquirer*, 5 April 1836, p. 4; Elizabeth McCraw, "Trenton," Virginia Historical Survey, 25 May 1937, Library of Virginia; William Shepard, "Buckingham Female Collegiate Institute," *William and Mary Quarterly* (April 1940), 169.

5   "Slate River School" (Incorporated), *Richmond Enquirer*, 16 March 1839, p. 3; "Slate River School," *Richmond Whig*, 15 January 1841, p. 3; Shepard, "Buckingham Female Collegiate Institute," *William and Mary Quarterly* (April 1940), 169.

6   Joanne L. Yeck, "A Noble Idea: Buckingham Female Collegiate Institute," *"At a Place Called Buckingham"* (Kettering, OH: Slate River Press, 2011), 65–79; Lulie Patteson, "Buckingham Female Collegiate Institute," *Felixville: A Forgotten Villages in Cumberland County Virginia and Other Sketches* (Farmville, VA: *The Farmville Herald*, 1967), 25–39; Shepard, "Buckingham Female Collegiate Institute," *William and Mary Quarterly* (April 1940), 167–193; William Shepard, "Buckingham Female Collegiate Institute," *William and Mary Quarterly* (July 1940), 345–368.

7   Rosa G. Williams, "Site of Humanity Hall," Virginia Historical Survey, 14 August 1937, Library of Virginia.

8   *Richmond Enquirer*, 7 December 1824, p. 3. The newspaper announced: "Married—On Thursday [December 2nd], Mr. Elijah G. Hanes, to Miss Mary Jarman Brown, daughter of Garland Brown, all of Buckingham County." See Ibid. In an article for Charlottesville's *The Daily Progress*, Lulie Patteson stated that Elijah Hanes married a Miss Baughan of Hanover County. To date, nothing more is known of this marriage. See Lulie Patteson, "Elijah Hanes Set Lofty Standards," *The Daily Progress*, 12 June 1958.

9   "Humanity Hall Academy," *Richmond Enquirer*, 11 December 1832, p. 1; "Humanity Hall," *Richmond Enquirer*, 18 December 1830, p. 4; "Humanity Hall Academy," 8 December 1843, p. 2; Williams, "Site of Humanity Hall"; Patteson, "Humanity Hall Academy," *Felixville*, 19–21.

10   "Rev. Robert Ryland," *University of Richmond*, accessed August 2014, http://urhistory.richmond.edu/people/Ryland.html.

11   "Humanity Hall Academy," *Richmond Enquirer*, 11 December 1832, p. 1.

12   "Humanity Hall Academy," *Richmond Enquirer*, 25 December 1834, p. 4.

13   "Humanity Hall Academy," *Richmond Whig*, 8 December 1843, p. 2.

14   "Humanity Hall Academy," *Richmond Whig & Public Advertiser*, 21 November 1854, p. 1; "College Presidents," *Randolph-Macon College*, accessed November 2014, http://www.rmc.edu/offices/president/college-presidents.

15   *Richmond Whig & Public Advertiser*, 21 January 1840, p. 2. Mary Hanes' death announcement read: "On Jan. 13, at Humanity Hall, in Buckingham County, age --, Mrs. Mary J. Hanes, consort of Elijah Hanes." See Ibid. This date conflicts with the transcription of the gravestone made in 1937. See Elizabeth McCraw, "Hanes Cemetery," Virginia Historical Inventory, 10 February 1937, Library of Virginia.

16   Ibid. Elizabeth McCraw located the Hanes graveyard at "2 miles northeast from Davidsons School House on Route #613, thence 200 yards east in a field." See Ibid.

17   Ibid.

18   Rosa G. Williams, "Hanes Cemetery," Virginia Historical Inventory, 16 July 1937, Library of Virginia. Garnett Williams located the Hanes graveyard at "2.9 miles northeast of Nuckols, Virginia, on Route #613. Cemetery on east side of highway." Ibid.

19   Federal Population Census, Buckingham County, Virginia, 1840.

20   "Humanity Hall Academy," *Richmond Enquirer*, 18 December 1846, p. 3.

21   Judith Leake Ayres was the daughter of the Methodist minister Rev. John Ayres and shared Methodist convictions with Elijah G. Hanes. Some Hanes family genealogies give Judith Leake Ayres' sister, Martha, as a third wife of Elijah G. Hanes; however, in 1850, an unmarried Martha remained with her father, Methodist clergyman John Ayres, while Judith is already Mrs. Hanes and will be named in Elijah's will as his wife. See Federal Population Census, Buckingham County, Virginia, 1850; Rosa G. Williams, "Will of Elijah Garland Hanes," Virginia Historical Inventory, 1 January 1938, Library of Virginia.

22   Roger G. Ward, *Land Tax Summaries & Implied Deeds, 1841–1870, Volume 3* (Athens, GA: Iberian Publishing Company, 1995), 124–125.

23   "Humanity Hall Academy, Removed," *Richmond Enquirer*, 31 December 1847, p. 3.

24   Harry Stuart Holman, *The Holmans of Virginia* (Privately printed, Third Edition, 2012), 45–46, 57–58.

25   "Whig Meeting in Buckingham," *Richmond Whig*, 16 January 1849, p. 1. Col. E.G. Hanes is mentioned along with other Buckingham County Colonels, some who served as Colonels in the Buckingham County Militia, e.g.: Col. John M. Harris, and others who were called Colonel as a "title of courtesy," including Hanes. See Ibid.

26 Methodist Episcopal Church, South. Virginia Conference. Lynchburg District. Buckingham Circuit (Buckingham County, Va.), Record book, 1852-1881, 32944b Miscellaneous reel 1042, Library of Virginia; Rosa G. Williams, "Hanes Chapel," Virginia Historic Inventory, 6 January 1838, Library of Virginia; Patteson, "Elijah Hanes Set Lofty Standards."

27 Williams, "Hanes Chapel;" Margaret A. Pennington and Lorna S. Scott, *The Courthouse Burned—," Book I* (Buckingham, VA: Historic Buckingham, Inc., 2002), 124. In 1869 and 1870, the "Class" at Hanes Chapel included Elijah G. Hanes' widow and several descendants, including the Ayres and Eldridge families. See Methodist Episcopal Church, South. Virginia Conference. Lynchburg District. Buckingham Circuit (Buckingham County, Va.), Record book, 1852-1881, Library of Virginia.

28 "Humanity Hall Academy," *Richmond Enquirer*, 27 December 1850, p. 1.

29 "Humanity Hall Academy," *Richmond Whig & public advertiser*, 21 November 1854, p. 1; "Apple Hill For Sale," *Richmond Whig*, 19 September 1856, p. 1.

30 *Richmond Whig & public advertiser*, 21 November 1854, p. 1. The original office still stands in the yard.

31 "Fourth Of July At Humanity Hall Academy, Buckingham," *Richmond Whig*, 7 July 1854, p. 2.

32 "Humanity Hall Academy, Buckingham, Va.," *Richmond Whig*, 19 August 1856, p. 4.

33 Ibid.

34 Ibid.

35 Federal Population Census, Buckingham County, Virginia, 1850; "Humanity Hall Academy," *Richmond Enquirer*, 27 December 1850, p. 1; Garland B. Hanes, *The Men of Randolph-Macon College and the Civil War*, accessed August 2014, http://rmccivilwar.blogspot.com/2012/01/garland-b-hanes-class-of-1854-ab-and.html.

36 James C. Hanes, *The Men of Randolph-Macon College and the Civil War*, accessed August 2014, http://rmccivilwar.blogspot.com/2013/02/james-c-hanes-class-of-1855-ab-and.html.

37 "Affairs in Buckingham," *The Daily Dispatch*, 13 December 1858, p. 1. Elijah G. Hanes' last will was recorded at Buckingham Courthouse after the fire in 1869. In it, he bequeathed 1,049 acres, which included the Humanity Hall Academy buildings, to his wife, Judith, to be divided among his children after her death. See Buckingham County Will Book 1, pp. 106–107; Rosa G. Williams, "Will of Elijah Garland Hanes," Virginia Historical Inventory, 1 January 1938, Library of Virginia.

38 "Humanity Hall Academy," *Richmond Whig*, 15 November 1859, p. 4.

39 "Humanity Hall Academy," Broadside 1861: 51, Virginia Historical Society.

40 Ibid.

41 "Garland B. Hanes," *The Men of Randolph-Macon College and the Civil War*. According to a brief biography, "Garland Brown Hanes enlisted as a captain on May 29, 1861 in Co. F of the 20th VA Infantry, and later was transferred to Co. A of the 57th VA Infantry. Hanes was promoted to major on April 15, 1862. In September of 1862, a letter to the Secretary of the Treasury asking for employment is marked 'employed,' so he presumably left his regiment prior to that (there are indications he was hospitalized for a time in 1862) and then served in the confederate bureaucracy." See Ibid.

42 "2nd Regiment, Virginia Artillery," accessed May 2014, https://familysearch.org/learn/wiki/en/2nd_Regiment,VirginiaArtillery. The 2nd Regiment of the Virginia Artillery disbanded in May of 1862 due to the Conscription Act and was assigned to Company A of the 22nd Battalion Virginia Infantry. See Ibid. According to a brief biography, James C. Hanes "was drafted as a private into Co. A of the 57th VA Infantry on October 18, 1864. He was captured on April 1, 1865 at Five Forks, VA and sent to the prison camp at Point Lookout, MD on April 5, 1865. Hanes was released on June 13, 1865 after taking the oath of allegiance. After the war, Hanes returned to farming in Buckingham county, where he also served for many years as superintendent of instruction for the public schools." James C. Hanes' oath of allegiance describes him as 5' 9", with dark hair, hazel eyes, and a fair complexion. See "James C. Hanes," *The Men of Randolph-Macon College and the Civil War*.

43 "Peter Fletcher Ford," *The Men of Randolph-Macon College and the Civil War*, accessed August 2014. http://rmccivilwar.blogspot.com/2013/09/peter-fletcher-ford-class-of-1860-am.html. According to a brief biography, "Ford, known as Fletcher, enlisted as a corporal on May 29, 1861 in Co. F of the 20th VA Infantry, which later became Co. A of the 57th VA Infantry. On February 28, 1863, he was in temporary command of the company. He was promoted to 2nd lieutenant on July 30, 1862. Ford was killed on July 3, 1863 during the Battle of Gettysburg." In 1860, he earned his Master of Arts degree at Randolph-Macon. See Ibid.

44 Federal Population Census, Buckingham County, Virginia, 1860.

45 "Garland B. Hanes," *The Men of Randolph-Macon College and the Civil War*.

46 "Humanity Hall Academy," *Richmond Whig*, 26 May 1868, p. 3.

47 Virginia Department of Education, *Virginia School Report: Second Annual Report of the Superintendent of Public Instruction* (Richmond VA: R.F. Walker, Superintendent Public Printing, 1872), 210.

48 Patteson, "Humanity Hall Academy," *Felixville*, 19–20.

49 Ibid.

50 Clipping files, Housewright Museum, Buckingham Court House, Virginia. According to Buckingham historian Lulie Patteson, Rev. James J. Spencer (1840–1919) was another pupil at Humanity Hall Academy who went on to distinguish

himself. Spencer served in the Confederate army and was a popular Baptist minister in Buckingham County and environs. See Lulie Patteson, "Thrice a Volunteer," *The Farmville Herald* (28 April 1932), 8.

51   Joanne L. Yeck, "The Woodsons of Buckingham County," Mss6:1 W8687:4, Virginia Historical Society.

Robert Henry Miller, C.S.A.
(Courtesy Sandra Carrington Nelson and John Stuart Clayton, Jr.)

Capt. Robert Henry Miller and Life at Millwood

In 1900, Robert Henry Miller and his wife, Eugenia, were living at Millwood, in Buckingham County. Eugenia's son, Andrew Bryant, and her mother, Mary Frances (Phillips) White, were also with them.[1] That year, on May 15th, Capt. R. H. Miller was awarded a pension from the State of Virginia for his service during the Civil War. His annual allotment was $15.00. The sixty-six-year-old applicant complained of a dislocated arm and general bad health. "My spine gives way and cannot hold out to work," Miller wrote in his application. He claimed only partial disability.[2]

In 1908, at seventy-four, Miller reapplied for assistance. He suffered from gastric, hepatic, and renal problems, as well as shortness of breath which he attributed to exposure during the war. He wrote that his condition was aggravated by "the hardship of the war prison life being held in retaliation for the prisoners at Andersonville, Georgia." W. B. Pettit, the doctor who evaluated Miller for his pension application, considered the condition permanent.[3]

Miller's war experience was grueling, though not unique. Many men from Buckingham gave as much; many gave their lives. Robert was twenty-seven years old when he enlisted as a Sergeant 1st Class on June 6, 1861, joining Company C, 44th Regiment, Virginia Infantry. The educated son of Buckingham planter, William Armistead Miller, Robert quickly advanced and was promoted to Full Lieutenant 1st Class by May 1, 1862. He was wounded at Sharpsburg, Maryland and taken as a prisoner of war at Spotsylvania Court House on May 12, 1864. Held at Belle Plain, he was transferred to Point Lookout, then to Fort Delaware. There Miller joined the ranks of what would become known as the "Immortal 600."[4]

On August 20, 1864, the Federal steamer, *Crescent City*, carried 600 Confederate officers from Fort Delaware to Hilton Head where they waited for a stockade to be completed on Morris Island, four miles across the harbor from the south end of Charleston, South Carolina. During the journey, the

Confederate and Masonic Reunion, Buckingham County, 1908
(SCOTTSVILLE MUSEUM, SCOTTSVILLE, VA)

While attending the dedication of the Confederate Monument at Buckingham Court House, Civil War veterans and Freemasons posed for this photo taken by Scottsville-based photographer William E. Burgess, who printed it and sold it as a postcard.

prisoners existed on a few crackers, with occasional bits of salt beef or bacon. On September 7th, the officers were delivered to the Federal stockade. Housed in A-frame tents, they were given pitiful rations and were tortured by sand fleas and mosquitoes. Exposure to the elements meant scorching sun and pounding thunderstorms. This was accompanied by forty-five days of constant shellfire as the Federals and Confederates battled over Charleston Harbor. At last, the surviving men were transferred to Fort Pulaski in Savannah, Georgia.[5]

Following Robert E. Lee's surrender at Appomattox Courthouse, Miller took the Oath of Allegiance on June 15, 1865, at Fort Delaware. In 1905, one of the captives at Morris Island, John O. Murray, wrote a book entitled *The Immortal Six-Hundred*. The name stuck and their story took on legendary proportions.[6]

After four years of war and many months as a prisoner, Miller began what must have been a very long journey home to Buckingham County. Returning in the summer of 1865, he found his wife, Agnes, sick with tuberculosis. She died that December, age twenty-nine, leaving her husband with four young daughters to rear and a farm to reorganize.[7]

Like so many men from Buckingham who fought for the Confederate States of America – whether they joined the Buckingham Institute Guards, the Buckingham Leaches, the Buckingham Yancey Guard, or Travis Rifles (Miller's Co. C, 44th Regiment) – Miller was ill-prepared both for the cruelty of the long war and for "the world turned upside down" he faced when he returned to his home on Randolph's Creek.[8]

ಯಲ

Born on October 19, 1833, Robert Henry Miller was the youngest child of William "Armistead" and Elizabeth "Betsy" H. (Pittman) Miller.[9] Their home was at Millwood, in the northeastern part of Buckingham County, near the Cumberland County border. They were among Buckingham's slaveholding, planter elite and the family expectation was that Robert and his brothers would live as their father had, either at Millwood or at similar plantations.[10]

In 1832, just prior to Robert's birth, a neighboring plantation was auctioned from the estate of Samuel Woodfin. Its description conjures a pleasant picture of life along Randolph's Creek:

Elizabeth H. (Pittman) Miller (Photograph and digital restoration by Robert Harris, Portrait Courtesy Bell Family Collection)

EXECUTOR'S SALE – On Friday the 17th February next, will be sold to the highest bidder, on the premises, that valuable tract of land, late in the occupancy of Samuel Woodfin, dec'd of Powhatan, lying on Randolph's creek in the county of Buckingham, adjoining the lands of William A. Miller, Edward Baber, Poindexter P. Smith, Elijah G. Haynes (sic) and others, containing 578 acres, one half or more of which is believed to be in woods and good tobacco land, upon a credit of one, two and three years, the purchaser giving bond with approved security, and a deed of trust to procure the payments – This land lies about five miles from New Canton, and three miles of Brown's mills, on said creek. Also, the crop of corn, fodder, &c., the stock of horses, cows, oxen, hogs, plantation utensils &c. upon a credit until the 25th of December next, the purchaser giving bond with approved security for all sums over five dollars, and for all sums of five dollars and under, cash will be required.

BY THE EXECUTORS.[11]

The estate was purchased by James Woodfin, who would be Robert Miller's neighbor for decades to come.

The Miller family valued education for both their sons and their daughters, as did most planters in Buckingham County. Robert attended Elijah G. Hanes' Humanity Hall Academy, located at nearby Physic Springs.[12] His brothers, John and Jesse Scott Miller, became physicians.[13] Their sister, Mary Marshall Miller, attended the prestigious Edge Hill School, in Albemarle County, operated by Thomas Jefferson's grandson, Thomas Jefferson Randolph, and his wife, Jane Hollins Nicholas, daughter of Governor Wilson Cary Nicholas.[14]

In the autumn of 1846, Robert was not quite thirteen years old when his father died at Millwood. A man of means, Armistead Miller was known beyond the confines of his county; notices of his death appeared in the *Richmond Enquirer* and the *Richmond Whig*.[15] His widow, Betsy Miller, was left in charge of at least two farms and more than twenty-five slaves.[16]

The 1850s were fruitful, fulfilling the promise of the antebellum agrarian ideal. Robert Henry Miller was groomed for this life. As expected, he grew into his father's place, eventually buying out his siblings and becoming the squire of Millwood, where he managed over 900 acres, extending from Randolph's Creek to the road to Cartersville and Mt. Zion Baptist Church, where the family worshiped.[17] He was about twenty-one years old when he married Agnes Scott Johnson. Settled at his ancestral home, they celebrated the birth of four daughters, Kitty, Elizabeth Agnes (Bettie), Nannie Franklin, and Arianna.[18] In 1860, Millwood was valued at $4,000. Eighteen slaves, worth $10,000, lived in four dwellings.[19]

Then the war came. Robert enlisted early, leaving Agnes in charge of the children, the farm, and about twenty slaves. Jesse Bagby, who was the family's overseer in 1860, may or may not have remained in Buckingham to help Agnes manage the farm.[20]

Robert Henry Miller survived the war, though he was much compromised by his experience. Agnes' death in 1865 compounded his sorrows. He was, however, one of the more fortunate veterans; he managed to retain his farm. Sometime before 1870, he married a widow, Eugenia Demenoucourt (White) Bryant of Cumberland County. She brought two sons with her to Millwood, Willie C. and Andrew J. Bryant.[21] The nearby village of Gilliamsville provided basic services. There, William J.C. Goode ran a store and served as postmaster.[22] Life at Millwood was, in some respects, stable once again.

※※※

Following the Civil War, the transition from a slave-based labor force to hired labor was unique to each Buckingham County plantation. Still, patterns emerged. Many of the oldest African Americans remained in place, often dependent on the generosity of their former owners. The ambitious, unfettered, and fit frequently left for cities, including Richmond, Lynchburg, and Charlottesville. Often couples, typically a man who had worked in the fields and his wife who may have long been a family's cook or housekeeper, continued in their former occupations, raising their emancipated and free-born children at the only home they had ever known.[23]

Over the next five decades, Robert Henry Miller faced a vastly changed society in Buckingham County and the fates of his former slaves fit this overarching pattern, though each had their own particular story.

In 1944, Nannie Franklin (Miller) Goodman, Robert and Agnes Miller's third daughter, dictated an oral history, remembering the slaves at Millwood. On the 1860 slave census, the Millers' laborers and servants were enumerated as cold facts. Nameless statistics, these individuals populated Nannie's childhood, living intimately with her, her sisters, and her parents.

60-year-old male, black	50-year-old female mulatto
45-year-old female, black	40-year-old female, mulatto
22-year-old female, black	17-year-old female, black
12-year-old female, mulatto	7-year-old female, mulatto
30-year-old male, black	13-year-old male, mulatto
5-year-old male, mulatto	4-year-old female, mulatto
2-year-old male, mulatto	2-year-old female, mulatto
2-year-old male, black	1-year-old female, mulatto
1-year-old female, mulatto	45-year-old female, black[24]

Scant as they are, Nannie's memories, dictated over eighty years after this census was made, provided names and histories to the enslaved at Millwood. Born on February 8, 1859, for Nannie, these African Americans would remain "Uncles," "Aunts," and "Mammies," their names and status forever linked as in the days before emancipation.[25] In Nannie's words:

> *"Aunt Annie attended the table and Mary Lou helped her."*
> *"Aunt Polly was the milker."*
> *"Martha Ann was the nurse. . . ."*
> *"Little Maria and her husband lived near the smoke house to guard the meat."*[26]

Nannie went on to recall that John was the family's butler and that beloved Old Uncle Dick "was buried under the apple tree in the white folks burying ground – not the negroes graveyard."[27]

During the years immediately following emancipation, the neighborhood along Randolph's Creek remained fundamentally intact and a significant number of former Miller slaves stayed on in Buckingham County, including Maria Toney. Nannie remembered that "Aunt" Maria was born between 1813 and 1815 and that she was chosen as a "house girl" when Robert Henry Miller's oldest brothers were boys. According to Nannie, when William Armistead Miller's estate was divided and Robert purchased Millwood, he also bought Maria "off the stump" when the Miller property was auctioned in 1860.[28] Also known as "Big Maria," she was still with the family at the end of the Civil War. At fifty,

Slave Births at Millwood

Between 1853 and 1865, the Commonwealth of Virginia collected slave births from the counties. The records are not complete, and the amount of information preserved varies significantly from county to county. For example, Buckingham County's clerk consistently recorded more information than the clerk across the James River in Fluvanna County. During this period, Capt. Robert H. Miller reported the following slave births at Millwood:

Birth	Mother	Date
Judy	Maria	20 November 1857
William	Polly	22 May 1858
(male)	Kitty	20 December 1858
Louisa	Mariah	23 September 1859
Sarah	Polley	28 December 1859

Kitty, who is not mentioned in Nannie Goodman's oral history, also had a daughter, Susan, whose death was reported on December 21, 1858, the day after her son was born. Susan was three years old when she died of cancer in Cumberland County. Maria/Mariah is likely "Aunt Maria," who was "bought off the stump." Polley is probably "Aunt Polly," who married William Watson. Nannie Goodman did not recall Polly's daughter, Sarah, who was living with the Watsons in 1870; however, Sarah's birth fits neatly between William (May 1858) and Mary (born about 1860). Judy and Louisa, mentioned in Nannie Goodman's oral history, were two of the youngsters who fell asleep while cleaning cotton.

Maria had little hope of finding work elsewhere; she and her husband remained at Millwood.[29]

Before the war, Maria married Primus Toney, once owned by Millwood's neighbor, James "Jim" Woodfin.[30] Marriages between slaves were frequently maintained across plantations, as was the case with Primus and Maria. These so-called "abroad marriages" were common in central Virginia. In 1860, Woodfin owned thirty-three slaves, one of whom was probably Primus Toney. That year, Woodfin's personal property, which included his slaves, was valued at $35,000. His 578-acre plantation was worth $10,000.[31] Woodfin was clearly prosperous and, in 1859, he got a new lease on life when he married Mary Ann Beckwith of Cazenovia, Madison County, New York. James was past fifty; Mary Ann was twenty-two, just a year older than Woodfin's son, James E. Woodfin.[32]

Census data supports Nannie's memory that the Toneys stayed to work at Millwood. In 1870, they were enumerated just three households from the Millers, likely living on Miller land, where Maria had spent all of her adult life. The sixty-year-old Primus labored on the farm, while the fifty-five-year-old Maria kept house. Nannie pointed out that Maria and Primus could have left Millwood, but that Primus stayed and farmed for Capt. Miller, eventually dying on the farm.[33]

Maria told Nannie that it was "Old Misses," Mrs. William Armistead Miller, who "took her for a house girl, and hid her to keep 'Ole Marse' (William Armistead Miller) from whipping her. Lee Hudgin's father was overseer for Wm. A. Miller and had charge of the negroes – made them work & disciplined them by whipping when necessary." Maria became indispensable in the Miller household; thus, when Armistead Miller died, Robert purchased her from his father's estate.[34]

The Toneys had several children, including a son named Dick, who left Millwood after the Civil War. According to Nannie, "Dick Toney married and lived in Powhatan [County]. At Primus' death Dick came for Aunt Maria." Indeed, Dick Toney returned to Buckingham and collected his mother. By 1880, she was living in Goochland County with Dick's family. Dick was forty-five years old and the widowed Maria was sixty-eight.[35]

Nannie went on to recall that "Mammy" Harriet Jones, the cook for two generations of Millers at Millwood, was born about 1815. As Nannie put it,

Hannah Patterson with Virginia Mahon, c.1915 (LINDA HOPE DOERGER COLLECTION)

Hannah Patterson lived and grew old near Mount Zion Baptist Church in the immediate neighborhood of Millwood. Her home plantation is unknown, though she likely would have associated with the Miller family slaves. Born in December of 1853, "Aunt Hannah," as she was known in the neighborhood, acted as a midwife, assisting Dr. Perkins Glover during the birth of seven babies for Blanche and Everett Mahon. Throughout her life, Hannah considered the Mahons "her" children. According to the 1910 census, Hannah gave birth to seventeen children of her own. That year, only three were still living. At eighty-eight, Hannah remained in her home, assisted by her extended Mahon family.

"Harriet was Elizabeth Pittman Miller's cook and had lived with Capt. R. H. always." Miller purchased Harriet from his father's estate, maintaining important continuity at Millwood. About the time of Robert's birth, Harriet married Pleasant Jones, raising their three daughters at Millwood. Pleasant, also known as "Grand Daddy," was the property of Mr. P.P. Wilson.[36]

After the war, the Joneses and two of their daughters remained in Buckingham, also living not far from the Millers. Nannie recalled the Jones girls by name and occupation. Polly married William Watson, who was the property of James Woodfin. Annie married Charlie Lightfoot. Lilian went North when she was young. In 1870, the Watsons and the Lightfoots were living in Buckingham County, adjacent the Joneses, not far from James Woodfin. Polly, born in about 1835, had been the Miller's "milker" and now had seven children. Annie, born about 1850, had attended the Miller's table and was the mother of two daughters.[37]

In 1870, no domestic servant resided in the mansion house at Millwood to help Eugenia Miller with the housework; however, Mary Jones lived next door. Occupied as a "domestic servant," it is probable that the thirty-year-old Mary Jones worked as Eugenia Miller's cook and/or maid.[38]

The fate of John, the butler, is not recounted by Nannie Goodman; however, it is clear from her memory of him that he was a commanding presence in the Miller household. Once, when Nannie's little sister, Arianna, cried at dinner, "John threatened to have her sent away from table."[39]

Nannie went on to observe, "Old people spoiled children and negroes." She gave an example of one young slave named Rosa who would pester Mary Marshall Miller's husband, Charles Davis. According to Nannie, Rosa would climb up in his chair, scratch his head, and threaten to "slap his jaws if he did not keep still."[40]

After the Civil War, as many freed men and women left Millwood as stayed in Buckingham. Nannie related that "Aunt" Mary went to live in Richmond. Sidney's brother, Ann P., and Mary Lou all joined Mary in the city. Mary Lou, who once helped at the Miller's table, married Solomon Wood and went to Richmond with the others. Nannie said that Mary Lou used to pray, "Lord bless Marse Robert and the children." It should be noted, however, that when Mary Lou had the opportunity to leave Millwood, she did so.[41]

The youngest emancipated individuals, Jimmie, Judy, Nancy, and Louise, "had gone before"– presumably to Richmond.[42] Even as small children, their lives were far from easy. Nannie related:

> Capt. Robert H. Miller had an overseer by the name of Jesse Bagby (Jennie Bagby Philips' uncle) who was hard on the negroes. When the small girls went to sleep at night while picking seed out of cotton by fire places in Marse Robert's bedroom, Uncle Jessie said "Jude. Jude. Jude wake up there." Judy said "yessa Marse yessir." Nancy & Louise would go to sleep sometimes too.[43]

Exhausted by plantation work, Judy, Nancy, and Louise, like Mary Lou, felt no magnetic pull to remain at Millwood and sought a better life in the city.

Buckingham County after the hunt, c.1900. From Left to Right: Wesley Taylor White (b. 1854), Afton Putney White (b. 1879), and Robert Henry Miller (b. 1834). (COURTESY JIM COOKE, SHIRLEY MCMICHEN COLLECTION)

Robert Henry Miller lived out his days at Millwood, dying of cancer on October 1, 1915; he is buried Mt. Zion Baptist Church, a stone's throw from his life-long home.[44] On March 13, 2010, a ceremony was conducted at his gravesite, commemorating his military service. A beautiful bronze cross was placed on his grave, similar to those given by the Confederacy during the war. A volley of muskets fired. Civil War reenactors arrived on horseback. Musicians played the beloved old songs. Speeches were made. A male soloist passionately sang the plaintive strains of "The Minstrel Boy." The weather was perfect and, nearly 100 years after his death, Miller received a lovely tribute.[45] When the musket smoke cleared and the voices were stilled once more, Robert Henry Miller's simple marker remains a lasting comment for a long and eventful life:

Capt. R.H. Miller

Born Oct. 19, 1833

Died Oct. 1, 1915

He was a Confederate Soldier, and a member of Mt. Zion Baptist Church.

Gone But Not Forgotten.

Asleep in Jesus.

NOTES

1   Federal Population Census, Buckingham County, Virginia, 1900.

2   Robert H. Miller, Confederate Pension Application, Library of Virginia.

3   Ibid.

4   See Kevin Conley Ruffner, *44th Virginia Infantry* (Lynchburg, VA: H.E. Howard, 1987).

5   See Mauriel Phillips Joslyn, *Immortal Captives: The Story of 600 Confederate Officers and the United States Prisoner of War Policy* (Shippensburg, PA: White Mane Publishing Co., 1996).

6   See John Ogden Murray, *The Immortal Six-Hundred* (Winchester, VA: The Eddy Press Corporation, 1905).

7   Jeanne Stinson, *Buckingham County, Virginia Death Records, 1853–1868* (Athens, GA: Iberian Publishing Co., 2000), 126. In the death records, Agnes is misspelled as "Agnus" and Robert Henry Miller is misidentified as "Richard Miller." See Ibid.

8   Eugene A. Maloney, *A History of Buckingham County* (Buckingham, VA: Historic Buckingham, 2014), 107–112. Maloney lists the men in Company "K," 4th Regiment, Virginia Calvary, Company "F," 20th Regiment, Virginia Infantry (Buckingham Institute Guard), Company "E," 21st Regiment, Virginia Infantry (Buckingham Leaches), Company "C," 44th Regiment, Virginia Infantry (Travis Rifles), and Company "D," 56th Regiment, Virginia Infantry (Buckingham Yancey Guard). A Robert Miller appears with the Buckingham Leaches. No Miller is listed for Company C, 44th Regiment. Maloney's source was muster rolls stored at Buckingham Courthouse. Ibid., 109.

9   Janice J. R. Hull, *Buckingham Burials, Volume II* (Westminster, MD: Willow Bend Books, 2002), 133.

10   Joanne L. Yeck, "Millwood: A Miller Plantation in Buckingham County, Virginia," Mss6:1 M6193:8, Virginia Historical Society; "Descendants of Francis McCraw and Mary Woodson," Unpublished manuscript, n.d., Jean DeNoon Cable Collection.

11   *Richmond Enquirer*, 4 February 1832, p. 1. The Miller and Woodfin families were connected in Cumberland and Powhatan counties as well as in Buckingham; James Woodfin's Buckingham land had once belonged to the Miller family. The land in Samuel Woodfin's estate was owned by Thomas Miller of Powhatan County, who conveyed it to Edward Carrington, who sold to Jesse Miller, who then sold it to Samuel Woodfin. See *Virginia Argus*, 13 June 1806, p. 4.

12   Mary Marshal Miller to Robert Henry Miller, letter, 29 June 1845, Miller Family Papers, Mss1 M6196 c, Virginia Historical Society.

13 Robbie J. Oliver, "Additional Miller Family History," unpublished manuscript, 22 March 1973, Harry S. Holman Collection; Harry Stuart Holman, "The Miller Manuscript," *The Virginia Genealogist* (January–March 1977), 25–27.

14 Miller Family Papers, Mss1 M6196 c, Virginia Historical Society.

15 *Richmond Enquirer*, 29 September 1846, p. 4; *Richmond Whig & public advertiser*, 11 September 1846, p. 1. The notice in the *Richmond Whig* read, "Died – At his residence in Buckingham County, on Sept. 2, in his 60th year, William A. Miller, leaving wife and several children." Ibid.

16 Federal Population Census, Buckingham County, Virginia, 1850; Slave Census, Buckingham County, Virginia, 1850; Agricultural Census, Buckingham County, Virginia, 1850.

17 Garnett Agee Williams, "Mt. Zion Cemetery," Virginia Historical Inventory, 12 February 1937, Library of Virginia; Rosa G. Williams, "Mt. Zion Baptist Church," Virginia Historical Inventory, 9 February 1937, Library of Virginia; Margaret A. Pennington and Leona S. Scott, *"The Courthouse Burned—," Book I* (Buckingham Court House, VA: Historic Buckingham, 2002), 147.

18 Federal Population Census, Buckingham County, Virginia, 1850, 1860.

19 Slave Census, Buckingham County, Virginia, 1860.

20 Federal Population Census, Buckingham County, Virginia, 1860.

21 Federal Population Census, Buckingham County, Virginia, 1870. Eugenia outlived her second husband, dying on September 28, 1924 in Cumberland County, Virginia. See Miller Family Genealogy, Ruby Talley Smith Collection.

22 Federal Population Census, Buckingham County, Virginia, 1860; Margaret A. Pennington and Leona S. Scott, *"The Courthouse Burned—," Book II* (Buckingham Court House, VA: Historic Buckingham, 2002), 70–71. The Gilliamsville post office was established on July 20, 1875, with William J. C. Goode as postmaster, and operated until October 15, 1914, when the service was moved to New Canton. See U.S. Appointments of U. S. Postmasters, 1832-1971, ancestry.com, accessed August 2014, http://search.ancestry.com/search/db.aspx?dbid=1932.

23 This summary is based on the author's research concerning various families living in Buckingham County as well as work done by the Central Virginia History Researchers. See African American Families Database, accessed September 2014, http://www.centralvirginiahistory.org/.

24 Federal Slave Census, Buckingham County, Virginia, 1860.

25 Nannie Franklin (Miller) Goodman, "Negroes at Millwood when Capt. R.H. Miller married Eugenia White (2nd wife)," dictated to Robbie J. Oliver, unpublished manuscript, 1944, Betty Duncan Collection. Nannie Franklin (Miller) Goodman

died on February 3, 1953 and is buried in the Mt. Zion Baptist Church cemetery in Buckingham County. See Hull, *Buckingham Burials, Volume II*, p. 124. Robbie Oliver, Nannie's niece and granddaughter of Robert Henry Miller, was born on July 14, 1890 and died in Culpeper, Virginia on July 5, 1979. She is buried in the cemetery at Mt. Zion Baptist Church. Ibid.; Social Security Death Index, 1935-Current, ancestry.com.

26   Goodman, "Negroes at Millwood."

27   Ibid. Nannie also mentions that Sidney, George, Sookey, and their daughter, Cindy, were brought from Goochland County by Capt. Miller's first wife. See Ibid.

28   *Richmond Whig*, 27 July 1860, p. 1.

29   Goodman, "Negroes at Millwood."

30   Ibid. In 1850, James Woodfin purchased 22 ½ acres on Randolph's Creek from the trustees for Rebecca Toney. It is possible that Woodfin also purchased Primus from the Toney family. See Roger G. Ward, *Land Tax Summaries & Implied Deeds, 1841–1870, Volume 2* (Athens, GA: Iberian Publishing Company, 1995), 325. Toney is a familiar name in northeastern Buckingham and Fluvanna counties. In 1850, there were at least four Toney households in the neighborhood of Millwood. In the 1830s, John W. "Jack" Toney of Fluvanna County owned the ancestors of Dr. Carter G. Woodson, including his father, James Henry Woodson, and his grandfather, Carter Woodson. See Joanne L. Yeck, "Carter G. Woodson: Deep Roots in Buckingham County," *"At a Place Called Buckingham"* (Kettering, OH: Slate River Press, 2011), 80–93.

31   Roger G. Ward, *Land Tax Summaries & Implied Deeds, 1815–1840, Volume 2*, p. 399; Federal Population Census, Buckingham County, Virginia, 1860. Millwood, by comparison, was valued at $4,000. Ibid.

32   *Richmond Whig & public advertiser*, 21 June 1859, p. 4. The notice informed Virginians that the couple had been married in New York on June 7, 1859 by Rev. William Clark. Ibid. James and Mary Ann Woodfin started their own family and, by 1870, had four children. See Federal Population Census, Buckingham County, Virginia, 1870. James Woodfin's first wife was Judith. In 1859, their daughter, Susan B. Woodfin, married James C. Hanes, son of Elijah G. Hanes, founder of Humanity Hall Academy. Dr. John C. Blackwell, President of Buckingham Female Collegiate Institute, performed the ceremony. See Randy Kidd and Jeanne Stinson, *Lost Marriages of Buckingham County, Virginia* (Athens, GA: Iberian Publishing Co., 1992), 188.

33   Federal Population Census, Buckingham County, Virginia, 1870.

34   Goodman, "Negroes at Millwood."

35   Federal Population Census, Powhatan County, Virginia, 1880.

36   Goodman, "Negroes at Millwood." To date, P.P. Wilson's plantation has not been located.

37   Ibid.; Federal Population Census, Buckingham County, Virginia, 1870. Nannie Goodman recited the names of many of the Watson children, indicating she may have been especially close to the family. Most of them were living with their parents in 1870. The names in bold were recalled by Nannie; the others appeared on the 1870 census: **Martha A.** [b. abt. 1853], **Pleasant** [b. abt. 1856], **Buck**, Willis [b. abt. 1858], **Mary** [b. abt. 1860], Nancy, Harriet [b. abt. 186-], Jane [b. abt. 1867], and **Melissa** [b. Nov.1869].

38   Federal Population Census, Buckingham County, Virginia, 1870. In 1870, Mary Jones was married to Essex Jones, age thirty-seven, a boatman. Ibid.

39   Goodman, "Negroes at Millwood."

40   Ibid. Mary Marshall Miller married Charles Davis in about 1848 and was given three slaves as a wedding gift. Rosa may have been one of them. See Ibid.

41   Ibid.

42   Ibid.

43   Ibid. In 1860, Overseer Jesse Bagby (60) was enumerated with the Millers. With him is Mary E. Bagby (22), likely his daughter. See Federal Population Census, Buckingham County, Virginia, 1860. Judy (b. 20 November 1857) and Louise (b. 23 September 1859) must have gone to Richmond with adults. Their mothers are listed in the slave birth records as Maria and Mariah. Perhaps this is the "Aunt Mary" whom the others followed to Richmond. See Leslie Anderson Morales (Editor), *Virginia Slave Births Index: 1853-1865, Volume 4: M-R* (Berwyn Heights, MD: Heritage Books, 2008), 144.

44   Hull, *Buckingham Burials, Volume II*, 133.

45   "Captain R. H. Miller Southern Cross Dedication, program, Mt. Zion Baptist Church, New Canton, Virginia, 13 March 2010.

Dr. George W. Bagby (Courtesy The Dietz Press)

In those early days Buckingham was, as it is to-day, a typical Virginia county. It was settled from the east, mostly of the English cavalier and the Huguenot elements. The large old plantations, owned by the old type of Virginia gentleman, now long since passed away, were easy centres of a society whose culture and elegance was not surpassed in Virginia.

The county, lying as it does at the foot of the Blue Ridge, its surface broken now and then with mountain spurs, is one of natural beauty. With the cultivation of the Old World, its hills could be made as beautiful as those of Southern France, and its long river bottoms as fertile as any in the world. Here, in this natural continuation of the great Virginia valley, peopled with the best element of the Old Dominion, George Bagby was born and spent his boyhood days. Here, in the very heart of Virginia, he came in contact with the real, true spirit of the State, and learned the life whose mouth-piece he was for nearly half a century.

"A Lover of Virginia," *The Richmond Dispatch,* 7 July 1901.

Buckingham County's Mark Twain: George W. Bagby

I ask no man's pardon for what must seem to a stranger a most exaggerated estimate of my State and its peoples. In simple truth and beyond question there was in our Virginia country life a beauty, a simplicity, a purity, an uprightness, a cordial and lavish hospitality, warmth and grace which shine in the lens of memory with a charm that passes all language at my command.[1]

George W. Bagby

In 1938, The Dietz Press of Richmond, Virginia published a new edition of *The Old Virginia Gentleman and Other Sketches* by Dr. George W. Bagby, marking the 50th anniversary of the author's death. The Executive Committee of the Virginia Historical Society announced the publication as the long anticipated work of "the celebrated humorist and man of letters" who served as Corresponding Secretary and Librarian of The Virginia Historical Society from 1859 to 1868 and as a member of its Executive Committee from 1859 to 1870.[2]

Well-known Richmond novelist Ellen Glasgow commented on the new edition, "The vital warmth and humanity of the writing will give this book a permanent place in the life and literature of Virginia. Some books do not grow old with the years, and these essays seem as fresh to me nowadays as they did when I first read them."[3]

Ellen M. Bagby, the author's daughter, edited the essays. The memorial edition proved extremely popular and, in 1943, it was followed by another edition. Ellen M. Bagby noted in the preface:

> The remarkable response of the public to the 1938 edition of *The Old Virginia Gentleman* (now exhausted) and the continued demand for the works of Dr. Bagby, justifies a fourth edition, which, while

embracing all of the material in the previous volume, will have the addition (by special request) of "The Southern Fool—A tough subject treated in a tender way." This was an address delivered before the South Carolina Press Association in 1877. It was after hearing this lecture that the distinguished Dr. Hunter McGuire said of Dr. Bagby: "He is a man one hundred years ahead of his time."[4]

One of Virginia's favorite historians and journalists, Douglas Southall Freeman, wrote a new introduction to the 1938 edition which he called "George W. Bagby, Patriot."[5] In it, Dr. Freeman informed his readers that Bagby's mother, Virginia Young Evans, was the "daughter of fine, intellectual Buckingham stock."[6] This circumstance of his mother's birth is how George William Bagby (1828–1883) came to be born in Buckingham, in the southeastern part of the county near the Cumberland County border. In August of 1828, Virginia (Evans) Bagby returned to her father's plantation to have her first child, a common custom in those days. Her husband, George Bagby, stayed behind in Lynchburg, minding his store. Young George's birth was quickly followed by that of his sister, Ellen. In 1834, their fragile mother died and the two children were partly raised by their aunt, Mrs. Elizabeth Hobson, who lived just across the county line in Cumberland.[7]

This simple, rural upbringing profoundly influenced George W. Bagby and, eventually, his literary style. Aunt Betsy's "good eatings" set a standard that city eats never attained. Lazy days in antebellum Virginia gave the future essayist plenty of time to absorb the smallest details of plantation life.

Decades later, in "Bacon and Greens," a very grown up George Bagby insisted that Virginians are defined by their eats. "In point of fact," he wrote, "the native Virginian is different from all other folks whatsoever, and the difference between him and other folks is precisely the difference between his bacon and greens and other folks' bacon and greens." The only perfect bacon and greens were to be found in Virginia and the secret, Bagby insisted, was in the bacon. That is because "our hogs are not penned up, but are allowed the free range of the fields and forest."[8]

After attending so-called "field schools" in both Buckingham and Cumberland counties, George was sent north to school, according to his father's wishes. At ten, he attended Edgehill School in Princeton, New Jersey, then transferred to Hurlbut School in Philadelphia, then attended Delaware College, finally matriculating at the University of Pennsylvania, earning a degree in medicine in 1849.[9] This lengthy, lonesome separation from home fed Bagby's longing for Virginia. He would spend the rest of his life talking and writing about the land and the people he deeply loved.

When George returned to Lynchburg, he showed little or no interest in medicine. He was drawn to journalism and, in 1853, he and his friend, George Woodville Latham, published the *Lynchburg Express*, launching Bagby on a lifelong career as an author, editor, publisher, and successful lecturer. In 1857, he moved to Washington, D.C., where he worked as a correspondent and honed his skills as a humorist. His breakthrough came when two articles were accepted by *Harper's New Monthly Magazine* and, in 1858, the *Southern Literary Messenger* published the first of his eight fictional and humorous letters written from "Mozis Addums," letters addressed to "Billy Ivvins" in "Kersvil, Buckingame Cty, Ferginny." Billy Evans' surname remembered Bagby's mother's family and Curdsville was a very real place in Buckingham County, Virginia. Why or how Bagby picked Curdsville to represent "typical" small town Virginia is lost to history.[10]

These satiric letters, written in phonetically-spelled colloquialisms, catapulted Bagby to "instant" popularity. Based in a tradition of dialect humor and stories of "local color," they poked fun at the backwoods boys of Virginia and, eventually, became the bane of Bagby's existence. The popular "Mozis Addums" series seemed to be all his readers wanted, overshadowing his diverse writings. Contrary to his readers, Bagby's literary peers viewed him differently and, in June of 1860, he became editor of the *Southern Literary Messenger*, which described itself as "a magazine devoted to literature, science and art." His salary was $300 per year. To make ends meet, he supplemented income by acting as associate editor of the *Richmond Whig*, contributing editor of the *Richmond Examiner*, and accepting correspondent jobs with out-of-state papers.[11] He also held offices with the Virginia Mechanics Institute, the Richmond Library Association, and the Virginia Historical Society.[12]

Bagby announced his vision for the *Southern Literary Messenger* in the monthly column afforded him, "Editor's Table," stating:

Lucy Parke Chamberlayne, 1858 (COURTESY THE DIETZ PRESS)

This portrait of the future Mrs. George W. Bagby epitomized her husband's ideal Virginia belle who would one day be the ideal wife and mother. In "The Old Virginia Gentleman," Dr. Bagby wrote:

Brightest by far of the memories of those days, that seem to have been passed in some other planet, is that of the Virginia mother, as I have so often seen her, in the midst of her tall sons and blooming daughters. Her delicacy, tenderness, freshness, gentleness; the absolute purity of her life and thought, typified in the spotless neatness of her apparel and her every surrounding, it is quite impossible to convey. Withal, there was about her a naivete mingled with sadness, that gave her a surpassing charm. Her light blush, easily called up when her children rallied her, as they habitually would, about her old-fashioned ways and her ignorance of the world, was something never to be forgotten. Sunlight, flushing with faint rose-tints the driven snow, could scarcely more excite the rapture of admiration. Her pride in her sons, her delight in her daughters, her lowliness and her humility—for she was least among them all, and they were as yet too young and full of bounding life to revere and worship her as she deserved—who shall, who can fitly tell of these things?

'A FEAST OF FUN'

Dr. G. W. BAGBY

WILL DELIVER A LECTURE,

ENTITLED

THE DISEASE CALLED LOVE

At _____

On _____ · Evening, _____ 187_

At _____ o'clock.

ADMISSION FIFTY CENTS.

Tickets for Sale at _____

OPINIONS OF THE PRESS.

From the Lynchburg Republican.

"Dr. Bagby on Wednesday of last week treated our people to his serio-comic lecture, and the burthen of his discourse was where." Never having analyzed this subject as a matter of art, we are unable to pronounce whether the Doctor's views were orthodox or otherwise. With his chief authority, Barton, a cynical old rascal and hater of women, we have some familiarity, and we protest, in the name of our lady readers, against any verdict upon love obtained upon the evidence of such a creature. Barton, indeed! Things have come to pretty pass! Barton, the miserable reprobate! But we will allow our injured friends to repress their own indignation. It contained equal wealth and aptness of illustration, equal force and felicity of expression, and equal harmony in bleeding of detail. If Dr. Bagby is not a man of genius, we give it up. The parlor scene in "Love" was worthy of Dickens in his best days, and the lecture itself was worthy of a large patronage."

From the Charlottesville Chronicle.

"Our friend, Dr. Bagby, the author of the admirable satire, "The Virginia Editor," delivered his lecture on "Love" in this place on Thursday evening. We have not laughed more for a number of years than we did on this occasion; and the audience generally seemed to enjoy the lecture exceedingly. We thought a knot of students in the gallery would go into fits over one or two points; and the girls, they giggled. We were particularly struck with the kicked young man under the window of his lady love, and thought the allusion to his cleaning his flagstaff a very happy touch. The allusion to the red-headed girl took the house by storm. We think the universal feeling among the audience when the lecture closed, was 'go on.'"

From the Lynchburg Virginian.

"Dr. Bagby's lecture on the 'Disease Called Love,' was delivered last night to a large and intellectual audience. The evident pleasure which it afforded them, as evinced by the hearty applause and merriment which it elicited, is the best commentary on its merits. As a humorous lecture, it is an entire success, and fully sustains the high reputation of the lecturer."

From the Annapolis, Md. Gazette.

"We had the pleasure of listening to the lecture delivered by Dr. Geo. W. Bagby, of Virginia, in the Hall of the House of Delegates, on Tuesday last. The inspiration of his lofty eloquence, riveted the closest possible attention, and the rich veins of humor interspersed throughout elicited frequent applause. His subject was 'The Disease called Love.'"

From the Prince Georgian, Maryland.

"The audience was in large part composed of ladies. The production was replete with the most original comicalities, and a vein of irrepressible humor ran from the first word to the last—the auditory being held in a state of uncontrollable merriment almost throughout its delivery. It was relished by all as an unusual treat."

Letter from Richmond.

"The Hall of the House of Delegates was packed last evening to hear Dr. Bagby lecture on "The Disease Called Love." Strange to say, some of our most venerable citizens—men of the highest social position, were crowded around the platform, some of them actually sitting on it, and they all enjoyed the lecture, if possible, more than the young people, who were of course delighted."

Clemmitt & Jones, Printers, Richmond.

Broadside, c. 1870 (Library of Virginia)

We desire especially to obtain home-made, purely Southern articles – tales, stories, sketches, poems that smack of the soil. We want the tone of the Messenger to be something different from the common run of magazines – we want it to be as distinct in character and style as are our people and institutions. We wish its pages to reflect the spirit of the South, as something separate if not superior to that of all other climes and countries whatsoever.[13]

Soon, "separate" and "superior" would become fighting words. While editor of the *Southern Literary Messenger*, Bagby became a staunch supporter of the formation of the Confederacy, thus politics invaded much of his writing. On April 22, 1861, he joined the Confederate Army. Stomach trouble and a generally fragile constitution caused his discharge in September of that year. He lingered in Richmond until the bitter end, fleeing on the same train that carried President Jefferson Davis out of the capital city. After the war, Bagby, his wife, Lucy "Parke" Chamberlayne, and their six children returned to Richmond, where he struggled once more to make ends meet. Then, in the winter of 1865–1866, his lecture, "Bacon and Greens or the Native Virginian" was a thunderous success, first in Richmond and then throughout Virginia and Maryland.[14] Bagby had found his post-war calling. Engagements as a lecturer and humorist not only provided much needed income for his family, but also were held for the benefit of the Virginia Historical Society and the Southern Historical Society, founded in 1868–1869 to document Southern history, beginning with the recent conflict.[15]

In 1870, when Virginia was readmitted to the Union, George W. Bagby became State Librarian as part of his duties as Assistant to the Secretary of the Commonwealth. He continued writing and appeared frequently on the lecture circuit. Broadsides announced that his entertaining evening discussing "The Disease Called Love" was "A Feast of Fun." Admission was a hefty $.50. Undoubtedly bombarded to speak for many worthy causes, Bagby raised money for such diverse groups as the Charlottesville Cornet Band and the library fund.[16] Like his better-known counterpart, Mark Twain, George W. Bagby the humorist entertained audiences North and South.

In 1875, when Bagby spoke at the Cooper Institute in New York City, he impressed northern audiences with his humorous "The Negro and his Peculiarities." The lecture consisted primarily of personal reminiscences of the South before the war. A review in *The New York Times* stated, "Dr. Bagby is a man of culture, and rendered his lecture highly entertaining, imitating the voice and dialect of the negro admirably."[17]

In 1877, Bagby penned his best-known and most enduring essay, "The Old Virginia Gentleman." In it, he presented a Virginia that is all charm and no mosquitos. He paints the landscape with what was already a nostalgic brush, describing in vivid detail the approach to an ancient and honorable central Virginia farm. It might be in Cumberland or Prince Edward or Buckingham. Everything in his picturesque canvas has its place, its purpose. Importantly, he begins, the Virginia Gentleman's "house was not jammed down within two inches and a half of 'the main, plain road.'"[18] A stranger would never guess that a beautiful homestead lay at the end of a turning out, no bigger than a rut. The cousins and the cousins of cousins, however, knew where that rut led and it "drew you like a magnet."[19]

Then came the ride through the woods, the more timber the better. Here the boys shot their squirrel and the hogs ran free. The Negroes, Bagby insisted, "can't be healthy without wood, nor enjoy life without pine-knots when they go fishing at night."[20] Once through the forest, the view opened up to fields of waving wheat and plumed and tasseled corn. Clover covered the hills and broad leaf tobacco was abundant. Cows chewed their cud and sheep were peaceful. It was a bucolic scene worthy of Constable, an ode to the country living that shaped Bagby. How he mourned these stately mansions of dusky red or mellow grey and their dilapidation following the War Between the States. "The soul," he wrote, "has fled."[21]

"The Old Virginia Gentleman" began as a lecture to benefit the Virginia Historical Society. Dr. Bagby explained his goal in his original introduction to his collected sketches:

> My hope was that its delivery throughout the State might awaken in our people a just pride in its Past, which with all its faults, has had no equal since Greece gave to the World that splendor which will live

when the sun dies. That pride aroused, I hoped they would revivify a society representing the history of the oldest and greatest of American States.[22]

In 1879, Bagby published *Canal Reminiscences: Recollections of Travel in the Old Days On The James River & Kanawha Canal.* The coming of the railroad was about to extinguish canal transportation and Bagby was inspired to write a brief memoir, praising the lazy days of the canal, recalling the initial blasting of rock to create the waterway in 1835.

First, he waxed nostalgic about the "good old days" of the flatboats on the river. Those James River batteaux, he wrote, were "picturesque craft that charmed my young eyes more than all the gondolas of Venice would do now. True, they consumed a week in getting from Lynchburg to Richmond, and ten days in returning against the stream, but what of that? Time was abundant in those days."[23]

He went on to describe his first trip to Richmond. For a ten-year-old boy who had barely made it to Warminster in Nelson County and had only imagined Cartersville on the James River in Cumberland County, Virginia's capital was a revelation.

> In 1838, I made my first trip to Richmond. What visions of grandeur filled my youthful imagination! That eventually I should get to be a man seemed probable, but that I should ever be big enough to live, actually live, in the vast metropolis, was beyond my dreams. For I believed fully that men were proportioned to the size of the cities they lived in. I had seen a man named Hatcher from Cartersville, who was near about the size of the average man in Lynchburg, but as I had never seen Cartersville, I concluded, naturally enough, that Cartersville must be equal in population. Which may be the fact, for I have never yet seen Cartersville, though I have been to Warminster, and once came near passing through Bent-Creek.[24]

During Bagby's school years in the North, the James and Kanawha Canal between Richmond and Lynchburg was completed and, upon his return to

Virginia, Bagby took his first ride on a packet boat. Forty years later, the sights and sound of impressionable youth were still vivid in his mind:

> At last we were off, slowly pushed along under the bridge on Seventh street; then the horses were hitched; then slowly along till we passed the crowd of boats near the city, until at length, with a lively jerk as the horses fell into a trot, away we went, the cut-water throwing up the spray as we rounded the Penitentiary hill, and the passengers lingering on deck to get a last look at the fair city of Richmond, lighted by the pale rays of the setting sun.
>
> As the shadows deepened, everybody went below. There was always a crowd in those days, but it was a crowd for the most part of our best people, and no one minded it. I was little, and it took little room to accommodate me. Everything seemed as cozy and comfortable as heart could wish. I brought to the table, - an excellent one it was, - a school boy's appetite, sharpened by travel, and thought it was "just splendid."
>
> Supper over, the men went on deck to smoke while the ladies busied themselves with draughts [checkers] or backgammon, with conversation or with books. But not for long. The curtains which separated the female from the male department were soon drawn, in order that the steward and his aids might make ready the berths. These were three deep, "lower," "middle" and "upper;" and great was the desire on the part of the men not to be consigned to the "upper." Being light as a cork, I rose naturally to the top, clambering thither by the leathern straps with the agility of a monkey, and enjoying as best I might the trampling overhead whenever we approached a lock. I didn't mind this much, but when the fellow who had snubbed the boat jumped down about four feet, right on my head as it were, it was pretty severe. Still I slept the sleep of youth. We all went to bed early. A few lingered, talking in low tones; and way-passengers, in case there was a crowd, were dumped upon mattresses, placed on the dining tables....

To this day you have only to say within my hearing trahn-ahn-ahn, to bring back the canal epoch. I can see the whole thing down to the snubbing post with its deep grooves which the heavy rope had worn. Indeed, I think I could snub a boat myself with very little practice, if the man on deck would say "hup!" to the horses at the proper time.[25]

"God Bless the Old Virginia Negro"

"The Old Virginia Negro" was one of the illustrations included in the 1938 edition of The Old Virginia Gentleman and Other Sketches. (Courtesy The Dietz Press)

Bagby lived many years in his beloved Richmond which he saw as a shining citadel in his youth. This lovely, romantic ode to Richmond is Bagby at his best:

> [H]owever bold and picturesque the cliffs and bluffs near Lynchburg and beyond, there was nothing from one end [of] the canal to the other to compare with the first sight of Richmond, when, rounding a corner not far from Hollywood [Cemetery], it burst full upon the vision, its capitol, its spires, its happy homes, flushed with the red glow of evening. And what it looked to be, it was. Its interior, far from belieing its exterior, surpassed it. The world over, there is no lovelier site for a city; and the world over there was no city that quite equalled it in the charm of its hospitality, its refinement, its intelligence, its cordial welcome to strangers. Few of its inhabitants were very rich, fewer still were very poor. But I must not dwell on this. Beautiful city! beautiful city! you may grow to be as populous as London, and sure no one wishes you greater prosperity than I, but grow as you may, you can never be happier than you were in the days whereof I speak. How your picture comes back to me, softened by time, glorified by all the tender, glowing tints of memory. Around you now is the added glory of history, a defense almost unrivalled in the annals of warfare; but for me there is something even brighter than historic fame, a hue derived only from the heaven of memory. In my childhood, when all things were beautified by the unclouded light of "the young soul wandering here in nature," I saw you in your youth, full of hope, full of promise, full of all those gracious influences which made your State greatest among all her sisters, and which seemed concentrated in yourself. Be your maturity what it may, it can never be brighter than this.[26]

On November 29, 1883, Dr. Bagby died in his Richmond home and was buried in the city's Shockoe Hill Cemetery. There his long-term companions include Chief Justice John Marshall and Buckingham County's own Peter

Francisco. Nestled above the James River, time has stopped for George Bagby and he was spared the march of progress which erased the Old South.

☼☙☼

There is no question that some of Dr. Bagby's writings have stood the test of time better than others. When he writes that Virginia's slaves were "the happiest peasantry this world has ever seen," it is clear that Bagby writes with rose-colored vision.[27] Yet, "My Uncle Flatback's Plantation," "Fishing on the Appomattox," and "Corn-Field Peas" continue to evoke the many charms of 19th century central Virginia. Through the mid-20th century, Bagby's writings elicited praise from reviewers. In a preface to the 1910 edition of *The Old Virginia Gentleman*, Southern "local colorist" Thomas Nelson Page called Bagby "A Virginia Realist" and found the title essay to be enduring – "the most charming picture of American life ever drawn."[28] He ranked Bagby next to Edgar Alan Poe as "the most original of all Virginia writers."[29]

In 1944, reviewer James Southall Wilson still found Dr. Bagby realistic, lacking in sentimentality. In his review of the fourth edition of *The Old Virginia Gentleman*, Wilson wrote:

> His Virginia is not the glamorous legend of Thomas Nelson Page nor the more universalized and modern Virginia of Ellen Glasgow. It is not the stately Virginia of Washington nor the catalogued Virginia of the antique dealers and the professional genealogists. The Virginia that Dr. Bagby realizes so evocatively in his sketches is the Virginia of the Civil War days and after, when the ideals of "Baronial Virginia" were still remembered. It is a friendly and a homely land and people. Bagby had none of the eviscerated refinement that spread like a blight over the land with its post-war poverty. He likes apple jack and is not ashamed to have suffered from chigoes. He prefers the Virginia word and the Virginia way of saying it. He is a Virginian: "tharfo he kin affode to talk as he blame chooses." That delightful arrogance with a twinkle is true Virginian. It gives the raciness that is part of the Bagby charm.[30]

It was perhaps Douglas Southall Freeman who best summed up George W. Bagby's contribution to Southern literature:

> His monument was his work. The gentlest, most gracious life of his day he had described with understanding. Human nature he had plumbed to its depths. Rollicking laughter of the servants and quaint speech of the farmer he had preserved. The pathos of a great struggle he had enshrined. All the beauties of a beloved countryside he had painted in his pages. His high powers, creative, original and diverse, had been given where he wished them to be spent—for Virginia.[31]

NOTES

1 George W. Bagby, "The Old Virginia Gentleman," *The Old Virginia Gentleman, and Other Sketches* (New York, NY: Charles Scribner's Sons, 1910), 44.

2 "Memorial Edition of the Old Virginia Gentleman," *Virginia Magazine of History and Biography* (January 1939), 85. The Virginia Historical Society was founded in 1831 and did not occupy its own building until 1893. Located at 707 East Franklin Street in Richmond, it was known as the Lee House, because it was the wartime home of Gen. Robert E. Lee's family. See "History of the VHS," accessed August 2014, http://www.vahistorical.org/about/history_vhs.htm.

3 "Memorial Edition of the Old Virginia Gentleman," *Virginia Magazine of History and Biography*, 85. Ellen Glasgow, a popular writer of her day, won a Pulitzer Prize in 1942 for her novel, *In This Our Life*. See "Ellen Anderson Gholson Glasgow, 1873-1945," *Documenting the American South*, accessed August 2014, http://docsouth.unc.edu/southlit/glasgowbattle/bio.html.

4 George W. Bagby, *The Old Virginia Gentleman and Other Sketches* (Richmond, VA: Dietz Press, 1943), Kindle Location 35; James Southall Wilson, "*The Old Virginia Gentleman and Other Sketches* by George W. Bagby," *William and Mary Quarterly* (January 1944), 86-89. The 1943 edition was followed by a fifth edition in 1948 which includes a personal memoir of Dr. Bagby written in 1889 by Kate Burwell Bowyer. See John Melville Jennings, "*The Old Virginia Gentleman and Other Sketches* by George W. Bagby," *Virginia Magazine of History and Biography* (January 1949), 96-97.

5 George W. Bagby, *The Old Virginia Gentleman and Other Sketches* (Richmond, VA: Dietz Press, 1938); G. Glenwood Clark, "*The Old Virginia Gentleman and Other Sketches* by George W. Bagby," *William and Mary Quarterly* (April 1939), 253–255.

6 Douglas Southall Freeman, "George W. Bagby, Patriot," in *The Old Virginia Gentleman and Other Sketches* by George W. Bagby (Richmond, VA: Dietz Press, 1943), Kindle Location 173.

7 Joseph Leonard King, Jr., *Dr. George William Bagby: A Study of Virginian Literature 1850-1880* (New York, NY: Columbia University Press, 1927), 1–6. Dr. Bagby's birth date is uncertain, recorded as both August 13 and August 25, 1828. See Ibid., 1. For an affectionate biographical tribute see "A Lover of Virginia," *The Richmond Dispatch*, 7 July 1901.

8 Bagby, "Bacon and Greens," *The Old Virginia Gentleman* (1910), 46.

9 King, *Dr. George William Bagby*, 5–6; Brendan Wolfe, editor, "George William Bagby (1828–1883)," *Encyclopedia Virginia*, accessed August 2014, http://www.EncyclopediaVirginia.org/Bagby_George_William_1828-1883.

10 Wolfe, "Bagby," *Encyclopedia Virginia*.

11   Ibid.

12   Freeman, "George W. Bagby, Patriot," Kindle Location 224.

13   "Editor's Table," *Southern Literary Messenger* (June 1860), 467, accessed August 2014, http://quod.lib.umich.edu/m/moajrnl/acf2679.0030.006/471:14?page=root;rgn=full+text;size=100;view=image.

14   Edward S. Gregory, "George William Bagby," in *The Old Virginia Gentleman, and Other Sketches* by George W. Bagby (New York, NY: Charles Scribner's Sons, 1910), xvii–xxx.

15   According to the first issue of the *Southern Historical Society Papers*, "The object proposed to be accomplished is the collection, classification, preservation, and final publication, in some form to be hereafter determined, of all the documents and facts bearing upon the eventful history of the past few years, illustrating the nature of the struggle from which the country has just emerged, defining and vindicating the principles which lay beneath it, and marking the stages through which it was conducted to its issue. It is not understood that this association shall be purely sectional, nor that its labors shall be of a partisan character." See: Rev. J. William Jones, D. D., "Editorial Paragraphs," *Southern Historical Society Papers: Vol. 1, January-June 1876* (Richmond, VA: Johns & Goolsby, Printers, 1876), 41, accessed August 2014, http://en.wikisource.org/wiki/Southern_Historical_Society_Papers/Volume_01.

16   Broadsides, 187-: 5, 1880: 8, 1880: 11, Virginia Historical Society.

17   "The Negro Race. Lecture by Dr. George W. Bagby, Of Virginia–Its Destiny To Gradually Dwindle Away–The Signs of Decadence," *The New York Times*, 21 April 1875.

18   George W. Bagby, "The Old Virginia Gentleman," *The Old Virginia Gentleman* (1910), 1.

19   Ibid, 2.

20   Ibid, 3.

21   Ibid, 6.

22   "Memorial Edition of the Old Virginia Gentleman," *Virginia Magazine of History and Biography*, 85.

23   George W. Bagby, *Canal Reminiscences: Recollections of Travel in the Old Days On The James River & Kanawha Canal* (Richmond, VA: West, Johnston & Co., 1879), 8–9.

24   Ibid., 12.

25   Ibid., 15–17.

26   Ibid., 24–26.

27   Bagby, "The Old Virginia Gentleman," *The Old Virginia Gentleman* (1910), 42.

28 Thomas Nelson Page, "A Virginia Realist," in *The Old Virginia Gentleman* (1910), xii. Partial to Dr. Bagby's tone, Page himself wrote what are now regarded as nostalgic and revisionist poems, stories, and novels, idealizing the Old South. According to the *Encyclopedia Virginia*, "In the context of the great social upheaval following that war, stories like Page's hugely influential 'Marse Chan' (1884) promoted the image of an Old South replete with gracious aristocrats and loyal servants and a New South fraught with turmoil but ready for reconciliation with the North. This nostalgic, revisionist version of history was embraced with gusto by both northern and southern readers, and its vestiges remain even today in popular concepts of the South." See "Thomas Nelson Page (1853–1922)," *Encyclopedia Virginia*, accessed August 2014, http://www.encyclopediavirginia.org/Page_Thomas_Nelson_1853-1922.

29 Page, "A Virginia Realist," vii–viii.

30 Wilson, "The Old Virginia Gentleman," *William and Mary Quarterly*, 88.

31 Freemen, *The Old Virginia Gentleman* (1943), Kindle Location 361.

(LIBRARY OF VIRGINIA)

Alexander Moseley, Editor of the Richmond Whig, *is buried at Willow Lake, the Buckingham County home of his grandparents, Robert Peter Moseley (1732–1804) and Magdalena Guerrant (1740–1826). There, the children of his colleague, James Hamden Pleasants, marked Moseley's grave with the following epitaph:*

> An eminent patriotic and wholesouled Virginian. The distinguished Editor for many years of the Richmond Whig, of splendid scholarship, courage, independence and ability. A man of rare simplicity, purity and selflessness, noble in his impulses, and steadfast in his friendships as in his principals. *Quis Desiderio Sit Pudor Aut Modus. Incorrupta Fides Midaque Veritas.* This stone is raised by the children of John Hamden Pleasants to the memory of their Father's friend and their own.

The Man behind Alexander Hill: Alexander Moseley

Between 1809 and 1810, two Alexander Moseleys were born. Distant cousins, they were both reared in Buckingham County, Virginia and, over time, their biographies became confused.

The older of the two, born on June 10, 1809, was the product of prominent Buckingham families. His parents were Col. Robert Moseley and his second wife, Elizabeth "Betsey" Putney, whose mother was a Fearn. Like many citizens in Buckingham County, he had more than a touch of French Huguenot blood; his Moseley grandmother was a Guerrant. A lifelong bachelor, he grew up to become the Editor of the *Richmond Whig*.[1]

The younger, whose full name was possibly Alexander Marshall Moseley, was born on July 22, 1810, in Powhatan County, Virginia. He grew up to be an attorney, practicing at Curdsville and at Gravel Hill, Buckingham County.[2]

One of these two men became the founder of "Alexander Hill," a tract of land in northwestern Buckingham gifted to newly emancipated slaves. Some accounts have attributed the gift to Alexander Moseley, Esquire of Gravel Hill; however, he was not a planter and never owned numerous slaves. By 1860, he owned just a two-year-old girl and a one-year-old boy, making him a very unlikely candidate for the man behind the community established at Alexander Hill.[3]

In fact, it was Alexander Moseley, Editor of the *Whig*, who made this remarkable gift to his former servants. His biography is fairly typical of a man of his station, giving no hint of this very atypical gesture that would affect many lives and one small corner of Buckingham County.

۞

Alexander Moseley grew up not far from Buckingham Court House where his family included an older brother, Robert Ellis Moseley, several half-siblings, and an abundant collection of cousins. Just days before his eighth birthday his father, Col. Robert Moseley, died and his mother, Elizabeth, was left in charge of the education of her sons. The specifics of young Alexander's early education are not known. Eventually, he joined his cousin, Henry Ellis Guerrant, at Washington College, then transferred to the University of Virginia. His brother-in-law, John M. Harris, acted as his guardian at matriculation in 1828.[4] Along with a few other students, Moseley was among the first to challenge the right for students to live "off campus."[5] He studied broadly, covering Ancient Languages, Modern Languages, Mathematics, Moral Philosophy, and Law.[6] Importantly, while at the University of Virginia, he developed a taste for journalism as editor of the *University Magazine*.[7]

In the summer of 1831, he graduated, acknowledged by the Schools of Moral Philosophy, Political Economy, and Law.[8] After completing his degrees, Moseley briefly practiced law, which did not suit him.[9] Soon he found himself drawn towards writing and politics and, in October of 1835, the socially and politically conservative young man joined the staff of Charlottesville's *Virginia Advocate* as an assistant editor. In those days, newspapers and politics went hand in hand. The *Advocate* supported state's rights, was anti-Jackson and, as such, was read by the men who would eventually join the Whig party.[10]

Living and working in Charlottesville, Alexander Moseley found his voice, which was not always discrete. In fact, one cousin wrote that he could be "very warm in his cause against power and corruption."[11] Moseley's heated opinions resulted in a challenge to a duel with fellow University of Virginia graduate and then Democrat, Alexander Rives. Intelligence prevailed, however; Rives refused the challenge and Moseley lived to write another day.

The next step in Moseley's career was aided by his politically-minded, Whig-oriented, Buckingham County cousin, Thomas Moseley Bondurant, founder of the *Richmond Whig*. On July 29, 1836, Alexander Moseley quit the *Virginia Advocate*, moved to Richmond, and joined the editorial staff of Bondurant's newspaper.[12] He was devoted to the *Whig* and would work there, off and on, for the next thirty-five years.

During 1845–1846, Moseley took an extended leave from politics and the newspaper business. In June of 1845, joined by traveling companion James Bowdoin of New York, Moseley embarked on a grand tour of Europe. Six months of his travels are preserved in diaries. His classical education prepared him well to appreciate the ancient cultures, art, and architecture he saw in England, France, and Italy.[13]

He found London's Belgrave Square "the most splendid and fashionable in the city."[14] Westminster Abbey, wrote Moseley, "repaid me for my visit across the Atlantic. . . and the thousand historical associations connected with the place were an ample remuneration. The whole will live in my memory many a day."[15] In Paris, at Notre Dame, he felt the presence of Julius Caesar who "had his camp nearby." The site of an ancient temple of Jupiter, Moseley wrote, "[it is] the first time my foot has trodden the ground known to have been consecrated to the worship of Jove."[16]

In Italy, Pompeii was being excavated and Moseley found the archeology fascinating.[17] In Rome, he marveled at the Vatican's Apollo Belvedere, despite its fall from critical grace. It impressed him "more than any piece of sculpture I ever saw. It seems to remind me of some divine being that I had known in my dreams. I returned to it again and again."[18] In Florence, he met contemporary sculptors, including the American, Thomas Crawford, whose equestrian statue of George Washington would eventually stand on the capital grounds in Richmond, Virginia.[19] Moseley even noted that he shopped for "the Virginia ladies," who might have included his mother, sisters, or his niece, Amanda Harris, who would name one of her sons Alexander Moseley Bolling.[20]

Moseley's sojourn undoubtedly changed him and, on his return, he took time to assimilate all he had seen, heard, and done. Seeking escape from city life in Richmond, the world's bustle, and the often emotional sphere of journalism, he went home to Buckingham. He remained a bachelor, initially living alone. In about 1847, he purchased 1,700 acres from R. B. Patteson, located on the James River, at Sycamore Island, fifteen miles northwest of Buckingham Courthouse.[21] There he enjoyed the life of a country gentleman, living in "elegant ease."[22] Valued at $13,000 and home to twenty-nine slaves, the farm consisted of 600 improved and 1,150 unimproved acres. Growing mixed crops and tobacco, Moseley also kept a large flock of sheep.[23] The challenges and excitement of the world of journalism soon drew him back to Richmond and, in 1848, he returned to his position as Editor at the *Whig*, only to retire once again in July of 1850.[24]

In 1853, he added Fish Pond plantation to his holdings. Situated in Nelson County, east of Warminster, it was a spectacular James River property. The farm was named for a private pond created from the river where the country squire could swim or fish. The James River and Kanawha Canal ran through the property and lock keepers were among Moseley's neighbors.[25] In addition to farming, he operated a steam mill to cut lumber and a grist mill which not only ground corn, but also produced products such as plaster.[26]

From the comfort of Fish Pond, Moseley could enjoy the view across the river to Sycamore Island and western Buckingham County where extended Moseley families owned large estates, including Wheatland and Willow Lake.[27] Fish Pond was an antebellum ideal. His commodious house sat high on the hill, crowning a "spacious lawn, full of native trees." It was made for entertaining and gracious hospitality.[28]

In 1937, Annie Harrower described the home for the Virginia Historical Inventory:

Fish Pond, Nelson County, Virginia (LIBRARY OF VIRGINIA)

It is a "T" shape, fifteen room house, frame, with a brick foundation.... A full length one story porch across the front, with a small one on the top in center with fancy balusters. There are two other small porches at sides. The house is covered with slate. Three brick chimneys. The house has three entrances from the front. The fireplaces are small, with low mantels and some carvings.[29]

If only those porches could talk!

By 1860, Moseley shared his home with his twice-widowed mother, Elizabeth Guerrant, and his two Walker nephews.[30] Living with them were a free mulatto man, Henry Bradley (born in New Kent County), and a free black man, John Harris (born in Buckingham County), probably the John Harris, Sr., later a grantee at Alexander Hill.[31] Moseley's wealth was calculated at $100,000, $70,000 of which was represented, in part, by his fifty-six slaves, who lived in thirteen dwellings at Fish Pond and Sycamore Island.[32]

ಐಲ

During the Civil War, Moseley returned once again to journalism and the *Whig*. His contribution to the paper's success was significant. Journalist Thomas Cooper DeLeon praised the newspaper in his memoir, *Four Years in Rebel Capitals: An Inside View of Life in the Southern Confederacy from Birth to Death*.

> [The] *Richmond Examiner* and *Whig* might have taken rank alongside of the best-edited papers of the country. Their literary ability was, perhaps, greater than that of the North; their discussions of the questions of the hour were clear, strong, and scholarly, and possessed, besides, the invaluable quality of honest conviction. Unlike the press of the North, the southern journals were not hampered by any business interests; they were unbiased, unbought and free to say what they thought and felt. And say it they did, in the boldest and plainest of language.[33]

Inventory of Negroes at Sycamore Island, Buckingham County, Virginia, 1857 (RECORDS OF THE SYCAMORE ISLAND AND FISH POND PLANTATIONS, 1856–1858, ROBERT ALONZO BROCK COLLECTION, BR 137, THE HUNTINGTON LIBRARY, SAN MARINO, CA)

Inventory of Negroes at Fish Pond, Nelson County, Virginia, 1857 (RECORDS OF THE SYCAMORE ISLAND AND FISH POND PLANTATIONS, 1856–1858, ROBERT ALONZO BROCK COLLECTION, BR137, THE HUNTINGTON LIBRARY, SAN MARINO, CA)

1857 Inventory of Negroes: Fish Pond and Sycamore Island

<u>At Fish Pond</u>

Cely, Nelson, Annie, John, William, Monroe, Tom, Peter, Jr., Infant girl, Peter Sr., Jack, Henry,

Reuben, Woods' Sam, and John Harris, free man of color.

<u>At Sycamore Island</u>

Old Jess, Young Jess, Taze, Old Amy, Young Amy, Liddy, Old Lize, Bill, Peter, Young Lize, Moly, Infant, Isaac Curd, Mary Ann, Henry, Sam Goodwyn, Charlotte, Jim (died), Eliza, Amanda, Nelly, Sandy, Wyatt, Betty, Gabe, Nelus, Clarissa, Winston, Silva, Aaron, Susan, Albert, Sam J., Cary Ann, Phil, Frank Taylor [?], Manuel.

<u>Deaths 1858</u>

January 9: Jim, age about 19, son of Sam Goodwyn, congestion bowels, after a week's illness

May 25: Child of Anny [Amy ?], age 11 mos., teething, sickly since birth

May 27 & 28: Child of Clairissa, aged 4 mos, over laid

<u>Births 1858</u>

Clairissa – died
Susan
Bettie

During 1857–1858, Alexander Moseley's kinsman, Ellis W. Putney, managed Fish Pond and Sycamore Island. A surviving plantation journal preserves Putney's records, including two "Inventory of Negroes" dated 1857. Among them are some of the men and women who, a decade later, will own and occupy Alexander Hill. According to the Library of Virginia, "It is unclear whether the Ellis Washington Putney who maintained the first half of this plantation record is Ellis Putney, Sr., born about 1812, or Ellis Putney, Jr., born about 1836, both in Buckingham County, Virginia." Moseley's mother, Elizabeth "Betsey" (Putney), was the daughter of Ellis Washington and Frances "Fanny" (Fearn) Putney.

The slave inventory was, at least in part, organized by family. In 1870, Isaac Curd and his family lived very near to Alexander Hill. His wife, Mary Ann, and son, Henry, both appeared with him on the Sycamore Island slave list. After 1858, their family continued to grow. Before 1870, the Curds had at least four more children, including a son named Alex. In 1870, Sam Goodwyn was living in Buckingham County, James River District, not far from Alexander Hill. With him are his wife, Charlotte, Amandy A. (who appears on the 1857 slave list as Amanda), Sandy, and Wyatt.

Ultimately, the war brought an end to the only way of life Alexander Moseley had ever known – one of privilege and relative security at the top of the social ladder. Like many members of the planter class, he experienced significant financial losses during the war. As a result of overwhelming debt, on October 15, 1866, he deeded Fish Pond to his cousin, Alexander Joseph "Sandy" Bondurant. The price was $40,000 – in gold.[34]

Alexander Moseley assessed his new life and the future of his former servants. With emancipation realized and Fish Pond sold, both he and many newly freed men, women, and children had lost their home. Moseley devised a plan to provide at least some of them with land to work, giving them a solid start in the New South.

On January 1, 1867, a remarkable deed was executed in Buckingham County. The tract of land consisted of 346 acres. The deed transferred Moseley's property to nine "men of color," including Gabriel Palmer, who would become the pastor of Alexander Hill Baptist Church, the first African-American Baptist church in Buckingham County. The others were Emanuel Wayne, Emanuel Moseley, Cornelius Palmer, Winston Palmer, Peter Scott, Jesse Moseley, Sr., John Harris, Sr., and Samuel Braxton. The tract was located at the headwaters of Ryan's Creek just west of Glenmore. On the deed, a church was noted at the tip of Emanuel Wayne's land on Nicholas Cabell's Ferry Road. In the center of the property, on Emanuel Moseley's lot, there was a saw mill.[35] The place became known as Alexander Hill.[36]

The men of Alexander Hill were on their own to work their land, grow their church, and care for their families. When the census was enumerated in 1870, all of the grantees remained on their land in James River Township. The relative value of their lots was recorded: Manuel Wain (sic), $86.00; Manuel Moseley, $88.00; Gabe Palmer, $114.00; Cornelius Palmer, $84.00; Peter Scott, $40.00; Jesse Moseley, $60.00; Samuel Braxton, $30.00; Winston Palmer, $84.00; and John Harris, $74.00.[37]

The 1870 census also reveals that Alexander Moseley provided a new beginning for far more than just nine men. Together with their wives, children, and extended families, they were a ready-made community. After Emancipation, some of Alexander Moseley's former slaves and grantees recorded their pre-1865 marriages with the Freedman's Bureau.[38] They included:

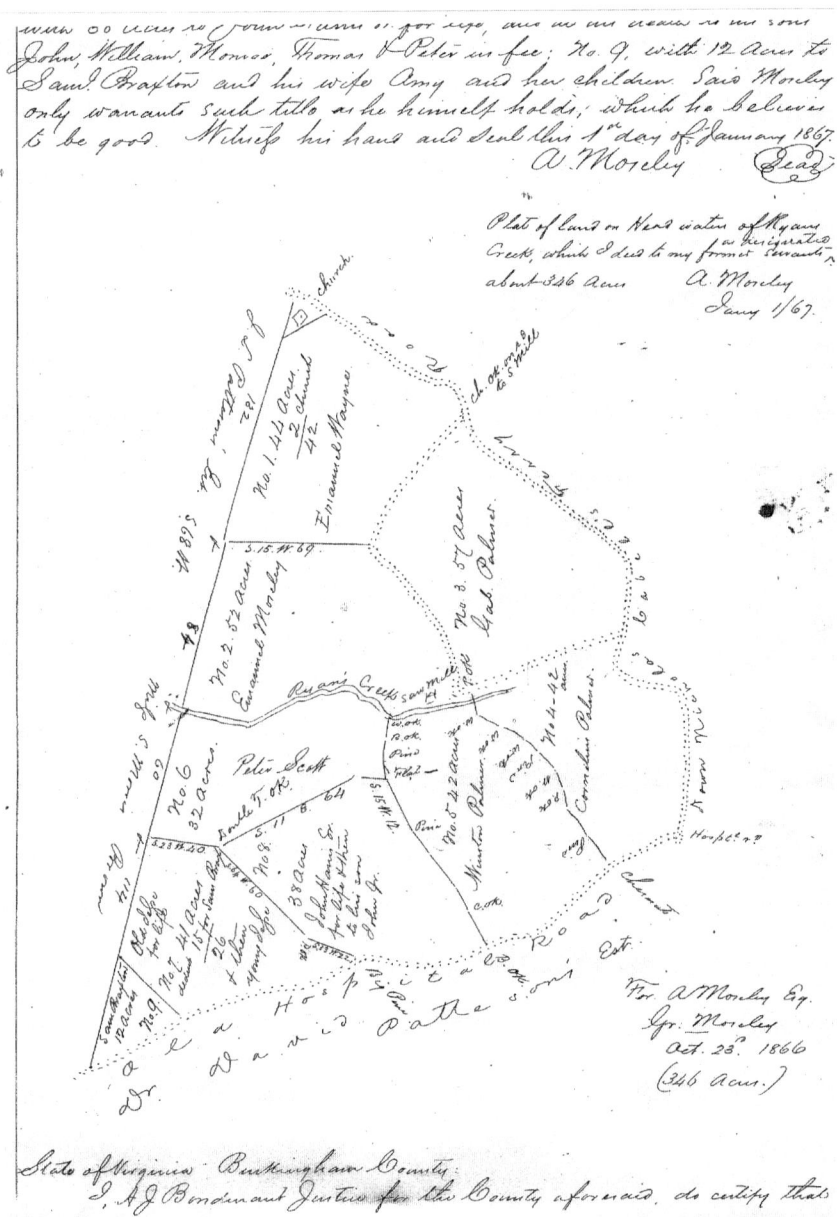

Alexander Hill Deed, 1866 (BUCKINGHAM COUNTY RECORDS, BUCKINGHAM, VA)

Sam Braxton and Amy Mosley
   (n.d.) Alex. Moseley, Nelson Co.[39]
Isaac Curd and Mary Ann Scott
   1850 On Farm Alex. Moseley, Nelson Co.[40]
John Harris and Eliza Scott
   1864 Alex. Moseley, Nelson Co.[41]
Jesse Moseley and Amy Jones
   25 December 1859 Alex. Moseley, Nelson Co.
Jesse Moseley and Lydia Palmer
   27 December 1864 Alex. Moseley, Nelson Co.[42]
Cornelius Palmer and Selina Woodson September
   1857 Alex. Moseley, Buckingham Co.[43]
Gabriel Palmer and Lydia Moseley
   27 October 1862 Alex. Moseley, Nelson Co.[44]

The Palmer family included three grantees, Gabriel, Cornelius, and Winston, all of whom could read and write.[45] Who were these literate Palmers who married women belonging to Alexander Moseley? The 1867 deed identifies them as former servants of Alexander Moseley, but were they all slaves?

Oral history maintains that Gabriel Palmer's wife, Lydia (a.k.a. Lidia and Lettie), was once the property of Alexander Moseley. She may be the woman named "Liddy" on Moseley's 1857 slave list.[46] According to Buckingham resident, Bob Parson, who compiled a history of Alexander Hill Baptist Church, "Gabriel Palmer was a free black who lived near the Moseley plantation."[47] If he is the Gabe on Moseley's 1857 slave list, was he freed prior to Emancipation? In 1870, the forty-year-old "Gabe" Palmer was described as a farmer. If he was already preaching, the census taker did not make note of it. Ten years later, however, Palmer's occupation would be given as "preacher." The church building identified on the 1867 deed indicates that Alexander Hill Baptist Church may have been more than a grove church by that date.[48]

In 1870, grantee Cornelius Palmer was living with his wife, Susan, and five children. While no Cornelius appeared on Moseley's 1857 slave list, it does include a Susan.[49] Winston Palmer, age twenty, is living nearby with his wife,

Alexander Hill Baptist Church (Photo Courtesy of William Q. O. Shelton)

Pamelia, and two children. Moseley's 1857 slave list recorded a Winston, between age twelve and sixteen.[50]

According to tradition, Cornelius Palmer founded Alexander Hill School.[51] Edward Lomax taught there, beginning a long and illustrious career in Buckingham County. In 1870, Edward Lomax and his family lived near the John Harris family at Alexander Hill; Lomax was enumerated as a twenty-one-year-old mulatto.[52] By 1886–87 and perhaps before, Edward and his wife, Josephine, held "First Grade Certificates" and were teaching in a "colored school" at Buckingham Court House. Together, they would go on to become leaders in the Buckingham County schools, conducting training institutes for African American teachers.[53]

In 1870, the remaining grantees were all residing at Alexander Hill: "Manuel Wain" (Emanuel Wayne); "Manuel" Moseley; Peter Scott, with his wife, Adeline, and their four children; the seventy-five-year-old Jessie Moseley, Sr. and his wife, Emma; and Samuel Braxton, with his wife, Emma, and their six children.[54]

Sixty-year-old John Harris, Sr.'s household was especially large. It included Kizia Harris, his wife, Abby Harris, Louisa Knight, and six more children, the youngest of whom was named Alex. Interestingly, the gift of land to John Harris, Sr. was "for life" and upon his death his thirty-eight acres were to go to his sons John, William, Monroe, Thomas, and Peter. By 1870, young John Harris, age thirty, and William Harris, age twenty-eight, were established in separate households, living with their families adjacent John, Sr.[55]

Following the community over the next ten years, there were births, deaths and no doubt an exodus or two, yet Alexander Hill appears to be a stable community. Rev. Gabriel Palmer preached. Winston Palmer died, leaving Pamelia a widow with five children to rear. Jesse Moseley, Jr. named his sixth child Alexander Moseley. Peter Scott and Samuel Braxton, both in their forties, headed substantial families. The Braxtons supported twelve children. John Harris, Sr., Gabe Palmer, Manuel Wayne, Manuel Moseley, and Jesse Moseley all farmed their own land.[56]

The success of Alexander Hill demonstrates that Alexander Moseley's faith was not misplaced when he established nine free men of color on land they could call their own. He believed in their abilities and they believed in themselves. The Palmers, the Moseleys, Emanuel Wayne, Peter Scott, John Harris, Sr., and Samuel Braxton took their gift and soared with it, providing a community for their children and their grandchildren.

‍ ಬಾಂ

And what of Alexander Moseley, Editor? By 1868, without a farm to manage, he returned to Richmond and worked at the *Whig*. He resided at 703 East Franklin Street, not far from where Gen. Robert E. Lee once lived, and, later, on 8th Street beyond Leigh Street, near the city springs. In early 1871, once again Moseley retired, purchasing a farm in New Kent County, Virginia at Dispatch Station and whimsically calling it "The Shanty." Ten years later, he died there on August 30, 1881, of a congestive chill.[57] According to one obituary, Alexander Moseley "contentedly spent his declining days in fishing, in reading, and in entertainment of his friends, who found in 'The Shanty,' as he called it, a hospitality as genuine, if not as sumptuous, as he dispensed in the days of his wealth at 'Sycamore.'"[58]

Alexander Moseley, Editor

On September 1, 1881, Richmond's *The Daily Dispatch* ran both a news article and an editorial concerning the death of Alexander Moseley. The first praised his scholarship and his "incisive and aggressive" writing, calling him "a man of genial temperament, loving good company and ever ready to serve his friends." This man, who created Alexander Hill, counted many African Americans among them. The editorial read as follows:

Death of Alexander Moseley, Esq.

A remarkable man was ALEXANDER MOSELEY, Esq., whose death is announced elsewhere in our columns this morning. He was for many years connected with the Richmond *Whig* when that journal was enjoying its highest reputation – when JOHN HAMPDEN PLEASANTS was its editor, and when it was a power, not only in Virginia but in the United States; but he seemed never to know that he was himself of the most elegant, most interesting, and most classic writers of his day and generation. Yet he was all this. We have often thought that he was the finest writer in Virginia. Perhaps we were mistaken; but all who have read his editorials will concede that he has left in Virginia no superior as a writer.

Mr. MOSELEY must have been an extremely diffident man. Those who knew him best (or personal acquaintance with him was but slight) say that he was as unpretending as he was learned. He was a true patriot, strongly attached to his native State; a sincere friend; a lover of nature; and altogether a man worthy of the respect and confidence of the whole community. Few men have wielded so much influence in this State. He died full of years and full of such honors as attached friends could confer – the only kind of honors which he esteemed.

Alexander Moseley, Esq. of Gravel Hill

Alexander Moseley, possibly Alexander Marshall Moseley, was born on July 22, 1810, in Powhatan County, Virginia, the son of Spotswood Lewis Moseley and his first wife, Mary Marshall. Sometime before 1817, the family moved to Buckingham County. On August 30, 1837, Alexander married Emeline J. Brown and in 1850 they were living on the Willis River in Buckingham's District 2 with their children, George B. Moseley, three years old, and Mary V. Moseley, one year old. The 1850 agricultural census credits him with 200 acres of land, 150 of which were cultivated. This Moseley residence was not far from Samuel Morris' farm and Buckingham White Sulphur Springs, in the southeast corner of the county. Alexander Moseley's wealth was valued at $1,200. He owned nine slaves, six of whom were children.

Later in the decade, the Moseleys joined Emeline's Brown family at Gravel Hill, living in the so-called Brick House. Beverly A. Brown, age seventy-two, headed the household. In the spring and summer of 1859, Moseley ran a series of advertisements in the *Richmond Whig*:

ALEXANDER MOSELEY,

ATTORNEY AT LAW,

Has changed his location from Curdsville, to Gravel Hill, Buckingham and continues to practice in the County and Circuit Courts of Buckingham, Cumberland, Prince Edward and Appomattox.

Address, Gravel Hill, Buckingham county, Va.

Alexander Moseley was a busy and respected attorney. Over the years, he acted as agent or trustee for many of the county's oldest families, such as Pratt, Heustis, Miller, Ayres, Jones, Sims, Tapscott, and Booker. By 1860, however, Alexander Moseley's personal property had dwindled along with his real estate. His personal property was valued at $4,000, which included two slaves, a two-year-old girl and a one-year-old boy.

Alexander Moseley's health failed dramatically. On April 30, 1870 he was admitted to Western State Lunatic Asylum in Staunton, Virginia. Fifty-eight years old, his education was described as "liberal" and his diagnosis was "overtaxed energies." It was noted by the administration that his first cousin, J. J. Brown, had died insane. After over two years of confinement, Moseley died at the Asylum on October 11, 1872. His death was recognized that year at the meeting of the Bar of Buckingham County. Robert T. Hubard, Jr., Esq. delivered an eloquent eulogy for three of its members who died in 1872: Alexander Moseley, Archer W. Vaughan, and Nicholas F. Bocock.

Resolved, That in the death of Alexander Moseley, Esq., in October, 1872, we have lost a warm-hearted friend and a legal associate second to none in his devotion to his profession, his laborious efforts to discharge its duties and his familiarity with the whole practice of the law.

NOTES

1   Harrison Moseley Ethridge, "Alexander Moseley, Editor of the Richmond Whig" (master's thesis, University of Richmond, 1967).

2   See Leila Eldridge D'Aiutolo, Warren L. Forsythe, William S. Hubard, and Mary Carolyn Mitton, *The Descendants of William Moseley 1605/1606–1655 of Norfolk, Va., Book I* (Privately published, 2000), 306–307, 426–427. In the 1870s, several notices in the Richmond newspapers referred to the Editor of the Whig as Alexander M. Moseley and A.M. Moseley, further adding to the confusion of the two men.

3   Slave Census, Buckingham County, Virginia, 1860.

4   John M. Harris married Alexander Moseley's half-sister, Evelina Ann Moseley, on October 30, 1823. See *Richmond Enquirer*, 7 November 1823, p. 3.

5   Ethridge, "Alexander Moseley," 3–7.

6   "A Catalogue of the Officers and students of the University of Virginia, 1828–1829, 5th session," accessed August 2014, http://xtf.lib.virginia.edu/xtf/view?docId=2005_Q4_2/uvaBook/tei/z000000106.xml; "A Catalogue of the Officers and students of the University of Virginia, 1829–1830, 6th session," accessed August 2014, http://xtf.lib.virginia.edu/xtf/view?docId=2005_Q4_2/uvaBook/tei/z000000107.xml; "A Catalogue of the Officers and students of the University of Virginia, 1830–1831, 7th session," accessed August 2014, http://xtf.lib.virginia.edu/xtf/view?docId=2005_Q4_2/uvaBook/tei/z000000108.xml.

7   "Death of Alexander Moseley, Esq.," *The Daily Dispatch* (Richmond, VA), 1 September 1881, p. 1.

8   *Richmond Enquirer*, 29 July 1831, p. 3.

9   "Death of Alexander Moseley, Esq.," *The Daily Dispatch*.

10   Ethridge, "Alexander Moseley," 8; *Virginia Advocate*, 9 October 1835. Published during 1827–1860, the *Virginia Advocate* was a weekly paper. See Chronicling America: Historic American Newspapers, Library of Congress, accessed August 2014, http://chroniclingamerica.loc.gov/lccn/sn84024689/.

11   Letter, Col. William Moseley of Buckingham County, Virginia to Col. John Moseley of Jessamine County, Kentucky, 22 May 1836, Moseley files, Housewright Museum, Buckingham, Virginia. Bennett Henderson Young described Col. John Moseley in *A History of Jessamine County from its Earliest Settlement to 1898*, "This gentleman was born in Buckingham county, Virginia, in 1760, and settled in Jessamine in 1793. He served in the Revolutionary war, and was a gallant soldier. He enjoyed the distinction of having reared the largest family ever known in Jessamine—he had three daughters and eighteen sons. He was extremely popular in his neighborhood, and his descendants in Jessamine are very numerous and still live in the immediate neighborhood where their

brave and prolific ancestor settled." See "Biographical Sketches of Prominent Citizens of Jessamine County," accessed April 2014, http://genealogytrails.com/ken/jessamine/jessamine_bios.html.

12   *Richmond Whig & public advertiser* 1833-1867, Chronicling America: Historic American Newspapers, Library of Congress, accessed August 2014, http://chroniclingamerica.loc.gov/lccn/sn84024658/.

13   Alexander Moseley Diary, Alexander Moseley Papers, 1837-1880, Accession 25787, Library of Virginia.

14   Ibid., 3 December 1845.

15   Ibid., 25 November 1845.

16   Ibid., 12 December 1845.

17   Ibid., 13 January 1846, 27 January 1846.

18   Ibid., 10 February 1846.

19   Ibid., 31 March 1846. Thomas Crawford (1814–1857) was born in New York City. In 1835, Crawford moved to Rome, Italy where he became a leader among American expatriates living there. His impressive statue of George Washington, which stands outside Virginia's State Capitol, survived the city's fire in 1865. See Barbara C. Batson and Tracy L. Kamerer, *A Capital Collection: Virginia's Artistic Inheritance* (Richmond, VA: Library of Virginia, 2005), 14–19.

20   Alexander Moseley, Diary, 25 February 1846.

21   Roger G. Ward, *Land Tax Summaries & Implied Deeds 1841–1870, Volume 3* (Athens, GA: Iberian Publishing Company), 197–198. Sycamore Island was adjacent the expansive farm of elder statesman Charles Yancey. In 1850, Yancey's farm was worth $55,000. Alexander Moseley's land holdings in Buckingham County are particularly difficult to trace. In addition to the fact that the original deeds were burned in the 1869 Buckingham Courthouse fire, there were at least three adult Alexander Moseleys living concurrently in Buckingham County: Alexander Moseley, editor; Alexander Moseley, lawyer; and Alexander Trent Moseley. Over the years, their records have been conflated.

22   "Death of Alexander Moseley, Esq.," *The Daily Dispatch*, 1 September 1881, p. 1.

23   Federal Population Census, Buckingham County, Virginia, 1850; Agricultural Census, Buckingham County, Virginia, 1850; Slave Census Buckingham County, Virginia, 1850; Buckingham County Land Tax, 1855, Library of Virginia. When Alexander Moseley moved his residence to Nelson County, he retained part of Sycamore Island. During 1864–1869, he still owned 500 acres in Buckingham County. See Buckingham County Land Tax, 1864–1869, Library of Virginia.

24   Ethridge, "Alexander Moseley," 32–47, 55.

25   Annie L. Harrower, "Fish Pond," 5 November 1937, Virginia Historical Inventory; Annie L. Harrower, "Fish Pond Office," 5 November 1937, Virginia Historical Inventory, Library of Virginia. The first owner was likely Dr. David R. Patterson who established the farm sometime prior 1829 when he died at his residence. See *Daily Richmond Whig*, 9 October 1829, p. 3. Plantation records kept for Fish Pond during 1857 note that Moseley owned 1,065.71 acres of which 70.23 acres were associated with the James River and Kanawha Canal Co. See Plantation records: Sycamore Island and Fish Pond, 21, Robert Alonzo Brock Collection, The Huntington Library, San Marino, California. This acreage was reduced. From 1863–1866, Moseley paid land tax on 468 1/4 acres in Nelson County. See Nelson County Land Tax, 1863–1866, Library of Virginia.

26   Ethridge, "Alexander Moseley," 71; Industrial Census, Nelson County, Virginia, 1860, Library of Virginia. In 1857, Alexander Mosley expanded Fish Pond, purchasing 465 acres from Samuel and Sarah J. (Harris) Allen of Buckingham. Sarah was the niece of Moseley's brother-in-law, John M. Harris. See Nelson County Deed, Allen to Moseley, recorded 23 February 1858, Joanne Yeck Collection.

27   Garnett Agee Williams, "Wheatland," 14 April 1936, Virginia Historical Inventory, Library of Virginia; Elizabeth McCraw, "Wheatland," 17 November 1937, Virginia Historical Inventory, Library of Virginia; Janice J. R. Hull, *Buckingham Burials, Volume I* (Alexandria, Virginia: Hearthside Press, 1997), 379–382. The dwelling house at Wheatland has been restored and, in 2013, it was owned and occupied by Don Moseley.

28   Annie L. Harrower, "Fish Pond."

29   Ibid.

30   Federal Population Census, Nelson County, Virginia, 1860. Sometime before 1820, Elizabeth (Putney) Moseley married Daniel Guerrant, who owned a tavern in Maysville, Buckingham County. In 1850, she was living with her daughter-in-law, Virginia Elizabeth (Bondurant) Moseley, Robert Ellis Moseley's widow. See Federal Population Census, Buckingham County, Virginia, 1850. Alexander Moseley's half-sister, Mary Ann (Moseley) Walker, died at her home near St. Marks, Florida on October 9, 1847. See *Richmond Whig*, 22 October 1847, p. 4.

31   Federal Population Census, Nelson County, Virginia, 1860. In 1860, John Harris, the free black man living at Fish Pond, was fifty years old. In 1870, the John Harris living at Alexander Hill was sixty years old. See Federal Population Census, Nelson County, Virginia, 1860; Federal Population Census, Buckingham County, Virginia, 1870.

32   Ibid., Slave Census, Nelson County, Virginia, 1860; Nelson County Land Tax, 1863.

33   T. C. [Thomas Cooper] De Leon, *Four Years in Rebel Capitals: An Inside View of Life in the Southern Confederacy from Birth to Death* (Mobile, AL: The Gossip Printing Company, 1890), 289.

34   "Gordon, Assignee v. Rixey, Assignee, and als.," *Cases Decided in the Supreme Court of Appeals of Virginia, Volume 76*, (Richmond, VA: R.F. Walker, 1883), 694–707. Alexander Joseph Bondurant (1836–1910) was the son of Thomas Moseley Bondurant (1797–1862) and Louisa "Marcia" Moseley (1799–1879). His parents were first cousins. In 1883, Fish Pond sold once again, this time to Col. Algernon Sidney Buford. According to Richmond's *The Daily Dispatch*, "The celebrated 'Fish Pond' estate, near Howardsville, Va., situated in Nelson county ninety-three miles above the city of Richmond, on James river, and containing, with Big Sycamore Island, 1,965 acres, was purchased on the 6th by Colonel A.S. Buford, president of the Richmond and Danville Railroad Company, at the price of $14,---. This estate was for many years the property of the late Alexander Moseley, Esq., and is well known as one of the most fertile and beautiful and healthy plantations in the lovely James River Valley." See *The Daily Dispatch*, 9 June 1883, p. 1.

35   Buckingham County Deed Book 1, pp. 272–274. On October 23, 1866, Alexander Moseley's cousin, Grandison Moseley of Willow Lake, surveyed the track and, on January 1, 1867, Alexander J. Bondurant, Justice of the Peace in Buckingham, witnessed the deed. On July 23, 1870, this significant deed was recorded in Buckingham County's new Deed Book 1. In 1871, the owners were taxed individually and Alexander Moseley retained 174 acres on Sycamore Creek. See Buckingham County Deed Book 1, p. 273. Today, the remains of Alexander Hill Baptist Church are situated on Route 655 (1171 Jerusalem Church Road), slightly south of where it appears on the plat. See Ibid.

36   It is notable that Alexander Moseley's first name was remembered rather than his surname. Oddly, there is no hill at the place. Was the name a nod to Israel Hill, the long-established free black community in Prince Edward County? See Melvin Patrick Ely, *Israel on the Appomattox* (New York, NY: Vintage Books, 2005); Margaret Thomas, emails to author, March 2013.

37   Federal Population Census, Buckingham County, Virginia, 1870.

38   Freedmen's Bureau Office Records, 1865–1872, Buckingham Virginia, FamilySearch, accessed August 2014, https://familysearch.org/.

39   In 1870, Sam Braxton was living at Alexander Hill with his wife, Emma, and their six children. See Federal Population Census, Buckingham County, Virginia, 1870.

40   Isaac Curd was not included among Alexander Moseley's grantees at Alexander Hill; however, in 1870, Isaac Curd, age forty-five, and his wife and Mary A., age forty, were living nearby in Buckingham County with their six children. See Federal Population Census, Buckingham County, Virginia, 1870.

41   In 1870, John Harris' wife, was enumerated in Buckingham County as Kizia and in Nelson County as Kissiah. The marriage record may be incorrect. He may have married twice. There was no Kizia listed in Alexander Moseley's 1857 slave list; however, there were two women called "Lize" and one named Eliza. See Federal Population Census,

Buckingham County, Virginia, 1870, 1880; Federal Population Census, Nelson County, Virginia, 1870.

42   In 1870, Jesse Moseley and his wife, Sylvia, were enumerated at Fish Pond in Nelson County, living adjacent A. J. Bondurant, owner of Fish Pond. By 1880, Jesse Moseley was living at Alexander Hill with his wife, "Sely," and seven children. See Federal Population Census, Nelson County, Virginia, 1870; Federal Population Census, Buckingham County, Virginia, 1880.

43   In 1870, Cornelius Palmer was living at Alexander Hill with his wife, Susan. They have a thirteen-year-old daughter, Louisa, indicating they were married about 1857. Selina may be a miss-recording of Susan or vice versa.

44   In 1870, Gabriel and "Lettie" Palmer were living at Alexander Hill. See Federal Population Census, Buckingham County, Virginia, 1870.

45   Federal Population Census, Buckingham County, Virginia, 1870.

46   Federal Population Census, Buckingham County, Virginia, 1870, 1880, 1900. From census to census, Lydia Palmer's age varies, along with the spelling of her first name. In 1900, she was living with her son, David Palmer. Her birth date was given as February 1846. See Federal Population Census, Buckingham County, Virginia, 1900.

47   P. Kevin Morley, "1865 Reflections A Historic Service Church Re-enacts Freedom Service," 1 May 2007, fredericksburg.com, accessed September 2014, http://fredericksburg.com/News/FLS/2007/052007/05012007/280305; Bob Parson, oral history, 2002, Alexander Hill files, Housewright Museum, Buckingham, Virginia. Bob Parson based his history on interviews with the church's oldest member, Mrs. Mildred Johnson (ninety-one years old at the time of the interviews), and others affiliated with the Alexander Hill Baptist Church. See Ibid.

48   E. Renée Ingram and Charles W. White, Sr., *Buckingham County* (Charleston, SC: Arcadia Publishing, 2005), 45. The congregation of Alexander Hill Church swelled to over 500 members. Eventually, some members split off and formed Warminster Baptist Church, located nearby and closer to the James River. Then, in 1896, others established Jerusalem Baptist Church, just down the road from Alexander Hill. See Ibid; Margaret Thomas to author, emails, March 2013.

49   Louisa Palmer, daughter of Susan and Cornelius Palmer, might be the child born to Susan in 1857–1858 at Fish Pond. See Federal Population Census, Buckingham County, Virginia, 1870; Leslie Anderson Morales (Editor), *Virginia Slave Births Index: 1853-1865, Volume 4: M–R* (Berwyn Heights, MD: Heritage Books, 2008), 211.

50   In 1870, a fourth Palmer household was headed by Julius Palmer who lived with his wife, Louisa, and a sixteen-year-old boy enumerated as Page Lomack (Lomax). See Federal Population Census, Buckingham County, Virginia, 1870.

51 Ingram and White, *Buckingham County*, 8. According to Ingram and White, the New York Freeman's Union Commission as well as the Freeman's Bureau financially supported the school at Alexander Hill. Ibid.

52 Federal Population Census, Buckingham County, Virginia, 1870.

53 Ingram and White, *Buckingham County*, 9.

54 Federal Population Census, Buckingham County, Virginia, 1870.

55 The 1870 census contains double entries for some of the former Moseley slaves, suggesting fluid movement between Fish Pond and Alexander Hill as well as within Buckingham County. John and Kizia/Kissiah Harris are enumerated both at Alexander Hill and in Nelson County adjacent A.J. Bondurant at Fish Pond. In Buckingham, they are listed with Louisa and James Knight and the Harris children. In Nelson County, the Harris children are also enumerated: Russ, Lydia, Cambridge, William, and the infant Alexander. Young Jesse Moseley and his family are enumerated in Nelson next to the Harrises, suggesting he is still working at Fish Pond. Louisa and James Knight are enumerated twice in Buckingham County, once with John Harris at Alexander Hill and once with Silvia Moseley (70), living not far from Julius Palmer. See Federal Population Census, Buckingham County, Virginia, 1870; Federal Population Census, Nelson County, Virginia, 1870.

56 Federal Population Census, Buckingham County, Virginia, 1880; Agricultural Census, Buckingham County, Virginia, 1880.

57 Ethridge, "Alexander Moseley," 96–129; *Alexandria Gazette*, 3 January 1871, p. 2.

58 *The Daily Dispatch*, 1 September 1881, p. 1.

Silhouette of Samuel Shepard (William G. Shepard Collection, The William and Mary Quarterly)

Preserving Buckingham County's Past: William Gamaliel Shepard

In the autumn of 1918, men across Buckingham County between the ages of eighteen and forty-five were registering with the Local Selective Service Board, facing the possibility that they might soon head to France and the trenches. William Gamaliel Shepard was among them. Twenty-one years old, of medium build, William had light brown hair and eyes. A native Virginian, he lived near Guinea Mills and was a pretty typical registrant save one detail; he was "self-employed" and gave his occupation as "literature."[1] In a county filled with farmers, William aspired to be a writer. He was determined and fulfilled his promise. In 1930, on the Federal population census, he gave his occupation as "writing," his industry as "author."[2]

William Gamaliel Shepard was born on August 25, 1897.[3] His parents were Miller Jones Shepard and Sallie Jane Gannaway.[4] "Willie" grew up in southern Buckingham County, near the Cumberland County line, on the family farm called Massinacac, named for the Monacan tribe that once occupied the area. His Virginia roots ran deep in a region steeped in history. His interest in and access to collected family papers would become the basis for his forthcoming articles.[5]

The Shepards and Gannaways valued a classical education. In the 19th century, the Shepard family had been directly involved in the founding of Buckingham Female Collegiate Institute and William's relations sent their daughters there to be educated. In keeping with this tradition, William attended college and expanded his experience through travel.[6]

As a budding man of letters, William read the *North American Review*, the nation's oldest literary magazine and, during 1917–1919, he wrote a series of letters to the magazine's Editor. These may be his first published writings.[7] The December 1917 issue includes a letter from William, which begins:

William Shepard's World War I registration card shows his occupation as "Literature," revealing that as early as 1917 he planned a career as a writer. (NATIONAL ARCHIVES AND RECORDS ADMINISTRATION, WASHINGTON D.C.)

As a new reader of THE NORTH AMERICAN REVIEW I desire to thank you heartily for your editorial in the August issue. It is a great relief to turn from the empty frothings of the newspaper editors to one who is capable of judging judicially of current events and with requisite vigor based on reason which the subjects of the day demand. *Vite!* should be our every-day slogan now at least.[8]

Flattering the Editor was a good strategy to get a letter published. Years later, William would write about the "Buckingham Literary Academy," founded by his ancestor, Col. William Evans (d. 1840), a reminder of how much Virginia gentlemen and Buckingham County planters appreciated a classical education and a life of the mind.[9]

William Evans was an omnivorous reader who kept his correspondents busy sending him books newly printed and imported from England. He was the instigator of the Buckingham Literary Academy which often met at his house near Curdsville. This creature of his interest had a small membership and the only names now known from extant scraps of the minutes note, the presence, while meeting at Traveller's Rest of "Yancey, Bolling, Patteson, Cabell, Shepard, Robertson, Eldridge, Howard." Political discussion was avoided at these causeries after one political session which ended [in] disastrous bickering.

Col. Evans himself kept the minutes, often copying prize poems into the minutes. No mention was ever made of the prize except the honor and this single illuminating entry – "Miss Eldridge read the prize poem, and thereafter was invited to attend the next meeting of the Academy and to the public dinner" – from which it seems that sitting down with such worthies was sufficient reward.[10]

William's appreciation for history extended to his family's direct participation in America's struggle for independence. In 1926, he applied for membership in the Sons of the American Revolution, based on the war record of

Travelers Rest, 1937 (LIBRARY OF VIRGINIA)

The Buckingham Literary Academy founded by William G. Shepard's ancestor, William Evans, met in private homes such as Travelers Rest. Once the home of the Horsley family and of Maj. Charles Yancey, this photo of the grand old Buckingham County house accompanied Garnett Williams' survey of the home for the Virginia Historical Inventory.

his ancestor, Lt. William Evans.[11] Concurrently, he submitted an article to the *William and Mary Quarterly*, in which he outlined the genealogy of "Shepard and other Buckingham Families." Published in April of 1926, he bemoaned the destruction of the Buckingham Courthouse in 1869, a refrain we continue to hear to this day. His writing, a bit flowery, is reminiscent of former times:

> If one were to attempt to connect up a long pedigree of a family in Buckingham it would be necessary to depend on affidavits of old inhabitants, who are rapidly going the way of all flesh and their precious recollections with them. In an old and settled country where a race has been long and gathered traditions family records are more accurate than in a new colony without much incitement to pride beyond being a good shot and a capable woodcutter. The families that were already prominent when coming to Virginia, for instance, had a tradition for local history and kept more complete accounts. Those accounts have largely disappeared in Buckingham.[12]

He concluded, saying:

> I should like to hear from anyone who has data on the families mentioned, particularly Evans, Gannaway, Shepard, Molloy, Yancey and Burwell. The identity of the Miss Yancey and Miss — Burwell and Miss — Woodson is especially desired. I hope those who can tell me interesting details will communicate with me at length at my address. Massinacac, Guinea Mills, Va.[13]

William Shepard's appeal was successful and in his subsequent article, "Shepard and Other Buckingham Families, Part II," he wrote:

> When I rushed into print in April 1926 with an article under the above heading I hoped my matter would be so imperfect and incomplete that those who read it would be goaded into indignant response. The result has been as I expected, minus the indignation, and I now have more authentic detail on all the subjects touched on in that issue of the Quarterly. The Buckingham county records are erroneously referred to in that article as destroyed excepting one old plat book, which was a typographical error: there were two. The personal and land tax books for the county are also in the State Library and have been found extremely valuable.[14]

In the second article, William interspersed old letters with his revised and expanded genealogy. Over the next decade, he would continue this practice of preserving, transcribing, and abstracting primary sources. The *William and Mary Quarterly* obliged by publishing them. In "Cumberland County, Virginia, Marriage Bonds" (1927), he noted the importance of documenting deteriorating records, writing: "So many of the old marriage bonds at Cumberland Courthouse are in a tattered condition I thought it might be useful to list those dating from the year 1800 backward to the year of the formation of the county."[15]

His published work included a transcription of an old memorandum book concerning "Some Buckingham Soldiers in the War of 1812" (1930), fragments of "Records from Old Jail at Cumberland C.H., Virginia" (1932), notations from a surviving militia book in "Buckingham County Courts Martial" (1932), and "Accounts of Buckingham Planters" (1933), in which John Gannaway paid Patrick Henry attorney fees, sold a Sorrel horse to a Jefferson, and paid Peter Francisco for shoeing a horse.[16]

While much of William Shepard's material came from his family papers, in 1934 he published a substantial two-part article, "Tobacco Inspection at Cartersville, Cumberland Co., Va., or Commonwealth vs. Dudley Street." He began by explaining the discovery and significance of the documents he transcribed:

> The ensuing depositions, found several years ago among the loose papers stored in Cumberland County jail, afford an unique commentary on the handling of tobacco in the year 1794, and give certain pleasing glimpses of the personalities of the deponents, all the more acceptable to the reader because of the monotonous drone of the formal question and answer in which the sparks of humanity are preserved. Apart from the very human bickering, the war of charge and countercharge, the bundle of stained papers contained matter of exceptional importance to the history of tobacco in Virginia.[17]

In 1935, William Shepard published more family letters, as well as excerpts from Samuel Shepard's diary, and, importantly, wrote a short history of Buckingham County which was included in *Today and Yesterday in the Heart of Virginia*, published by *The Farmville Herald*. Its comparative brevity likely reflects the paucity of Buckingham records rather than William Shepard's efforts.[18]

During 1937, William was an informant for several Virginia Historical Inventory surveys, including details about his family homes and papers.[19] He resided at 1001 High Street in Farmville, Virginia, and about this time married Lucy Irving (1903–1985), who was also the product of old Virginia families.[20] The couple moved to Daytona Beach, Florida, and over the years traveled extensively throughout Latin America with their only son, Lucius, who would become a writer as well.[21] The Shepards remained in Florida where William died in March of 1974.[22]

ACCOUNTS OF BUCKINGHAM PLANTERS
Contributed by William Shepard, Guinea Mills, Va.

John Gannaway the emigrant's accounts.

	£	s.	d.
1763 Debit			
To other items brought down	101.	9.	8
Settlement with T. Turpin, Feb.	6.	10.	3
1 gallon Rum		6.	6
Carriage 1 hhd. Tobo. & provisions for carter		14.	—
2 gallons molasses		8.	—
1 qt. Rum		1.	6
1 sursingle		3.	6
1 kerb Bridle		7.	6
R. Bolling	8.	3.	9
Cash Paid Samuel Shepard for 1 sett of books by him brought from England, to witt:			
1 Dictionary by Bailie			
1 sett of Wm. Shakspere			
E. Spenser's Fairy Queene			
1 sett of the Spectator			
1 sett of Mr. Defoe's books			
1 large Diary			
1 copy of Cervantes Don Quijote de la Mancha, for Zaida			
La Cid—do	6.	4.	2
To shoeing a mare, by Housewright	2.	—	
Patrick Henry, as attorney against Josias Jones in Buckingham		14.	6

*   *   *   *   *   *   *   *

Credit

	£	s.	d.
To 704 lb. Pork 22/—	7.	14.	10½
To sawing & grinding at my Mill	161.	8.	7¾
1 Bay Horse sold to H. Bell	6.	2.	—
1 Negro Pompey aged 24 sold to Benjamin Howard	175.	—	—
30 Bush. corn supplied to my Mill 2/6	3.	15.	—
12150 lb. Tobo. 20/—	121.	10.	—

*   *   *   *   *   *   *   *

1764 Debit

	£	s.	d.
To George Poindexter	11.	—	—
Dr. Allen for bleeding 2 Negroes & performing Post Mortem on Female do. thought to be poisoned by her Husband	2.	7.	—
12 yd. white Sheeting 2/—	1.	4.	—
1 Linen Handkf.		1.	10
A. Winston, supplies	7.	8½	
J. Jones for making Breeches	1.	4½	
1 Pewter Bason		10.	—
78 lb. Beef of Alex. Stinson 12/6		9.	9
1 Bottle Bateman's Drops		2.	6
2 lb. Raisens		2.	6
100 herrings		3.	—
2 lb. White Sugar		2.	6
5 Bush. Wheat 3/6		17.	6
1 pint Train Oyle			9
2 Jews Harps			4
1 Primmer			4

☙☗

William Shepard's final article for *William and Mary Quarterly* was his most significant contribution to the history of Buckingham County. Published in 1940, in this lengthy two-part article, "Buckingham Female Collegiate Institute," William explained his reliance on the papers of John Trent Gannaway and the Shepard family and apologized that he was not able to conduct more research before leaving Virginia. Despite this limitation, the family papers proved rich, enabling William to collect and transcribe an impressive number of primary documents concerning Virginia's first woman's college, turning them into a remarkably fulsome history. He detailed the Institute's magnificent building, credited the Buckingham gentlemen who created its library, described the talented faculty and administration, and explained the Institute's financial problems and ultimate demise during the Civil War. He also surveyed other private schools and academies in Buckingham which came and went during the 19th century.[23]

If this narrative of Buckingham Female Collegiate Institute had been William Shepard's only contribution to Buckingham County history, it would have been outstanding; however, he left much more . . . a rich potpourri of transcribed letters, reflections, and memories of Buckingham County plus a tradition of preservation and publication for future writers and historians to emulate.

"Buckingham Grand March" (LESTER S. LEVY COLLECTION OF SHEET MUSIC, SHERIDAN LIBRARIES, JOHNS HOPKINS UNIVERSITY)

William G. Shepard's two-part article which appeared in The William and Mary Quarterly and chronicled the founding, evolution, and demise of the Buckingham Female Collegiate Institute was his single most important contribution as a writer. This etching was featured on the sheet music for the "Buckingham Grand March," written by Arnaud Préot who taught music at the college. In 1857, the march was "composed and respectfully dedicated to the Directors of the Female Collegiate Institute of Buckingham Va." The drawing was executed by Rev. Henry James Brown, a Methodist minister and fellow instructor at the Institute. He also served as vice-president of its board. Rev. Brown studied with the renowned artist, Thomas Sully.

NOTES

1   William Gamaliel Shepard, World War I Selective Service System Draft Registration Card, accessed August 2014, http://search.ancestry.com/search/db.aspx?dbid=6482.

2   Federal Population Census, Buckingham County, Virginia, 1930.

3   Shepard, World War I Selective Service System Draft Registration Card.

4   Federal Population Census, Buckingham County, Virginia, 1900, 1930. According to the death certificate for Miller Jones Shepard, he was born on April 9, 1862 and died on March 1, 1936. Virginia death record, Library of Virginia.

5   William Shepard, "Shepard and Other Buckingham Families," *William and Mary Quarterly* (April 1926), 148–154.

6   Federal Population Census, Buckingham County, Virginia, 1940; William G. Shepard, SS Caledonian passenger list from Londonderry to New York, August 1928, Passenger Lists, ancestry.com. William Shepard was thirty years old at the time of this voyage.

7   *North American Review* is America's oldest literary magazine. See "*North American Review*," accessed August 2014, http://www.northamericanreview.org/history.

8   William Gamaliel Shepard, "Demosthenes, the War, and T. R.," *North American Review* (December 1917), 966–967.

9   William Shepard, "Buckingham Literary Academy," *Today and Yesterday in the Heart of Virginia* (Farmville, VA: *The Farmville Herald*, 1935), 210.

10   Ibid.

11   William Shepard, Sons of the American Revolution Application for Membership, Sons of the American Revolution Membership Applications database, 1889–1970, ancestry.com.

12   William Shepard, "Shepard and Other Buckingham Families," *William and Mary Quarterly* (April 1926), 148–154.

13   Ibid.

14   William Shepard, "Shepard and Other Buckingham Families, Part II," *William and Mary Quarterly* (July 1927), 174–180.

15   William Shepard, "Cumberland County, Virginia, Marriage Bonds," *William and Mary Quarterly* (October 1927), 282–291.

16   William Shepard, "Some Buckingham Soldiers in the War of 1812," *William and Mary Quarterly* (April 1930), 168–171; William Shepard, "Records from Old Jail at Cumberland C. H., Virginia," *William and Mary Quarterly* (January 1932), 39–40; William Shepard, "Buckingham County Courts Martial," *William and Mary Quarterly* (July 1932), 193–201; William Shepard, "Accounts of Buckingham Planters," *William and Mary Quarterly* (July 1933), 180–181.

17   William Shepard, "Tobacco Inspection at Cartersville, Cumberland Co., Va., or Commonwealth vs. Dudley Street," *William and Mary Quarterly* (July 1934), 181–202.

18   William Shepard, "Buckingham County," *Today and Yesterday*, 199–205.

19   William Shepard served as informant for several surveys, included: "Edgewood," "The Knob," "Letter of 1805," "A Letter by Samuel Shepard, Recommending a Slave for Church Membership in 1839," "A Friendly Letter," "A Letter by James O'Malley," "Papers Belonging to William Shepard," and "Willis Mountain," all submitted by field worker Elizabeth McCraw. See Virginia Historical Inventory, Library of Virginia.

20   Before the Shepards were married, Lucy Irving taught Spanish at Susquehanna University in Pennsylvania. See Federal Population Census, Snyder County, Pennsylvania, 1930; Katherine Dunn, "An Introduction to Lucius Shepard," accessed August 2014, http://www.sfsite.com/fsf/2001/dunn0103.htm.

21   In 1959, the Daytona Beach City Directory listed William Shepard as a freelance writer. See Daytona Beach City Directory, 1959, U.S. City Directories database, 1821–1989, ancestry.com. The Shepards' only child, Lucius Taylor Irving Shepard, became a prolific fiction writer, specializing in Science Fiction and Fantasy. See Dunn, "An Introduction to Lucius Shepard;" "Lucius Shepard," *The Encyclopedia of Science Fiction*, accessed August 2014, http://www.sf-encyclopedia.com/entry/shepard_lucius.

22   Federal Population Census, Volusia, Florida, 1940; William Shepard, Social Security record, ancestry.com. The 1940 census notes that William completed two years of college. His occupation is given as writer, his industry historical magazine. He noted an income of $500, supplemented by other income. The couple rented furnished rooms and at the time of the census had one lodger. See Federal Population Census, Volusia, Florida, 1940.

23   William Shepard, "Buckingham Female Collegiate Institute," *William and Mary Quarterly* (April 1940), 167–193; William Shepard, "Buckingham Female Collegiate Institute," *William and Mary Quarterly* (July 1940), 345–368. In 1933, Shepard published "Appended Data on Buckingham Female Institute" in *The Farmville Herald*. It supplemented Lulie Patteson's "Buckingham Female Collegiate Institute." See *Felixville: A Forgotten Village in Cumberland County Virginia and Other Sketches* (Farmville, VA: *The Farmville Herald*, 1967), 25–39.

Louise Harrison McCraw (Courtesy Estaline Anderson McCraw)

A Life of Service: Louise Harrison McCraw

In 1920, the *Richmond Times-Dispatch* ran a lengthy obituary for William Emmett McCraw of Buckingham County, a rare tribute to a man from a rural area.

William Emmett McCraw, the youngest son of Cary Harrison McCraw and Mary Gilliam, was born at "Elysian Grove," in Buckingham County, on April 20, 1846. At the age of 16 he became a volunteer in the Confederate army, serving with Company K, Fourth Virginia Calvary, and although a mere boy, he was known among his comrades as one of the bravest and most daring of Stuart's men. He was twice wounded, but as soon as he could lay aside his crutches he set out to fill again his place in the ranks, only to be turned back by the news of Lee's surrender. During the dark days of Reconstruction he met his difficulties like the soldier that he was and began to build a bright future on the saddened past.

In his early twenties he was married to his boyhood sweetheart, Miss Bettie Gilliam, of Buckingham also, and through the years of the their long and happy life the love which began in school days seemed only to grow and ripen as they fought the battle of life together. Before the end came this mutual affection had approximated perfection as nearly as is possible for a human emotion. Upon his children he lavished the love and devotion of which only a self-sacrificing nature, such as his, is capable. To the guest in his home he displayed always the hospitality of an old Virginia gentleman. Besides his widow he is survived by five children, Richard Miller McCraw, Edward Cary McCraw, Mrs. N. W. Kuykendall and Misses Bessie Edmonia and Louise Harrison McCraw.

Always interested in politics and prominent in political affairs, he held worthily several positions of trust, among which was that of deputy collector of internal revenue. In politics, as in every other phase of life, he championed the cause which he believed to be right and stood firmly for his convictions in the face of any opposition he happened to meet. In public his optimism, his cordiality, his loyalty and his integrity won for him a host of friends.

But it was in his church associations that he was able to render his most definite service to the God to whom he had consecrated his life. For fifty-six years he was a member of Enon Baptist Church, for a long period superintendent of the Sunday school, and for forty years clerk of the church. Always willing to bear more than his share of the burdens, and in every other way living the faith which he professed he set an example for his associates of Christian purity and fidelity. It was not strange that as he was nearing the end he should have had no fear of death.

On May 23, at his home, "The Pines," after a short but violent coughing spell, he breathed his last. He was buried with Masonic honors by the lodge of which at one time he had been treasurer for twenty years. The floral offerings, the last tribute paid him by his friends, both white and colored, gave further proof of the esteem and affection with which he was held in the hearts of all who knew him.

In death, as in life, he wore the expression of a good fighter – of one who had struggled for principles. In all the Scriptures there seem to be no lines more fitting to describe the end of his life than these: "I have fought a good fight. I have finished my course. I have kept the faith. Henceforth there is laid up for me a crown of righteousness."[1]

Though the obituary is not signed, it bears the style of Emmett's literary daughter, Louise Harrison McCraw, who though still living in Buckingham County at the time of her father's death, likely sent this loving, reverent, and romantic tribute to the Richmond newspaper. If so, it is among her first published works. In it, Emmett McCraw shines as a Christian paragon, an ideal of the characters Louise would one day create in her religious novels.

Louise Harrison McCraw was born in Buckingham County in February of 1893 at her family's home, The Pines, near Andersonville, in the southern part of the county. By the age of five, she was determined to become a writer. When one of her storytelling older sisters angered little Louise, she went to the vegetable garden, stamped her foot, and announced, "When I get grown, I'm going to write a book about how bad it is for older children to boss younger children."[2]

Louise was good to her word and became a writer. She started early. During 1904–1906, the youthful (and doubtless enthusiastic) Louise began submitting stories, poems, riddles, and recipes to the children's page of Richmond, Virginia's leading newspaper, *The Times-Dispatch*. Several were printed. The page, dedicated to *The Times-Dispatch* Children's Club (T.D.C.C.) was extremely popular and was featured in the newspaper's Sunday edition. Impressive headlines announced, "Our Children's Page Made By Children" or "This Page Made For And By T.D.C.C. Members." By 1908, the club had 5,000 members.[3]

In one published letter to the Editor, twelve-year-old Louise wrote:

Dear Mr. Editor,
I enclose the end of my story this week and hope it will be published. I have a pretty little spotted kitten named "Montague." I call him Monty for short. He is very young and I have to feed him on catnip tea. I haven't caught any fish yet, but I expect I will go fishing to-morrow.
Your friend, LOUISE HARRISON MCCRAW[4]

Louise was also a budding artist. In 1904, *The Times-Dispatch* printed her sketch of a "Morning Dove" and one of "A Prairie Hen."[5]

Her girlhood home at The Pines dated from the 18th century. The oldest section, built in 1798, was made up of three rooms stacked on top of each other – a basement, first floor, and second floor. Elaborated over the years, it burned in 1930.[6] The farm was an ongoing physical embodiment of Buckingham County's past, full of constant reminders of the economically devastating Civil War to which her parents were a direct, living connection. The Pines provided an atmosphere that would infuse Louise's novels to come. Her family and her church, Enon Baptist, instilled the cultural and spiritual values that would direct all of her life's work.

After graduating from the Woman's College of Richmond in 1911 with a Bachelor of Letters degree, Louise returned to Buckingham County and began teaching school.[7] In 1920, she worked as a grammar school teacher in Buckingham County and, sometime before 1925, she and her sister, Elizabeth "Bessie" Edmonia McCraw (1888–1941), moved to Richmond and lived in a boarding house on Park Avenue in the city's Fan District.[8] Bessie was educated at the Farmville State Teachers' College and, before moving to Richmond, she

(COURTESY ZONDERVAN PUBLISHING HOUSE)

Rev. James McConkey, co-founder of the Braille Circulating Library, was an inspiration to Louise McCraw. Her biography, James H. McConkey: A Man of God, *was published in 1939.*

taught for four years at the Cannaday Presbyterian Mission School in Floyd County, Virginia.[9] Later, she studied at St. Luke's Hospital Training School and worked as a hospital nurse.[10]

This might be the story of many sisters who moved from Buckingham County to Richmond in the early 20th century; however, once Louise was in the city, her career took a surprising turn. She had been deeply influenced by the writings of Rev. James H. McConkey, regarding him "above all other spiritual authors."[11] Rev. McConkey was a respected speaker, author, and publisher of Christian books. His work stressed practical Christianity and he spoke on such topics as "The Surrendered Life," "The Believer's Gift to God," and "The Dedicated Life."

Based in Pennsylvania, McConkey spoke periodically in Richmond. In early 1925, Louise, who had worked with the blind, approached him, suggesting that his books and pamphlets should be published in Braille. She informed him that in the United States alone there were 100,000 blind persons, many of whom could read Braille and, while various denominations produced literature in Braille, no evangelical Christian literature was available.[12]

Rev. McConkey agreed to the idea and insisted that volunteer offerings fund the Braille versions of his books. It quickly became clear that costs prohibited giving the volumes away and the idea of a lending library was born. Ultimately, Louise and McConkey would be identified as the co-founders of Richmond's Braille Circulating Library.[13]

In November of 1925, Richmond's Braille Circulating Library, the only Braille library in the world to circulate exclusively Christian material, was established and headquartered in a closet in Louise's rented room. Needless to say, she was a staff of one and quietly distributed the initial Braille printings of Rev. McConkey's books, *Faith*, *The Fifth Sparrow*, *The God Planned Life*, and *Chastenings*.[14] The Braille Library soon outgrew Louise's closet and, in 1927, moved to Richmond's Young Men's Christian Association (YMCA), with which McConkey was affiliated. Built in 1910 and located at Seventh and Grace Streets, the impressive facility included the area's first YMCA swimming pool.[15]

In the early years, Louise's job as Secretary was only part-time; she spent her afternoons at the YMCA fulfilling requests. Time was not the measure of her devotion and it became increasingly clear that she would dedicate her life to the Braille Library. As demand and the collection grew, her work became full-time, with support coming from part-time and volunteer workers who learned to type braille, creating new volumes for the library. Classes were taught at the Red Cross headquarters in the Richmond Trust Building. Miss Mattie Harris served as instructor, promising that "after relatively few lessons the students are able to begin work on books to add to the library."[16]

The *Richmond Times-Dispatch* covered the activities of the library on a regular basis, praising its international outreach. Despite the deepening worldwide Great Depression, the library's work grew steadily, distributing copies of James H. McConkey's books both in English and in translation. Letters of gratitude

Central YMCA, Richmond, Virginia (JOANNE L. YECK COLLECTION)

By 1927, the Braille Circulating Library was located at the Central YMCA in Richmond, Virginia. According to this postcard printed by Louis Kaufmann & Sons: "The new Central YMCA building in beauty of its architectural features and completeness of its equipment, is without a doubt one of the finest Association buildings in the US. Cost, fully completed and equipped, about $300,000, of this amount over $200,000 was subscribed by the citizens of Richmond in an enthusiastic campaign limited to 15 days, thus establishing a 'world's record.'"

arrived from around the globe – from Calcutta, where a "Mohammedan" teacher worked at the government school for the blind, to Cairo, where 400 blind persons read translations of the nonsectarian Christian literature at Moslem University. In China, material was circulated through the Chinese Braille magazine and, in Japan, through the Japanese Braille magazine.[17] China was the first foreign country served by the library and, after the rise of Communism, many of the library's volumes remained in the country.[18]

Louise was never shy about her faith or her work. From time to time she expressed her feelings in a letter to the Editor of the *Richmond Times-Dispatch*, just as she had as a girl from Buckingham. One entitled, "Who Made Woman A 'Lure and Temptation?'," appeared in the Saturday edition, printed on January 28, 1928. In it, she argued:

> No charge can be made against Christianity, which does not revert to its founder. If what Dr. Anspacher says of Christianity is true, then the fault is in its founder. It is an accepted fact that Jesus Christ was the first to place woman on equality with man. The stand He took in regard to the woman brought into the temple to be stoned was characteristic.[19]

Louise's letter resulted in a vehement rebuttal, signed by "Eve." Among other biting comments, Eve wrote, "I daresay Miss McCraw would be shocked if she would pick up the New Testament and read some of the writings of Paul on woman."[20] It would not be the last time Louise's words resulted in controversy and her belief in the equality of women would be reflected in her dual careers, as well as in her fiction.

By 1935, under Louise's direction, the Braille Circulating Library shipped Braille books to every state in the nation and to seventeen foreign countries.[21] The books were sent without charge to any blind person or institution requesting a volume. The U.S. Government mailed books free of charge within the United States and only required one cent postage for those going abroad.

Louise's practical faith fueled her work. "Some people think that if a person is blind, he will necessarily be religious. That's foolish," she said. "The blind are neither more religious nor less religious than any one else. Often they haven't been taught. Their opportunities are so much fewer that you'd expect them to be less religious."[22]

Eventually, the Library moved its headquarters from the YMCA to Richmond's Fan District; anyone who dropped in would find Louise hard at work. In 1941, a letter to the Editor of the *Richmond Times-Dispatch* described such an encounter. It was signed, simply, An Interested Rambler.

> Sir, – Recently while walking in one of the oldest and most historic sections of Richmond, I noticed just across the street the home of the Braille Circulating Library. Having no particular destination, I followed my impulse and entered. In a few minutes I was seated across the desk from the founder and secretary, and we were chatting as old friends. One had only to look into those clear blue eyes to know that here was one who puts "first things first," and serves humanity with sincerity and sympathy. . . .
>
> My visit came to an end all too soon; what seemed like minutes had really been an hour, so with apologies for having taken so much of the secretary's time, I stepped again into the street. As I continued my walk I thought here is a work directed against "soul erosion." The workers believe with Paul that every life should be "a pageant of triumph," and that the blind should have every opportunity afforded those with sight. Here is a work that deserves the interest and support of Christian people everywhere.[23]

Over the years, Louise received numerous letters, sometimes in Braille. She and her volunteers made personal friends of many readers. "If they want to write," said Louise, "we write back."[24] There were also many meaningful personal encounters. On a trip to England in 1954, at a school for the blind, Louise met Peter White, of Bristol, who had read braille since he was six years old and was reading two to three grade levels above his age. At almost eight years old, Peter became the youngest patron of the Braille Circulating Library. At the other end of the spectrum, many individuals in their eighties relied on the service. Louise knew well the library's sustaining value. Postage had increased, though. Now, for a three-cent stamp, the volumes brighten thousands of dark worlds around the globe.[25]

Louise traveled beyond Richmond to speak to the blind in Baltimore and to students in Michigan and Ohio.[26] By 1953, the library was producing Talking Books, distributed on records which required special equipment to play them. Circulation of Talking Books soon caught up with and surpassed Braille books. Louise remained the Library's only full-time employee and donations by friends of the Library continued to provide the only funding. To this day, the library has never solicited funds.[27]

℘⃝ɞ

Concurrent with her job at the library, Louise began writing books, primarily novels with religious themes. They proved very popular and, between 1934 and 1965, she found a place among Richmond's best-known authors.[28] Her first full-length, published novel, *Hearts That Understand* (Moody Press), was printed in 1936.[29] Dr. Harry Ironsides, pastor of Moody Memorial Church, Chicago, described the book saying, "It is dramatic enough to interest any lover of well-told tales, moving enough to sustain interest throughout and appealing enough to make a deep impression on the moral and spiritual nature.... I began to read it at bedtime and did not put it down until 2 o'clock in the morning."[30]

Likewise, Dr. James R. Graham, a Presbyterian missionary in China, found that the novel took on important contemporary issues and was an excellent vehicle to reach youthful readers. He noted, "Many young people will read an attractive story who could not be induced to read a Christian apologetic."[31] Dr. Robert C. McQuilken, President of the Columbia Bible College, Columbia, South Carolina, addressed the importance of religious themes in Louise's novels: "Most novels omit completely the thing that is most fundamental in human life – a man's relation to God; those that include it often give a perverted view. Miss McCraw, with a true view of life and Christ, has given a wholesome and real picture of what Christ can mean when the life is turned over for his guidance."[32]

Indeed, Louise Harrison McCraw had found her niche with her first full-length novel, an "attractive story" with a strong religious message. With rare exception, she never wavered. A short biography of Louise, written in 1949 and published in the *Richmond Times-Dispatch*, described her as "disseminating spiritual truth in a form more acceptable to people" than the "purely didactic."[33] It was as true of her tenth volume as it was of her first.

Spiritual and religious fiction was extremely popular at the time, particularly the work of Lloyd C. Douglas, whose national bestsellers included *Magnificent Obsession* (1929) and *The Robe* (1942). James Hilton (*Lost Horizon*, 1933) was successful first in England, then in America. Louise's blend of romance and religion, coupled with a woman's point of view, set her apart. She spoke to what became a devoted audience and her novels were popular book club selections.[34]

Hearts That Understand was set in the contemporary world of social services, sold widely, and became "the subject of considerable controversy." Ministers in Richmond passionately discussed the book. Rev. A.P. Williams, pastor of Barton Heights Methodist Church, used *Hearts that Understand* as a basis for a sermon, calling it "the best Christian novel," while two others severely criticized its contents.[35]

Local interest remained strong and, in the spring of 1937, Louise presented her novel to Circle One of the Woman's Missionary Society of Pace Memorial Methodist Church. The group met in a private home on Park Avenue in Richmond's Fan District; however, it was open to the public and the event was announced in the *Richmond Times-Dispatch*.[36] Her debut novel certainly made a splash and, over the years, the *Times-Dispatch* would generously continue to cover her work.

In the summer of 1937, the *Times-Dispatch* announced Louise's second novel, *Glorious Triumph*, complete with a charming photo of the author. A slight smile suggests a warm and friendly air. Her wavy, dark hair is modestly coiffed, pinned in the back in stereotypical librarian-style. Her clear blue eyes look directly at the camera. The article reports Miss McCraw's residence at 1106 Grove Avenue. These were simpler days in Richmond; Louise did not hide from her public. Perhaps, she even encouraged an eager young reader to knock at her door. She had stories to tell and a strong Christian message to impart. In any

Miss Louise McCraw
Novel To Be Published

Miss L. H. McCraw Writes Novel

(Courtesy Richmond Times-Dispatch)

case, she could always be found at the Braille Circulating Library, then still located at the YMCA.[37]

Her third novel, *Blue Skies*, published in 1938, took on the controversial issue of interfaith marriage. The book's release prompted a letter to the Editor of the *Richmond Times-Dispatch*. Written by a loyal reader in Philadelphia, Pennsylvania, Louise's audience was clearly vocal and had grown outside the Richmond area. Now described as a "popular Southern authoress," Louise had blended religion, romance, and a prickly topic, the relationship between

Christians and Jews. The story centered on the romance between the main character, Aaron Rothenberg, and Edith St. Clair, who though "cultured and refined as she is, nevertheless, is lacking in real understanding."[38]

Louise's next book was a departure, a biography of her colleague, Rev. James H. McConkey. Published in 1939 and written just two years after his death, *James H. McConkey, A Man of God*, proved popular and there were at least four editions.[39] Rev. McConkey had been a great inspiration to Louise and, with the assistance of his family, especially his nephew, W. McConkey Kerr, she wrote the biography. John McConkey was a native of Pennsylvania, studied at Princeton, and was named President of his class. He went on to study law, was admitted to the bar and was closely affiliated with the work of the YMCA. An invalid in his last years, he died at the age of seventy-nine.[40]

The Housewright Museum in Buckingham Court House contains a near complete collection of the novels of Louise Harrison McCraw donated by Pauline Peters Word. Nest Among the Stars *(1942) was published by Zondervan. Louise McCraw found her title in the book of Obadiah 1:4 – "Though thou exalt thy selfe as the eagle, and though thou set thy nest among the starres, thence will I bring thee downe, saith the Lord."* (Courtesy Historic Buckingham)

The biography was followed by *Shining After Rain* (1940). Set during the Civil War, the novel featured cousins fighting on opposite sides of the conflict. Published by Zondervan Publishing House, it was priced at $1.00, slightly under best-selling novels of the day. Rachel Field's historical romance, *All This and Heaven Too*, cost $1.39 and Phyllis Bottome's anti-fascist novel, *The Mortal Storm*, was priced at $1.29.

In 1937, Louise participated in the Virginia Historical Inventory, serving as an "informant" for her sister-in-law, Elizabeth B. (Watts) McCraw, a Buckingham County field worker for the WPA project.[41] As was the case for many of Louise's generation who grew up in the South, the lasting effects of the Civil War penetrated her childhood. She desired to keep those stories alive, both in fact and fiction, and helped preserve a Civil War-era letter written from Valley Mountain on August 28, 1861, by her cousin, Frank O. McCraw. He was one of seven sons of Thomas McCraw, survived the war, and lived to be an old man.[42]

While Louise continued her work for the Braille Circulating Library, she managed to write a book each year. Her novel, *Shining After Rain* (1940), was followed by *Does God Answer Prayer?* (1941), which analyzed all aspects of prayer, and another novel, *Nest Among the Stars* (1942).[43] Her next novel, *On the Wings of the Morning* (1943), was published by Fleming H. Revell Company of New York, London, and Edinburgh. The American News Company announced, "The latest work of a topnotcher in the field of clean fiction – the sort you can recommend without reserve. There is nothing goody-goody about Miss McCraw's stories."[44]

In 1946, *Crystal Sea* contained unmistakable autobiographical elements. Louise dedicated the novel as follows:

To Annie McCraw Anderson
The sister who told me stories of great books and led me into a love of literature.

Louise's heroine, Janet, leaves a rural life (very reminiscent of Buckingham County), first to attend college in the city and then to settle there, just as Louise and her sister, Bessie, had done. Set between the World Wars, Janet's early life was spent on an old-fashioned Virginia plantation. Louise employed familiar Buckingham surnames, including Hale and Bondurant, and locales such as

Plantersville and Hampden-Sydney College. Janet's Aunt Edmonia remembered a McCraw family name.

The *Richmond Times-Dispatch* ran a full review by J. Blanton Belk, who wrote: "Perhaps the casual reader of novels will have to be patient during some of the early pages but the reward will come as the larger plot develops. Love is not refined quickly and neither is faith. There are too few books of this character for young people. Perhaps it is because so few can look so deeply into a young girl's heart."[45]

By the 1950s, Louise Harrison McCraw had joined the ranks of Richmond's diverse community of writers. In May of 1951, Thalhimers, the city's impressive department store located at Seventh and Broad Streets, hosted an event

The Crystal Sea *(1949) was published by Revell and cost the contemporary reader $2.00. J. Blanton Belk, reviewing the novel for the* Richmond Times-Dispatch, *exclaimed, "Every young person in America could profitably read this quest for genuine love."* (COURTESY HISTORIC BUCKINGHAM)

celebrating local authors. Louise joined over forty writers for an informal buffet luncheon and chat with the public. Literary notables included: Dr. Douglas S. Freeman (*Robert E. Lee*), James Branch Cabell (*The Devil's Own Dear Son*), Ellen M. Bagby (who collected George W. Bagby's sketches in *The Old Virginia Gentleman*), Virginius Dabney (*Dry Messiah*), Rebecca Yancey Williams (*Vanishing Virginia*), and Mary Wingfield Scott (*Old Richmond Neighborhoods*).[46]

The Honor of Preston Reed (1952), published by Moody Press, was followed by *My Heart's at Liberty* (1961), and *It Shall be Forever* (1965). In addition to her novels, Louise also contributed to several evangelical journals, including *Sunday School Times* and *Moody Monthly*.[47]

Richmond's Fan District remained Louise's home and workplace. Her several addresses were typical of single women, who changed boarding houses or apartments, from time to time. In her retirement, Louise was named Executive Secretary Emeritus of the Braille Circulating Library Room, then located in Richmond's Fan District at 2700 Stuart Avenue, where it remains today.[48]

She died at her Buckingham County home on January 25, 1975. Services were held in Dillwyn, Buckingham County, at Dunkum Funeral Home. The family requested that in lieu of flowers, contributions be made to the Braille Circulating Library Room. She was buried in the family cemetery.[49]

Today, while print copies of Louise's books are scarce, her novels are still available from the Braille Circulating Library. Beginning with her debut, *Hearts That Understand*, the blind around the world continue to experience the inspirational romances created by a talented and determined girl from Buckingham County.[50]

NOTES

1   "William Emmett McCraw," obituary, *Richmond Times-Dispatch*, 29 May 1920, p. 6.

2   "Virginia Writers: Louise Harrison McCraw," *Richmond Times-Dispatch*, 14 August 1949, D-7.

3   "Supreme In Virginia. Strides Taken by *Richmond Times-Dispatch* Put It in Lead," *Shenandoah Herald*, 10 July 1908, p. 2.

4   *The Times-Dispatch*, 30 April 1905, p. 7.

5   "This Page Made For And By T.D.C.C. Members," *The Times-Dispatch*, 31 July 1904, p. 8; "This Page Made For And By T.D.C.C. Members," *The Times-Dispatch*, 25 September 1904, p. 8.

6   Elizabeth McCraw, "The Pines," Virginia Historical Inventory, 27 January 1937.

7   *The Times-Dispatch*, 2 June 1911, p. 9. The Woman's College of Richmond was founded as Richmond Female Institute and, later, became Westhampton, a Baptist college for women. Eventually, it was absorbed into the University of Richmond. See E.M., "Memorial Room Preserves Records of Richmond Female Institute," *Richmond Times-Dispatch*, 20 June 1937; "Westhampton College," accessed August 2014, http://wc.richmond.edu/traditions/history.html.

8   Federal Population Census, Buckingham County, Virginia, 1920; Federal Population Census, Richmond, Virginia, 1930; "Bessie Edmonia McCraw," obituary, *Richmond Times-Dispatch*, 22 January 1941, p. 24.

9   Cannady was one of the so-called Harris Mountain Schools. These Presbyterian mission schools were founded in 1913 in Floyd, Montgomery, and Franklin counties. Schools included Shooting Creek, Ferrum, Cannaday, Christiansburg, Buffalo Mountain, Sylyatus, Pippen Hill, Boone's Mill, Taylor's Mountain, Thaxton, Cave Mountain, Greenlee, Algoma, and Franklin. See "A Guide to the Harris Mountain Schools Collection, 1913–1961, Virginia Tech," accessed August 2014, http://ead.lib.virginia.edu/vivaxtf/view?docId=vt/viblbv00212.xml;query=.

10   St. Luke's Hospital, located in Richmond, Virginia, trained nurses from 1886–1935; it reopened later in the 20th century and closed again in 1986. See "Virginia Nursing History: Diploma Programs," Virginia Commonwealth University, accessed August 2014, http://www.nursing.vcu.edu/about/history/.

11   Louise Harrison McCraw, *James H. McConkey: A Man of God* (Grand Rapids, MI: Zondervan Publishing House, 1939), 122.

12   McCraw, *James H. McConkey*, 122–127.

13   "Circulating Braille Library Sends Volumes All Over World: Miss Louise McCraw at Y.M.C.A. Directs Work for Blind Readers," *Richmond Times-Dispatch*, 7 February 1937, p. 2; Lois Reamy, "Braille Library Here Supplies 18 Countries," *Richmond Times-Dispatch*, 3 February 1957, p. 2-C.

14   McCraw, *James H. McConkey*, 125. Initially, the collection consisted exclusively of McConkey's writings and functioned as a branch of McConkey's Silver Publishing Company. Gradually, the collection expanded, adding other authors of inspirational literature to the library's catalog. See "Braille Circulating Library Maintained," *Richmond Times-Dispatch*, 26 April 1929, p. 15; "Miss McCraw Will Review Novel Today," *Richmond Times-Dispatch*, 30 March 1937, p. 12; "Virginia Writers: Louise Harrison McCraw."

15   McCraw, *James H. McConkey*, 159; A Guide to the YMCA of Greater Richmond Records, 1854–2004, Library of Virginia. In 1942, the YMCA moved to its present location at East Franklin and North Foushee streets.

16   "Volunteers to Aid in Work: Books in Braille Sent From Richmond All Over World," *Richmond Times-Dispatch*, 12 July 1934, p. 6.

17   "Braille Library Supplies Books to Over 1,200 Blind Persons," *Richmond Times-Dispatch*, 3 December 1931, p. 2; Clarence Boyking, "Richmond Parade," *Richmond Times-Dispatch*, 8 May 1935, p. 2.

18   "'Talking Books' for the Blind Being Made in Richmond," *Richmond Times-Dispatch*, 30 August 1953, B-6.

19   Louise H. McCraw, "Who Made Woman A 'Lure and Temptation?'" *Richmond Times-Dispatch*, 28 January 1928, p. 4.

20   Eve, "Eve Insists Dr. Ansapacher Had Low-Down on Women," *Richmond Times-Dispatch*, 2 February 1928, p. 4.

21   "Circulating Braille Library Sends Volumes All Over World," *Richmond Times-Dispatch*, 7 December 1937, p. 2.

22   "Blind Seek Light: Braille Library Here Emphasizes Religion," *Richmond Times-Dispatch*, 15 June 1955, p. 7.

23   An Interested Rambler, "That the Blind May See," *Richmond Times-Dispatch*, 1 March 1941, p. 8.

24   Laurens Irby, "For Eager Hands: Richmond Braille Library Sends Out Bulky Volume," *Richmond Times-Dispatch*, 25 March 1956, D-1.

25   Ibid.

26   "Miss McCraw Will Address Blind Students," *Richmond Times-Dispatch*, 29 January 1947, p. 15; "Local Author to Give Talk in Michigan," *Richmond Times-Dispatch*, 26 October 1947, p. 15.

27 "'Talking Books' for the Blind Being Made in Richmond," *Richmond Times-Dispatch*, 30 August 1953, B-6.

28 "Thalhimers honors Richmond and Charlottesville Authors," *Richmond Times-Dispatch*, 18 May 1952, C-13.

29 Previously, McCraw had published a "popular gift book" titled *Starward* (Richmond, VA: Garrett & Massie, c.1934). Copies are preserved at the Virginia Historical Society and Small Special Collections, University of Virginia. Also see "Miss McCraw Will Review Novel Today," *Richmond Times-Dispatch*, 30 March 1937, p. 12.

30 "Virginia Writers: Louise Harrison McCraw."

31 Ibid.

32 "Louise McCraw Publishes Second Novel, Glorious Triumph," *Richmond Times-Dispatch*, 21 July 1937, p. 9.

33 "Virginia Writers: Louise Harrison McCraw."

34 Ibid.

35 "Barton Heights To Discontinue Night Service," *Richmond Times-Dispatch*, 2 August 1936, p. 8; "Miss McCraw Will Review Novel Today," *Richmond Times-Dispatch*, 30 March 1937, p. 12. The news article, "Miss McCraw Will Review Novel Today," does not reveal the nature of the controversy over her first novel.

36 "Miss McCraw Will Review Novel Today."

37 "Louise McCraw Publishes Second Novel, Glorious Triumph," *Richmond Times-Dispatch*, 21 July 1937, p. 9.

38 F. Harper, "Blue Skies and Romance," *Richmond Times-Dispatch*, 19 June 1938, p. 2.

39 McCraw, *James H. McConkey, A Man of God* (Grand Rapids, MI: Zondervan Publishing House, 1939); Third Edition (Pittsburgh, PA: Bethany House, 1939); Reprinted, Pittsburgh, PA: Silver Publishing Society, 1945.

40 "James McConkey (1858–1937): Devoted Writer," *Path 2 Prayer*, accessed August 2014, http://www.path2prayer.com/article/1141/revival-and-holy-spirit/books-sermons/new-resources/famous-christians-books-and-sermons/james-mcconkey-devoted-writer.

41 Joanne Yeck, "Ladies of the WPA: Chronicling Buckingham's Vanishing Past," *"At a Place Called Buckingham"* (Kettering, OH: Slate River Press, 2011), 143–157.

42 Elizabeth McCraw, "A war letter of 1861," Virginia Historical Inventory, 15 December 1937, Library of Virginia. Louise Harrison McCraw acted as an informant for at least two other surveys: "Site of Elysian Grove," 15 September 1937, and "The Pines: The McCraw Home," 27 January 1937, both written by Elizabeth McCraw. See Virginia Historical Inventory, Library of Virginia.

43   "Miss McCraw Writes Book," Richmond Daybook, *Richmond Times-Dispatch*, 11 November 1941, p. 6.

44   Allen R. Matthews, "Off the Bookshelves," *Richmond Times-Dispatch*, 31 October 1943, H-4.

45   J. Blanton Belk, "Looking Into the Soul of Youth," *Richmond Times-Dispatch*, 20 April 1947, D-7.

46   "Richmond Authors Will Have 'Day' On Wednesday," *Richmond Times-Dispatch*, 18 May 1951, A-9, III-1.

47   "Louise McCraw, Novelist, Worker for Blind, Dies," *Richmond Times-Dispatch*, 27 January 1975, B-2. According to one biographical sketch, Louise wrote short stories; none of these are known to survive. It is possible they appeared in religious journals and magazines. See "Virginia Writers: Louise Harrison McCraw."

48   "Louise McCraw, Novelist, Worker for Blind, Dies." As throughout its history, the Braille Circulating Library "does not charge for any of its services, incurs no debt, operates on a cash basis, receives no federal or state funding, but is sustained by concerned individuals, foundations, and churches. Few ministries have been in continuous operation for so long a period of time without an endowment or another source of funding. The Braille Circulating Library is truly a 'faith ministry'." See Braille Circulating Library, accessed August 2014, http://www.bclministries.org/.

49   "Louise McCraw, Novelist, Worker for Blind, Dies."

50   Library Catalog, Braille Circulating Library, accessed August 2014, http://www.bclministries.org/content/library-catalog.

About the Author

From an early age, historian Joanne Yeck was drawn to a career of writing and research. After earning her doctorate in cinema studies at the University of Southern California, she taught and wrote about film history for many years. She is the author of numerous articles concerning Classic Hollywood and American Popular Culture, and is the coauthor of *Movie Westerns* and *Our Movie Heritage*. Since 1995, her interest in Virginia history has become a full-time occupation. Years of research resulted in *"At a Place Called Buckingham"... Historic Sketches of Buckingham County, Virginia* (2011) which celebrated the county's 250th anniversary. In 2010, she was awarded a Jefferson Fellowship at the International Center for Jefferson Studies which supported her research for *The Jefferson Brothers* (2012), a biography of Randolph Jefferson. Her blog, Slate River Ramblings, attracts a growing community interested in Buckingham County and its environs. When not exploring the back roads of Virginia, she lives in Kettering, Ohio. Visit Joanne online at joannelyeck.com and slateriverrambling.com.